# THE TENT
## OF AVRAHAM

---

## GLEANINGS
### *from the*
## DAVID CARDOZO ACADEMY

---

*Edited by*

## NATHAN LOPES CARDOZO

*To*

*July · 2012*

*Jerry & Alice,*

*with love,*

*Nathan Lopes Cardozo*

מכון קרדוזו
DAVID CARDOZO ACADEMY

### URIM PUBLICATIONS
Jerusalem ◆ New York

*The Tent of Avraham: Gleanings from the David Cardozo Academy*
Edited by Nathan Lopes Cardozo

*Typesetting by Ariel Walden*
Printed in Israel
First Edition
I S B N : 978-965-524-114-3

Urim Publications, P.O. Box 52287, Jerusalem 91521 Israel

Lambda Publishers Inc.
527 Empire Blvd., Brooklyn, New York 11225 U.S.A.
Tel: 718-972-5449 Fax: 718-972-6307
mh@ejudaica.com

www.UrimPublications.com

This book is dedicated by

Mrs. Chana Yocheved Rozen-Newman

of Bloomfield Hills, Michigan

to the memory of the

*Lohamei haMahtarot* (underground fighters)

*of*

Etzel – The National Military Organization
in the Land of Israel

*and of*

Lehi – The Fighters for the Freedom of Israel

*Iyar 5772 – April 2012*

# Contents

# Introduction

MY DEAR WIFE, Freyda Rachel Lopes Cardozo-Gnesin, published a liber amicorum, a *festschrift* in honor of my 60th birthday. Many friends, including several major Jewish thinkers, contributed to it. There could have been no gift more beautiful than this, and it was a great moment of spiritual excitement when my grandchildren presented me with the book.

That festive occasion prompted me to contemplate my life story. There I was, the child of an assimilated Jewish family, who had lived in a non-Jewish world in Holland with only gentile friends. At the age of sixteen, I made a conscious decision to become a full member of the Jewish people. And there I was, forty-four years later, sitting with my wife, children and grandchildren – several with black *kippot*, others with colored; some with *peyot* and some without – and many friends who are all dedicated to Judaism and deeply in love with it.

How did *that* happen?

I went to non-Jewish schools my entire life, dreamed of becoming a philosophy professor (Spinoza!), ended up in England's Gateshead Yeshiva, a bastion of *Haredi* Judaism, and received my rabbinical ordination from some of the greatest East European Roshei Yeshiva. I then moved to Yerushalayim where I discovered Avraham Joshua Heschel, Franz Rosenzweig, Martin Buber, Rabbi Avraham Yitschak HaCohen Kook,

Rabbi Mordechai Yoseph of Isbitza (the *Mei HaShiloach*), Rabbi Eliezer Berkovits, and many others. In addition, I continued to read extensively on general philosophy.

In Israel, as well as on my lecture tours, I have met with some of the finest religious thinkers. Many have become my best friends and taught at the David Cardozo Academy in Yerushalayim, which was started as a think tank/laboratory and teachers training college with what is now called a "Cardozian" flavor. With the help of my dear friend and former educational director, Rabbi Francis Nataf, the academy was born out of my personal religious experience, my meetings with great religious souls, and my education in Jewish and non-Jewish philosophies.

It was some of these thinkers who were approached by my wife and asked to write essays for my 60th birthday. The great majority of them kindly obliged. Some of the written pieces were of a very personal nature; others were more academic and spiritual.

Rabbi Francis Nataf carefully read each essay, and we then decided which ones to include in this anthology. Some of the contributors were requested to rewrite or re-edit their essays to make them more suitable for a compilation of scholarly writings. Others could not do so because of time limitations. Still others were not included because their essays belong to a different writing genre.

The David Cardozo Academy is an unusual place. It is unlike a typical training college where people are merely instructed. In our academy, all members can speak their minds and neither teachers nor students have to worry about fitting in. Both come from varied backgrounds and ideologies and are encouraged to share their personal and often emotional struggles with Judaism: the ups and downs in their own Jewish religious lives; their doubts and their certainties; their frustrations as well as their moments of spiritual exhilaration. This has led to the most intriguing revelations from the inner souls of some of the finest Jews whom we are blessed with today. Discussions and battles in the classroom can escalate to heated exchanges and explosive disputes, and they have greatly contributed to a better understanding of diverse religious positions and personalities.

Some of the essays in this anthology reflect these personal battles. Others are of high intellectual standing and bring new insights into the great Jewish heritage.

My thanks go to all the contributors; to Rabbi Francis Nataf for going over the entire manuscript; to Daniel Sheer, our executive director, who was instrumental in finalizing the project; to Mrs. Esther Peterman, our dedicated secretary; to my son-in-law, Rabbi Chanan Atlas, who has been directing our programs at the Interdisciplinary Center (IDC) Herzliyah and in Ramat Aviv; to all of our think tank members; to Debby Katz and Channa Shapiro for their editing.

Special thanks go to my dear friend and mentor, Rabbi Dr. Norman Lamm, chancellor and former president of Yeshiva University. His constant encouragement and contribution to this anthology are invaluable.

I owe many thanks to Mrs. Ann Newman of Detroit who made this publication possible. Sincere thanks to my dear friends Michael and Hila Kagan for their support of all our programs. As usual, the Aron and Betsy Spijer Foundation in Holland was of great help.

I thank my dear wife Freyda Rachel who, together with all our children (in-law), made this happen. Her love and dedication, as well as theirs, are beyond description.

Special thanks to Tzvi Mauer of Urim Publications who agreed to publish this volume.

Finally, I thank the Lord of the Universe for the many miracles He has done and continues to do for all members of our family, and for granting my wife and me the great blessing of watching them grow into mature and proud religious Jews. In fact, we have recently been blessed with two great-grandchildren! May it continue!

Nathan Lopes Cardozo
Yerushalayim,
Iyar 5772, April 2012

Rabbi Dr. Nathan Lopes Cardozo

# The Beth Midrash of Avraham Avinu: Tentative Thoughts Towards a Jewish Religious Renaissance[1]

I     IDEOLOGY AND PHILOSOPHY

## INTRODUCTION

IN THE LAST several years, many upheavals have taken place in Israel that no one could ever have imagined. These upheavals also have far-reaching consequences for Diaspora Jewry and could entirely change the situation of the Jewish people throughout the world. It is unclear where Israel and the Middle East are heading, and it will take some time before a more peaceful era will really emerge. Still, we must look beyond this. We must prepare Israel and its citizens for the time when it will become crucial to make decisions about their identity and their connection to Judaism. While that connection at this point in time is, to say

---

1   The following essay is based on an inaugural lecture which was given in 2005 by Rabbi Dr. Nathan Lopes Cardozo at the opening of the Beth Midrash of Avraham Avinu as part of the David Cardozo Academy in Jerusalem of which Rabbi Cardozo is the founder and dean.

the least, ambivalent, it will one day become a matter of such importance that the refusal to address it will no longer be an option. Not only will it be decisive as far as the spiritual condition of Israel is concerned, but it will actually determine whether the State of Israel will continue to exist. Much of the upheaval taking place at this hour is due to Israel's lack of a Jewish spiritual direction and imagination. It will soon become evident that the physical survival of the State of Israel will one day become *so* dependent on Judaism that it will be necessary to bring the great teachings of this tradition to the Jewish people in a completely different light.

This, however, is not only true of the State of Israel but of the Diaspora as well. Major changes are also needed there to guarantee that Judaism again becomes the central raison d'etre for Jews. If this does not come about, the Diaspora Jewish community will further disintegrate and, in the years to come, no longer be able to survive as an important force within world Jewry. This may ultimately lead to a change of American policy towards Israel with far-reaching consequences. We must be prepared for this hour. It is to meet these challenges that the David Cardozo Academy is primarily dedicated.

### THE BETH MIDRASH OF AVRAHAM AVINU

There are two kinds of schools within Judaism, two types of *Batei Midrash*: The Beth Midrash of Moshe Rabbenu and the Beth Midrash of Avraham Avinu. Although both of them are integral parts of Judaism, the difference between them is critical.

Maimonides, in *Hilchot Avodat Kochavim* (1:1–3), states that Avraham Avinu started a movement of *emunah* (religious faith). While Maimonides sees Avraham's discovery of God as the result of philosophical contemplation, other interpretations do not believe that this was a purely intellectual discovery, but rather the result of an existential encounter with God. What Avraham discovered is not so much that God exists but that "God is of no importance, unless He is of supreme importance" (Abraham Joshua Heschel).

This discovery touched Avraham's entire personality and transformed him into a different human being. It infused him with a great amount of wonder for all existence and deep concern for the wellbeing of mankind. This was not just a matter of the mind but of the heart. As such he became the driving force behind a movement which turned the world on its head. An irresistible movement in which *emunah* (in this instance, deep religious faith), and *chesed* (kindness), became the central pillars. *Emunah* filtered through his very personality and initiated him into an, until then, unknown world. The far-reaching effect of this transformation becomes clear when we remind ourselves of Rashi's comment that Avraham was able to "convert" many of his contemporaries.[2] Why was he so successful in doing so? Was it because of his great intellect? Surely this must have played a role, but there is little doubt that it was mainly due to the kind of personality he had become. Those who are touched by God do not just add another dimension to their personality, but are completely transformed into different people, whilst maintaining their own individuality. Consequently such people are able to connect with others in ways that are not available to those who do not share the experience of God.

This may illustrate Avraham's impact on his surroundings. Confronted by the kind of personality he was, the world around him stood re-created, trembling in a new light, radiating a new spectrum of *colors*.

## Not Textbooks but Text People

Abraham Joshua Heschel once observed that we do not need more textbooks but rather more "text people." The difference between a student and a disciple is that a student studies the text while a disciple studies the teacher. It is the *middot tovot* (the exalted characteristics), the integrity and sensitivity that are the central components of successfully teaching a religious tradition. This is the *grundnorm*, the foundation, on which the Beth Midrash of Avraham Avinu stands: To teach so as to transform and inspire an upheaval in the soul. It is here that we find the roots of Judaism in their most essential form. What we have to understand is that Judaism started as an existential

---

2   *Bereshit* 12:5.

movement in which all that man does, thinks, feels and says is touched by the spirit of God.

### INCUBATION TIME, JUDAISM'S NON-HALACHIC START

Judaism did not start as a halachic tradition, as we know it today. It took hundreds of years before the Sinai revelation, with all its halachic implications, could take place and halachah become possible. Much had to happen prior to such an exalted moment. Halachah had to grow out of the Abrahamic experience. It is only *then* that the Beth Midrash of Moshe Rabbenu became possible. This is the Beth Midrash of halachic discussion and halachic decision-making. But such a Beth Midrash must first of all be grounded in the existential *emunah* orientation of the Beth Midrash of Avraham Avinu.

It took hundreds of years before there was a possibility for the Sinai revelation to have any impact. There had to be an incubation time in which concepts of *emunah* took shape and in which the spiritual foundations of Judaism could grow. The grandeur of the Jewish traditional *weltanschauung* had to first mature and find its way through actual faith experiences before it could turn into a halachic way of living. The Sinai revelation can therefore only be seen as the *re*

*sult* of the Beth Midrash of Avraham Avinu, which found its solidification in the halachic foundation of Sinai. It is here that the faith experiences of the generations before Sinai, starting with Avraham, were transposed into a practical spiritual way of living.

We can call these moments "root experiences" (Emil Fackenheim) since they had to become epoch making events, making an inroad in the subconsciousness of the Jewish people, laying the foundations for the halachah to make use of when the time had come for it to be revealed. They would permit a glimpse of a sphere in which an unrestricted power, the root of halachah, is at work. They somehow needed to destroy the security of all conventional knowledge and undo the normalcy of all that is ordinary. It is, above all, the abiding astonishments of these moments which are crucial. They must make every natural explanation deepen the wonder of the moment. No knowledge or cognition should weaken their astonishing quality.

## Aggadah and Halachah

What is crucial to comprehend is that halachic Judaism will not survive if it is not constantly reminded of and consciously connected to Avraham Avinu's Beth Midrash, and this matter has become a major problem in today's Jewish religious community. By way of explanation, we must take notice of the relationship between the halachah and the world of aggadah, the non-halachic teachings of the Jewish tradition as found in the Talmud and Midrash. What is the difference between these components of the Jewish tradition?

Halachah can inform man on how to act in any given situation, but it cannot provide insight into the quality of a given act or a sense of spiritual change that is the result of the performance of the halachic act. Aggadah is there to allow the unseen to enter the visible world, to go beyond the realms of the definable, perceivable and demonstrable. It allows us to begin to comprehend the infinite through the use of finite acts. It is a religious metaphor to enable us to form mental images of the indescribable.[3] It unfreezes the frozen world of the halachah, revealing the Divine flow behind it.

It is here that we understand the crucial importance of the Beth Midrash of Avraham Avinu. It is through *this* Beth Midrash that the whole aggadic world was formed and from which it draws its spirit. While halachah is explained as the system of codes and regulations that govern life, the Beth Midrash of Avraham Avinu enables man to formulate a *weltanschauung*, a worldview which gives man the ability to function on an existential, philosophical level, rather than solely on a concrete level. Although halachah is quite flexible in its very nature, the world of aggadah deals with the sum total situation of man that transcends the inherent limitations of every legal

---

3 See also Hayyim Nahman Bialik, *Halakah and Aggada*, trans. Julius L. Siegel (New York: Bloch, 1923), and Abraham Joshua Heschel, *God in Search of Man* (New York: Farrar, Straus, and Cudahy, 1955), chaps. 32, 33.

system. The Beth Midrash of Avraham Avinu, as represented by the world of aggadah insures that Judaism stays ever fresh. It is a far cry from theology or catechisms, as seen in other religions, in which the truth, through the introduction of dogma, has once and for all been finalized.

Aggadah is the result of the existential struggles of the great men of faith, in which matters are tested, discussed, thought over and reformulated, with the knowledge that *no* final conclusions have ever been reached or *could* be reached. After all, the early Sages of Israel realized that any attempt to do so would fail because creeds and dogmas can only be indications of poor attempts to convey what cannot adequately be expressed. To argue that there are definite fundamentals of faith is to undermine authentic religious faith in the same way that people would try to argue that musical notes are the fundamentals of music. They are not – they are only directions for the musician to follow, showing the way, but never "*das ding an sich*" (the thing unto itself). Dogmas can never become walls – they can only function as windows into a world beyond definitions.

## The Problem of Pan-Halachah

It is here that we encounter a major crisis in today's Judaism. Over the years, the distance between the aggadah and the halachah, the Beth Midrash of Avraham Avinu and the Beth Midrash of Moshe Rabbenu, has been growing. By now we are encountering an independent halachic world that has turned its back on the world of Avraham Avinu and therefore shows signs of disintegration. This is evident by the fact that nearly everything has been turned into a halachic issue, a kind of "pan-halachah." Today's Judaism has become over-halachized, rejecting nearly any dimension in which the spirit of man requires more than just a practical response to his problems and challenges. It has finalized faith-positions.

For halachah to stay healthy and authentic, it must draw its spirit from of the world of faith, as represented by aggadah and beyond. Specifically, it is crucial that in the case of faith, matters should remain fluid and not become static. In matters of the spirit and the quest to find God, it is not possible to come to final conclusions. The quest for God needs to be open-ended so that the human spirit has the opportunity to find its way through trial and discovery. The very fact that today we encounter a serious attempt to see halachah as the *only* expression of Judaism and the constant attempt by some halachic authorities to bring the spirit of Judaism back to finalized dogmas is a clear indication that even in matters of *hashkafah*, (Jewish religious philosophy), those very authorities try to "halachize" matters of faith. By doing so they rob Judaism of its vital flowing spirit. *What needs to be understood is that halachah is the practical upshot of un-finalized beliefs, a practical way of living while staying in theological suspense.* Only in that way does Judaism not turn into a religion that becomes paralyzed in awe of a rigid tradition or evaporates into a utopian reverie. This dynamism can only come about when Jewish beliefs consist of a fluid liquid that halachah then transforms into a solid substance. Halachah needs to chill the heated steel of exalted ideas and turn them into pragmatic deeds without allowing the inner heat to be cooled off entirely. Jewish beliefs are like shafts, which dart hither and thither, wavering as though shot into the air from a slackened bowstring, while halachah is straight and unswerving.

The fact that this matter is no longer recognized as crucial to the future of Judaism is more than worrisome. A plant may continue in apparent health for some time after its roots have been cut, but its days are numbered.

We do not suggest dismantling the Judaism of halachah – such a move would be suicidal – but we maintain that to allow Judaism to develop into a dry legal system in which the spirit takes a backseat will result in rigidity to such an extent that its very purpose will be completely undermined.

## Embryonic Judaism

This issue is crucial to the future of Judaism and Jewish identity. Only when we rediscover its essential spirit and try to find the world of the spirit *behind* the halachah are there good reasons to believe that many will re-engage Judaism. To do this, we need to search for Judaism in its *embryonic* form, before it became solidified in the Sinai experience. We are convinced that, through this, halachah can retrieve much of its spiritual power, making it more attractive and more in tune with the spirit of man. We should not, after all, forget that for several hundreds of years the "de-Abrahamization" of Judaism has been set in motion. This is the result of many factors beyond the parameters of this essay. All that we can say is that leaders such as Maimonides, Nachmanides, the Ba'al Shem Tov, Rabbi Yisrael Salanter, Rabbi Mordechai Yosef of Isbitza, Rabbi Samson Raphael Hirsch and Rabbi Eliezer Berkovits in our own days, all luminaries of the Jewish spirit, realized this in their times. While they made major contributions to overcome this problem, the overall situation of the Jewish people has drastically changed, and new initiatives are necessary. This is, first of all, due to the fact that the establishment of the State of Israel ushered the Jewish people into a completely new situation including Jewish self-determination. Secondly, the radical challenge to the religious faith of the Jew due to the Holocaust experience has been overwhelming and demands new original ways to respond to that challenge.

### THE EXISTENTIAL MEANING OF THE TALMUD

To discover the spirit of the Beth Midrash of Avraham Avinu, it will be necessary to approach the Talmud in that very spirit. Instead of viewing the Talmud in its conventional way, through the eyes of the great *lomdim* (Talmudic scholars) and halachic authorities, it will be necessary to take an existential approach to the text through which one can discover the different *weltanschauungs* that are at the root of the great Talmudic halachic disputes, such as those between Abbaye and Rava, or Beth Hillel and Beth Shammai. While the approaches of *chakirot* (Talmudic investigations), *pilpul* (Talmudic casuistry) and plain *pshat* (meaning of text) are of great importance, we are convinced that, as a religious text, the Talmud holds the religious foundations of Avraham's Beth Midrash as well. There can be little doubt that when we encounter the disputes of the *Tanna'im* and *Amora'im* (early and later Sages) we can see patterns of *hashkafot* (philosophies), to which each *Tanna* or *Amora* was dedicated. Therefore, it should be possible to trace these *hashkafot* throughout all their halachic positions. Their attitudes towards life, philosophy, good and evil are reflected in their halachic rulings. As such, they are manifestations of the multi-*colored* revelation at

Sinai based on the Talmudic principle of *"eilu ve-eilu divrei Elohim chayim"* ("these and those are the words of the living God").[4]

God endowed each of the sages with a spark of the multifaceted dimensions of Torah, and it is *those* dimensions that are reflected in their halachic positions. Due to the fact that each of these positions has gone through an incubation time starting with the faith of Avraham and ultimately finding its way to Sinai, it is in the Oral Torah, of which the Talmud is the main representation, that we are able to retroactively discover the foundations of the Abrahamic faith. It is, after all, the Talmud that gives us insight into how halachic positions came into existence. The great debates are representations of the "pre-thoughts" of the great halachic minds, in which they reveal their thought processes in the incubation phase before they were finalized into halachic positions. It is here that minority opinions become of great importance, and it is for this reason that they are mentioned. As a kind of an archetypal mind set, these debates reveal the subconscious motivations of the multitude of thoughts and existential experiences of faith since the days of the Beth Midrash of Avraham Avinu.

### New Halachic Options

Although beyond the scope of his essay, we believe it important to mention that it will be necessary to take a much closer look at the many minority and deflective opinions in the Talmud. These halachic opinions, although not accepted as normative, may very well hold the key to the spiritual needs of tomorrow's Jews. They may even function as alternative options for those who are not able to find much inspiration in the established halachah of today. In an age in which personal autonomy has become crucial, it may be a wise move by the rabbis to allow people to choose between many Talmudic halachic options. This may help to advance the healthy growth of many young people who are searching for new spiritual possibilities in which they will feel entirely at home.[5] Since halachic positions are, as we mentioned

---

4   *Eruvin* 13b.

5   This may be an "Orthodox" alternative to Humanistic, Reform and

earlier, often the outgrowth of the different faith positions of the earlier
Sages, much broader and diverse "faith options" for our future generations
may be possible in which many more people will find a satisfactory and
inspirational halachic life style. This is especially of importance since human beings are made of such variant *colorful* psychological ingredients that
it is very hard to see how all of them can actually live by one and the same
religious code.[6] In this way, traditional Judaism could offer many authentic
and diverse forms of Judaism without denying the divinity of the Torah and
authenticity of the Oral and Rabbinic tradition.[7]

## To Inherit Faith and the Need for Warfare

Most important is to become aware of the fact that one cannot inherit faith
and that one cannot receive the Jewish tradition in conventional ways. One
must earn and fight for it. To experience and to have faith, one needs bold
initiative and not casual continuity. Religious practice must never be rote
but should constitute a happening. Jewish commitment can only be genuine
when we struggle and fight to constantly rediscover it.

Every generation must find its own way to God and henceforth to the
Jewish tradition. Religiously speaking, would this not be the case, there
would be little reason for that generation to exist. What, after all, is the
meaning of human existence if not to reveal another dimension of His
multi-*colored* world and Torah, and hence to understand itself better? To
repeat what others have said and not to add to it is to claim that all knowledge about Him and His Torah has been exhausted and to insist that we are
merely replicas of our forefathers. Not only would that set a limit to His
omnipotence and the Torah, but it would lead to the desecration of His

---

Conservative Judaism.

6    This is no doubt the reason why Judaism could never be entirely defined and
why several religious lifestyles such as the different Kabbalistic, non-Kabbalistic,
Chassidic and anti-Chassidic communities came into existence.

7    The earlier mentioned observation of the Sages that "These and those are the
words of the Living God" (*Eruvin* 13b) is a clear indication of such a position.

name. To be God is to be a Being of infinite possibilities and a great amount of pluralism, which is reflected in all His creations.

We are obligated to discover Him in new ways, and we must find ways to advance that goal. This is the task that the David Cardozo Academy has set for itself – discovering the new in the old. It is far from easy. Spinoza's (with whom we have our differences!) last line is his *Ethics*: "All noble things are as difficult as they are rare," is most relevant. Still, with much courage and hard work, we will be able to do so.

To be religious is to live in warfare. It requires constant novelty. The need to struggle with Judaism's foundations while knowing that one is touching on religious truth and the awareness that one will never fully acquire or comprehend its full meaning is the only way to a genuine religious recognition.

But how does one accomplish this goal?

## AVRAHAM AVINU AS AN ARCHETYPE

This goal, we believe, is only possible when we walk in the footsteps of Avraham Avinu and place ourselves in his position. We will never be able to do this in the full sense, but we can *rediscover* what he already found. Simultaneously, we should add our own personal self to this process so that we are not just rediscovering Avraham's earlier found faith but also giving it a highly personal dimension. Doing so, we must be careful not to obscure the real idea of growth, which is not to leave things behind us, but to leave things *inside* us. As such, it is the task of every Jew to discover the archetypal Avraham in himself or herself and add his or her own self.

Just as Avraham Avinu discovered the fundamental pre-halachic forms of the Jewish faith on his own, so must we. And just as he was open for the Divine to enter and to make contact with him while he was in the process of making his discovery, so must we place ourselves in similar conditions. What needs to be done is to retroactively rediscover what it was that set Avraham on his spiritual path. As mentioned before, Avraham was not so much the discoverer of God's existence as he was trying to find the way to *experience* God in the here and now. *We* too are able to experience this by carefully implementing the categories through which the Torah sees the world.

But it is not only the Avraham within us which we need to discover but also all the other early biblical personalities. Yitzchak and Ya'akov and afterwards the Twelve Tribes all contributed to the "faith community" and added new dimensions to this pre-halachic lifestyle. By studying their lives and trying to identify with them we must experience a "pilgrimage through souls" until we discover our own religious dimensions.

### In Order to Refer

It is here that we recognize the uniqueness of the biblical approach to life. As Abraham Joshua Heschel teaches, while the Greeks learned in order to comprehend, and modern man learns in order to use, the Jews learned in order to refer. Avraham was the first figure to experience the biblical view of all life. He discovered God's presence by recognizing the sublime and the wonder and realized that the meaning of things is greater than can ever be expressed, and that the existence of the sublime cannot be conveyed in adequate ways. It can be sensed in every drop of water or grain of sand, but the attempt to express this recognition in a purely rational way inevitably fails. It is only by means of radical astonishment that we realize that it is total mystery on all levels that surround us. Once this is spiritually recognized and has overtaken our very being, God can enter into a relationship with us in a way similar to how Avraham experienced his relationship with God.

It is not the mystery *itself* that sets us on that road, but, as in the case of Avraham, it is by asking ourselves *what to do* with that mystery and by recognizing that something is demanded from us in relationship to that mystery. In that way two things are accomplished – the experience of God and an understanding of the vital importance of halachah. It is in this respect that the Beth Midrash of Avraham Avinu and the Beth Midrash of Moshe Rabbenu meet. The fact that man is capable of recognizing the *mysterium* of all existence, and that, on a practical level he is able to react, investigate and enjoy all that he has discovered, is fundamental to the appreciation of halachah. Halachah is a practical response to the faculty of standing in wonder. The fact that one can only take account of this faculty but cannot account for it, confronts man with another inescapable question. Does he deserve this faculty? The crucial question is actually whether he can make a claim on this faculty. The shattering truth is that he does not deserve this faculty and that he could not possibly deserve it. Nobody ever earned the right to live, to love and to enjoy. They are gifts not rewards. This confronts man with an existential embarrassment. What is needed is to give man not just a possibility to discharge this debt towards God but to realize that he is in *need* of doing so, as this will be the only way by which he will attain his dignity.

One needs to obey the One who gave. Only in *that* way is there some symmetry between the Giver and the receiver. The recognition that all man's faculties and that all existence are rooted in mystery obligates. This recognition becomes law in the life of the Jew. This is central to our Academy.

## THE WONDER OF JUDAISM

But it is not just the wonder about this world or about the grain of sand; it is above all *the wonder of Judaism* that we need to rediscover. It is Judaism's phenomenal quality, its broadness, its ability to radically refresh the human spirit, its transforming strength and, perhaps above all, its healthy attitude towards life that must be recognized. Because Judaism is a religion that deals so much with the day-to-day minutiae, in which every small issue becomes a major one, the overall grand picture often gets lost. One must be able to see the forest through the trees. Jewish education must focus on the all-inclusive insights and values of Judaism and not just on its many details.

## WHAT IS AUTHENTIC?

Still, it is not only in response to our world that Judaism provokes wonder. We also need to be engaged in wonder at Judaism's struggles, its worries and its constant search for new ways to explain itself. To do this properly we will face some painful issues. How do we recognize what is authentic and what is not? We will be forced to question some components, which are now seen as essential parts of Judaism, but may, after all, not qualify as such. There is little doubt that certain concepts and values entered the Jewish tradition via the backdoor that do not really belong.

These concepts are mainly found in the elucidation of the Jewish tradition and not in its essential structure, although it may be argued that certain halachic decisions by (contemporary) rabbis also do not always reflect Judaism's basic values. This matter, however, is extremely complex because, as we have already mentioned, Judaism fails to have a catechism or even a universally accepted system of dogmas. Not even Rambam's "Thirteen Principles of Faith" were ever officially accepted as binding. It will therefore be hard to state unequivocally what makes Judaism into Judaism. Here, a return to the Beth Midrash of Avraham Avinu may give us some direction. As mentioned before, it is in its incubation phase that we may find some clarity about the fundamentals of Judaism.

However, it may sometimes be necessary to question some so-called Jewish beliefs and even to suggest that they may need to be replaced by others. The need to break idols and to take down sacred cows is in itself a Jewish task that started with Avraham Avinu himself. We should therefore not be afraid to do so or at least to discuss the possible need for this. This may raise some eyebrows in certain religious circles and we will be accused by some of being controversial, which may well be true, depending on what one means by controversy. *Great controversies are also great emancipations.* They often clarify and enhance essential philosophies behind great traditions. It may be true that matters like these may never get finally settled, and this may very well be a great blessing, as it will prove Judaism's multifaceted nature and its unwillingness to be pinned down on every issue. Still, it is undeniable that there are some powerful beliefs within Judaism that cannot be circumvented and without which the very structure of Judaism would collapse. Matters like these must be very carefully considered.

## COHERENT PLURALISM

For this reason, it is important to mention that within our Academy, opposing views will be expressed and that religious pluralism will no doubt be part of its *weltanschauung*. We will not attempt on every occasion to reconcile all these views although it will be necessary to do so when it contributes to a more comprehensive picture. Pluralism is no doubt part of the Jewish tradition. Looking into the creation, it is clear that God Himself is a pluralist. Still, this does not mean that everything goes. There must be coherence in pluralism for it to have any value. Pluralism itself has its rules. As in a Rembrandt painting, many *colors* contradict each other but, together and within a certain order, they create not just coherence, but a painting of unprecedented beauty.

## II     THE ACADEMY

### THERE IS NO GREATER FAILURE THAN NOT TRYING

It is out of this notion that my philosophy and this Academy have slowly emerged. It is a slow process and it is far from solidified. What this means is that many of my thoughts are still in flux and that I am still searching. It is for this reason that I consider my lectures far from ideal. They should be more creative, focused and challenging. It is for similar reasons that I am not yet satisfied with many aspects of our Academy. It has not yet found its full existential shape and in many ways it still lacks enough originality and has not yet fully incorporated the spirit of the Beth Midrash of Avraham Avinu. I call on our teachers and students to join me in developing our Academy as a worthy representation of the world of the Abrahamic faith, searching for the authentic spirit of Judaism. We must in every way possible stay away from intellectual and spiritual dullness. That in our search we will sometimes make mistakes is certain, but we should never forget that by shutting the door to all error, truth will be shut out as well. There is no greater failure than not trying.

I am fully aware that such an approach and a need for exploration are not for everybody. For some people there is no need for all this because they are satisfied with the more established way in which Judaism is being presented today. I fully understand that. Perhaps we are in need of people who are great in their *emunah* without requiring all these intellectual and spiritual pursuits. But, simultaneously, we cannot continue to believe that Judaism can spiritually and intellectually survive without the concept of *chiddush* (novelty). We also cannot ignore the need to elevate Judaism to new dimensions, provoked by a new world which, more and more, challenges us to ensure that our relationship with God remains our primary concern.

### THE STUDENTS AND THE TEACHERS, HEARING AND RESPONDING

To start a movement, we need disciples and young people who are prepared to jump, like Nachshon ben Aminadav into the Reed Sea, into the sea of uncertainty but who also come with strong *emunah* in the greatness of Judaism. To do so, we primarily need to create a new generation of rabbis and teachers, women and men who are thoroughly acquainted and imbued with the spirit of the Beth Midrash of Avraham Avinu, who live with a flame in their souls. To reach that goal we need to rethink the purpose of education, its dimensions, its challenges and the relationship between teachers and students.

As such we must ask ourselves two serious questions: First, what does it mean to be a student? And second, what does it mean to be a teacher? To answer these questions is far from easy. On a superficial level the student needs to learn the art of listening, while the teachers should learn how to not merely speak, but above all how to respond. But both listening and responding are indeed an art, entailing many crucial layers, dimensions and challenges. Listening does not only mean to listen "to what has been said" but also to "what is alluded to," to "that which remains unspoken," and to "that which cannot be expressed in words."

Judaism realized this fact long ago. It is for good reason that we sing when we learn Torah. There is the *niggun* (melody) to *lernen* (the Jewish way of learning), a tune that cannot be expressed with words. After all, words take on a completely new meaning when set to music. In singing we perceive what otherwise is beyond comprehension. It is the art of bringing heaven down to earth. It is reaching out to a realm that lies beyond the reach of verbal capacity. Words often become slogans, even idols. But music is the refutation of human finality. One needs to become smitten by music and never recover, and so it is with learning Torah. A sentence without a tone, without a musical quality, is like a body without a soul. The secret of a good sentence is the creation of a total quality that corresponds to the deeper meaning of words. A song is the expression of the soul's nakedness. And that is what the student needs to learn – to put the words of the teacher to a tune. The Hebrew word "*lishmoa*" means "to hear" the whole spiritual background of what is being said, both with words and in their absence.

The task of the teacher is to set the tone, the intonation of what needs to be heard. He is like the *chazzan,* becoming a commentator to the words he sings. He must make sure that his community sings what he initiates.

But not just that – the teacher must also respond to the questions that the student does *not* ask, does not know how to ask, but needs to ask and is often scared to ask. Many people are unaware of the deep questions they have. Often they are repressed or hidden. One of the major reasons is that people fear asking questions when the possible answers may challenge their lifestyles or attitudes. As Abraham Joshua Heschel once said, "Man is a questioner but he lost the questions." Perhaps we should add "because he *wanted* to lose the questions."

Indeed, the teacher's task is to rediscover the question that hovers over the mind and heart of the student, but of which the student may not be consciously aware and may even fear.

## The Struggle of the Teacher

What is just as important is that the teacher shows his student that he *himself* struggles with questions. In certain Jewish religious circles, especially in some outreach programs, we have created a cult, making the impression that the teacher has all the answers and is expected to have all the answers. Not only is this impossible, but it is also undesirable. Those who do not continue to search can never become authentic teachers because teaching can only take place in an atmosphere of constant questioning. *The quest for certainty paralyzes the search for meaning.* Uncertainty is the very condition that impels man to unfold his intellectual capacity. A philosophy of intellectual finality has disastrous consequences for any spiritual and intellectual growth.

Often the impression is made that one merely needs to ask the teacher and everything will fall into place, and problems will cease to exist. Anybody who studied the Jewish tradition knows that this attitude is a complete misrepresentation of this very tradition. It is the ongoing search for the truth that stands out and that is at the core of Judaism. The task of the teacher is to show the direction in which the answer could be found, but not to give a final answer. Even when the teacher feels that he has a comprehensive answer, he must try to make the student discover it on his own, guided by the teacher's suggestions. In such a way the class also turns into a think tank, an approach that is at the core of our Academy. The teacher should take the steering wheel but he should invite his co-travelers to join him and get involved in the steering. It is true that there is not always enough time in the classroom to do so, but at least there must be the possibility for the student to continue thinking and arguing about that which he is learning beyond the classroom.

While it is true that in the sciences there is often the possibility of definite answers, this is not true in religious studies, general philosophy or spirituality. This may not be to the liking of all students, as some would like to see religion as a hardcore discipline not much different from science, but to those who have a keen insight into matters of faith and philosophy, it is clear that the only way to stay spiritually honest is to understand that matters like faith cannot be empirically tested. Would such a test be possible, much of the value of faith would be undermined. This is indeed the risk.

*There is no authentic life choice that is risk free.* All such decisions entail dangers and uncertainties. To live a life of faith is to be prepared to live a committed religious life due to an inner belief of the heart and not because there is absolute empirical certainty. I find it altogether scary when students tell me after a lecture that "everything has fallen into place." Instead, there is a constant need for questioning and rethinking one's beliefs, which is a crucial component of teaching. As I mentioned before, in many ways religion should be warfare – a fight against the indolence and callousness that stifle inquiry and make drifting with the current into the standard.

## THE UNHEARD MUSIC

There are, however, other problems. A teacher can be misunderstood. This may be due to the lack of clarity or the lack of sufficient explanation. There may be too much emphasis on one dimension of a topic and too little on another. But there is also a kind of misunderstanding that is not the result of a mistake by the teacher or a lack of proper understanding by the student but rather the result of a complete misrepresentation on an altogether different level. This misunderstanding is due to the fact that there is an existential "background" to nearly all teaching. It is this kind of latent background music that is unheard but keenly felt. It has been created over many years through discussions, observations, spirituality and emotional content accumulated around a teacher, the composition of the teacher's specific spiritual milieu. It is like a seashell to which you can apply your ear and hear the perpetual murmur of the distant waves that, while it cannot be fully identified, encompasses your whole being.

It is necessary for the student to hear this music while listening to the teacher, as it creates the spiritual frame in which any lecture takes place. If one does not experience this, one is incapable of understanding what the teacher is trying to convey. As such, there is the unique and immediate music that belongs to a particular lecture and there is the "sub-music," or underlying music, that runs through all lectures, whatever the topic. There is music on the surface and there is the music in the background. This is the task of a real school – to create music that plays and is heard throughout all the lectures. A particular lecture may not even touch consciously on this kind of music and has no intention of doing so, but it will still be transformed through this music. It is the general philosophy of the school, which is felt throughout, and it may give a completely different meaning to every lecture. Suddenly, everything stands in a different light and overthrows conventional interpretations.

## Leonard Bernstein and Glenn Gould

I am reminded of a famous controversy between two of the greatest musicians of our generation: Leonard Bernstein and Glenn Gould. It centered on Brahms's Piano Concerto No. 1 in D minor and took place at Carnegie Hall in New York on April 6, 1962. Uncharacteristically, Leonard Bernstein felt the need to speak to his audience before he conducted this concert in which Glenn Gould would be the pianist. His reason was that he totally disagreed with Glenn Gould's interpretation of the piano concerto. Bernstein then asked the rhetorical question of why he did not have one of his students conduct the concert. He responded that he was utterly fascinated with Gould's interpretation and wanted to be part of it. It had become a completely new musical experience and, as such, most innovative and refreshing, although Brahms, according to Bernstein, never had such an interpretation in mind! This is what musicians call the sportive element in music. What Gould did was set a completely new background to every part of the Brahms's piano concerto. All parts were set to a new tone, although not a note was changed. The outcome was not just masterful but thoroughly novel.

It is this ingenuity that needs to take place in a classroom. The words of the teachers may be conventional and, as such, of little novelty, but in light of a new spiritual setting, every word takes on an utterly new dimension.

One may argue that matters such as these are not really crucial to human existence and that we can do without Gould's interpretation. However, for those who understand that life is not about surviving but rather about constant re-creation and the need for adventure and experimentation so as to discover new dimensions within life, nothing is of greater importance. Living beings constantly move and grow, whereas, organic matter that fails to grow, shift and move, decays and eventually dies. So it is with man's spiritual life. The role of religion and those who teach is to facilitate the blossoming of the human soul and prevent man from descending into spiritual stagnation. This is the deeper meaning of Spinoza's observation that all noble things are as difficult as they are rare.

One must realize, however, that initially the student will not hear the music. His existential ear will have to become sensitive and slowly open up to this kind of music. The murmur, the spiritual undercurrent, must be activated and emerge from its shell before it can transform the student. This can only occur when the teacher himself, or herself, has been touched by this kind of spirit and has tapped into the music.

## ON BEING CONTROVERSIAL

There is little doubt that some will see our Beth Midrash of Avraham Avinu as controversial. Novelty has always been seen as a threat. The new always carries with it a sense of violation, a kind of sacrilege. Most people are more at home with that which is dead than with that which is different. This is most unfortunate. But to help Judaism move forward, it will sometimes be necessary to challenge well-established religious beliefs, and we will do so when we consider them problematic in relationship to a broader understanding of Judaism. Simultaneously, we may propose new insights that we believe will benefit authentic Judaism. We sincerely believe that such insights are completely within the framework of Judaism and, as I expressed earlier, of the greatest importance to the future of Judaism and its living spirit.

At the same time, we are aware of the great dangers that accompany the introduction of novel concepts. We should not be overanxious to encourage innovation in cases of doubtful improvement, where a brand-new mediocrity may replace well-established excellence.

After all, one does not discover new lands without consenting to lose sight of the shore from where one begins one's journey. Conversely, we should neither forget that men of new insights were often initially regarded as foolish only to earn acknowledgement of how right they were at a later date.

## RELIGIOUS KNOWLEDGE

What has been totally forgotten in many religious and rabbinic circles is that it is not simply the accumulation of facts that builds enduring knowledge. It is the complete identification with the *implied* meaning of that knowledge, its renovation and its continued development. *We must be careful not to drown in our knowledge and, because of that, become fearful of introducing new insights.* In that way, the simple accumulation of knowledge can suffocate us and prevent us from breathing fresh air. Such possibilities are not only unfortunate, but they go to the core of Judaism. We must be careful not to embalm Judaism, and claim that it is alive because it continues to maintain its external shape.

### MISGUIDED SCHOLARSHIP

What is just as important, if not more so, is to state that one should not approach Judaism as an academic discipline and deal with its sources in a purely scholarly way. We are profoundly unhappy that so much Jewish scholarship focuses on questions of philology, archaeology, or comparative studies without trying to understand the message and *religious* depth of the ancient texts. Sometimes one gets the impression that scholars, while reading and dissecting a text, are overtaken by a desire to kill it and its meaning instead of reviving it. This is a great tragedy. The academic world must realize that the need for "objectivity" in reading religious texts is a hopeless undertaking. Religious texts are rooted in a completely different world and their value will not be appreciated through this kind of scholarly approach. It is somehow like people who are *color*-blind looking at colors and consequently claiming that *colors* do not exist.

We also humbly protest against scholars who pronounce verdicts on authentic Judaism while having insufficient Jewish knowledge to do so. It is most disturbing that while they would not dare do so in regards to other disciplines, they take the liberty of doing so when discussing Judaism because of some superficial familiarity with its sources. The fact that this specifically happens among Jewish intellectuals of great standing is all the more disturbing. Just as the State of Israel is often judged by double standards, so too is Judaism. This is most unfortunate.

This does not mean that we deny that there is an important place for academic studies in relationship to Judaism, but it requires the scholar to have great humility and a sincere openness to its unique *religious* meaning.

## THE AWE OF HEAVEN

Let us return to perhaps the most important aspect of the Beth Midrash of Avraham Avinu – that is the issue of *yirat Shamayim*, and *middot tovot*. One of the greatest tragedies in Jewish education is that we have separated the teaching of Judaism from encouraging our youth to feel the presence of God in one's personal life and the constant privilege to transform oneself into a more dignified and sensitive personality. While we give much attention to Jewish knowledge and the correct understanding of, for example, the commentaries of Rashi and Tosafot, we fail to teach our students the insight that such knowledge has genuine value only when it leads to a greater awareness of God and a deeper appreciation for our fellow man.

Nobody can deny that Judaism finds itself today in a crisis that threatens to have devastating consequences. Instead of Judaism growing upwardly, it is becoming corpulent, growing in a horizontal way. The growth of adherence to halachah in the last few decades has clearly not been accompanied by a true religious revival. Genuine religiosity has nothing to do with the Yiddish expression of *frumkeit*.

This mistake is partially a result of the fact that we are sometimes more concerned about halachah than about God. At the same time, it is not uncommon that the *mitzvot bein adam l'Makom* are considered to be far more important than the *mitzvot* related to our fellow man. While it is common practice to emphasize *chumrot* (stringencies) and to encourage a strict observance of Shabbat and kashrut, we rarely see a parallel intensity when dealing with matters of human relationships. We may decide that we will only partake of *glatt* (strictly) kosher food, but we have forgotten that it may be more important that we are "*glatt* kosher" when it comes to the commandments regulating our relationship with our neighbor. Rabbi Joseph Breuer of the Washington Heights Kehilla in New York used to say: "Not just *glatt* kosher but also *glatt-yosher*, extremely *honest.*"

### As a Sefer Torah

When teaching these matters, we must make sure that we, as teachers and rabbis, reflect in our personal conduct that which we propose and teach in the classroom, as there is truly no better education than example. Thought and practice must illuminate each other. The mark of a *sefer kodesh* (holy book), says Rabbi Tzadok of Lublin, is that its author and the content of his book are one and the same. A teacher must be a living Sefer Torah and imbue his or her students with the aspiration that one day they will be able to live the kind of life that their teacher represents.

True, even the best teachers among us may sometimes fail, but we must immediately try again. A *Sefer Torah* which is *pasul* (ritually invalid), is still a Sefer Torah even when it needs *tikkun* (repair). A Sefer Torah must not be desecrated even when it cannot be used in the synagogue service. So it is with man. Even when man fails, he is still a "Sefer Torah." The greatest tragedy is when we stop longing to become a living "Sefer Torah." As long as the dream is alive, the changes necessary to reach that goal are within our reach.

This yearning has a direct relationship with Torah learning and with comprehending the Jewish tradition. One of the most remarkable teachings of Judaism is that it claims that one cannot think with clarity or properly understand a *sugya* (passage) in the Talmud when one's characteristics are not in tune with the honesty of the text. When one lives a bent life, one's thoughts are also skewed. All of us have the obligation to scrutinize ourselves and rebuild ourselves constantly. The need for self-discipline, humility, the pursuit of truth, the love for one's neighbor and the abhorrence of the hollow pursuit of honor, are not just theoretical ideals but values that, in accordance with Jewish tradition, must be implemented not only in the grand events of our lives but specifically in our most trivial moments.

Too few people realize that the way we close a door without properly looking to see if there is someone following us, whether we walk a guest to the door or not, whether we fold a towel after using it or leave it for another to pick it up, are the actions that reveal much about our inner self. Because all behavior takes place in the presence of God, nothing is insignificant and even our trivialities should aspire to holiness.

## Jewish Sensitivity

I am reminded of the illustrious "Alter of Kelm," Rabbi Simcha Zissel Braude, one of the towering personalities in the Mussar movement in the nineteenth century, who, while walking in the street, asked: "How one can walk on a road that has been built at the expense of much suffering by others?" On another occasion, the rabbis of Kelm used to disembark from their carriages so as to make it easier on the horses to reach the top of the hill in accordance with the prohibition of *tza'ar ba'alei chayim* (causing pain to animals). Refinement, *adinut haNefesh* (sensitivity to the soul and proper behavior), stood at the top of their spiritual agenda and everything was done in pursuit of this goal.

## Trivialization and *Zerizut B'menucha*

In our days the world experiences a trivialization of the human language. As religious Jews we must re-introduce refinement of language and the need for eloquent speech. "A man is hid under his tongue," says the proverb.

We must also practice *zerizut b'menucha* (eagerness to do a mitzvah while remaining calm). *Zerizut* (eagerness), after all, is a matter of the heart and the head and not of the feet. All of this is related to the famous verse in which God states: "I command you *today*." (*Devarim* 6:6) This, our commentators tell us, is not to say that we should see the *mitzvot* as given every day, but rather it must be understood as if each mitzvah was given today *for the first time.* One should never be content with previous understandings or experiences of a mitzvah. There is a need to constantly deepen a commandment, to make it new, and just like Franz Rosenzweig responded, when he was asked whether he used to lay *tefillin,* we must be able to answer: "Not yet!"

## Torah Leaders

There is a need to produce great Torah leaders, who fully understand this great challenge and lead the Jewish tradition back to its former *living* spirit.

Most "Torah leaders" of today are no longer aware of the tremendous spiritual challenges the Jewish people are encountering at this hour. They will only be able to do so when they are willing to look beyond the world of halachah and search for its spiritual components, which are to be found in the Beth Midrash of Avraham Avinu. As indicated by several *Midrashim*, Avraham's uniqueness was defined by his willingness to confront the enormous challenges of his generation and deal with them head on. He did not run away from them but instead studied them carefully and considered all the options of how to respond to them. He realized that he could only help his generation when he felt its pain as if it was his own. After all, one can only help one's fellowmen when one goes down to them and lifts them up. But we must be aware that just like a bird may think that it is an act of kindness to lift a fish in the air, so rabbinical leadership may be choking its followers thinking that they provide them with spiritual oxygen. The problem today is that most leaders are merely following out in front while failing to marshal the way we are going.

Simultaneously, leadership which does not show any doubt about its competence and which is incapable to voice its own religious reservations cannot be men of faith. They are but men of creed who cannot touch a soul in doubt. Avraham had little authority but a lot of authenticity. He was a great doubter and therefore authentic.[8] While authority is always dangerous, selfish, inexplicable, and strives on mysterious affairs in a dark privacy without explaining itself, authenticity takes place by daylight and is so genuine that one can't deny it when finding oneself in its presence.

It is the task of the *yeshivot* to introduce our future leaders to a different kind of curriculum than what they offer at this moment. They must make them realize that Jewish leaders need a much broader knowledge of Judaism than that which the best conventional *yeshivah* education can offer.

It would be wise to remind ourselves of an observation by the aforementioned Franz Rosenzweig: "... in being Jews, we must not give up anything, not renounce anything, but lead everything back to Judaism .... This

---

8   See, for example, Rabbi Mordechai Yosef of Isbitza, *Mei HaShiloach* (Jerusalem: Mishor Publishers, 1990), I:29 and II:19.

is a new sort of learning – a learning for which in these days ... he is the most apt who brings with him the maximum of what is alien."⁹ There is a need to reshape anything that is considered alien into a form that facilitates a better and deeper understanding of Judaism. This is a new kind of *teshuvah* (repentance). *Teshuvah* is not just a stage in life but a program for life. It is a process and not just an attempt to rectify something that has been out of order. It is a spiritual condition that belongs to the mechanism of Judaism itself.

For great Torah scholars to become leaders and Gedolei HaDor, there is a need to understand that which makes Rembrandt different from all other painters. What all of them take as subject of their canvases, Rembrandt uses as the raw material of his vision. Where the others see facts, he perceives hidden connections that link his preternatural sensibility to reality and transports all that he has religiously from the universal creation to the plane of a new creation. Without this sensibility there is no authentic art of the quality required. Rembrandt did not care what others had to say about his art and often violated the request of his clients. What he cared about was his inner liberty to go his own way. He realized that the purpose of art is *to disturb* and not to produce finished works, but to stop in exhaustion in the middle, for others to continue. Art has to be an autobiography of a human being in progress. Without this knowledge, no great Talmudic scholar can ever become a leader. Only when he becomes an artist can he create Torah law or give advice.

It is for this reason that our Academy is also a kind of think tank. We hope to take our students on roads not yet (or not enough) travelled. We want them to be part of the endeavor discussed here and to participate in our search. This mission demands courage and *yirat Shamayim,* and we will do our best to live up to both of these traits. Whenever possible, we will take Avraham Avinu as our example.

The Jewish people are standing at a crossroads that they have never experienced before. While Jews have often lived from crisis to crisis, they have

---

9   See "On Jewish Learning" in Nahum Glatzer, *Franz Rosenzweig, His Life and Thought* (New York: Schocken, 1970), 241.

never, since the destruction of the second Beit HaMikdash, experienced a situation in which they found their way back to their homeland and, having arrived there, become confused as to why they strove to go there in the first place.

Only when we drastically change direction and make sure that the educational approach of the teacher incorporates that which I have brought to the reader's attention, will it be possible for something of enduring importance to take place. We should not forget what Abraham Joshua Heschel said, which I quoted earlier: "We have too many textbooks and too little text people." Ultimately it is the integrity of the teacher that will be able to bring real change. We must prevent the study of Judaism from becoming solely an academic undertaking. We must make sure, by example, that it is an encounter with the world of religious experience which brings about a transformation in man. Only in that way can we make Judaism irresistible.

No doubt, this is far from easy. Indeed, "all noble things are as difficult as they are rare." But just as Avraham understood that there is no success without hardship, so too, there is no Judaism without the realization that many may succeed by what they know, or do, but few by what they *are*. It is only in the art of authentic being that there is a real future for the religious man.

Rabbi Dr. Norman Lamm

# Notes on the Concept of *Imitatio Dei*[1]

UNLESS IT IS granted that there is some common element that binds Creator and creature, some minimal resemblance between God and man that cries out for fulfillment, then He is so totally "other" that He does not really matter. If God and man cannot meet on the plane of moral character, then religion is completely deistic, man is utterly alone, and faith is nothing more than unprovable assent to a set of metaphysical propositions totally devoid of ethical consequences. Such a philosophical religion is unthinkable to the Hebrew mentality.

> It hath been told thee, O man, what is good and what the Lord doth require of thee: only to do justly and to love mercy and to walk humbly *with* the Lord thy God.　　　　　　　　　　　　　　　　　　　　　　　(*Michah* 6:8)

The ideals of justice and mercy and humility are not rationally arrived at or supported by man independently of his religious affirmations. Nor are they solely disembodied commands issued forth magisterially by the

---

1　This essay, which appeared many years ago in a now inaccessible volume, is dedicated to my dear friend and esteemed colleague, Rabbi Dr. Nathan Lopes Cardozo who is living proof of the concept of *imitatio Dei*.

Absolute out of the infinite recesses of His celestial heights. They are an invitation to man to *participate* in the Divine activity. God both appeals and commands. He tells us what is both "good" and "required": that we act "*with the Lord thy God*." (The phrase may be read to apply to all three antecedent elements – "to do justly" and "to love mercy" as well as "to walk humbly.")

The passage from *Michah* is reminiscent of the words of Moses at the end of *Devarim* 10:

> And now, Israel, what doth the Lord require of thee, but to fear the Lord thy God, to walk in all His ways and to love Him ... For the Lord thy God ... doth execute justice for the orphan and the widow and loveth the stranger ...

Michah uses the verb "*doresh*" – "require" or "demand"; Moses uses the gentler "*sho'el*" – "ask." Like Michah, Moses sees God as the model for human conduct. At the very beginning he indirectly implies the "withness," or fellowship, of man and God (*sho'el me'imach*, which literally means "asks from with you," rather than the standard *sho'el mi'mach*, "asks of you") and then explicitly commands the imitation of God: "to walk in all His ways." By means of the imitation of God, we learn to do that which neighborly love itself cannot teach us: to love the *stranger* and plead for the outcast and the disadvantaged. Thus, the retort of Ben Azzai to R. Akiva – who held that "thou shalt love thy neighbor as thyself" is "a great principle in the Torah" – that "'this is the book of the generations of man ... in the likeness of God made He him' [*Bereshit* 5:1] is a greater principle than that."[2]

The concept of man's creation in the Divine Image implies not only a new identity for man, but the possibilities of self-transformation. The Image immanent within him both represents and challenges him to transcendence. To put it pithily, the *imago Dei* is linked with *imitatio Dei*.[3]

---

2  *Sifra* 4. Both here and in JT *Nedarim* 9:4, only the first half of the verse is cited, but it is standard practice in rabbinic literature to quote the beginning of a verse when the middle or end is intended as the proof-text. So Ra'avad to *Sifra*, *loc. cit.*, and see *Torah Shelemah* to *Bereshit* 5:1, no. 1.

3  The concept of Imitation, of *hepu theo*, "go after God," was known to Plato. See

The Image is more than a metaphor for a metaphysical deposit of dignity which magically calls man forth out of the stifling uniformity of cosmic naturalness into a special place in Divine providence. It is a concept filled with ethical content, and one that is intimately connected with the supplementary notion of the Imitation of God.

God, for the Jewish mind, is a demanding, commanding, requiring, inviting, pleading God, and His implorations are directed to man to be "with" Him, to "follow" Him, to "walk in His ways." Anything less yields a God incommunicado, a *Deus absconditus*, eternally incarcerated in His absoluteness, and man abandoned to cosmic solitude, his religion ethically neutral and morally dumb, and hence spiritually sterile. Such a Deity cannot be imitated. He is more abstract and more sophisticated than the idolater's fetish, but not fundamentally different. Indeed, the psalmist conceives of the "imitation" of the pagan god as a curse: "They have ears but hear not; noses have they but they smell not ... neither speak they with their throat. They that make them *shall be like unto them*; yea, every one that trusteth in them" (*Tehillim* 115: 6–8). Not so with the personal God of Judaism. Image and Imitation are the bridge on which mortal man and his infinite Creator meet. And it is this bridge, this linkage, which gives Judaism its distinctive moral practicality.

The relationship between Image and Imitation must be approached in the context of a further analysis of the Image-idea. Upon reflection, it will

---

*Republic* 613a, *Theatetus* 176b, and elsewhere. Philo (*Migr.* 24, 132) quotes Plato approvingly, adding as a proof text, "And Abraham came near to God" (*Bereshit* 18:23), i.e., Abraham assimilated the Divine quality of pity and thus pleaded for Sodom. A similar interpretation is offered by the medieval Talmudist R. Eliezer of Metz, *Sefer Yereim* 3. The idea was known to both Islamic and Jewish philosophers. For references, see Sarah O. Heller Wilensky, "Isaac Ibn Latif – Philosopher or Kabbalist?," *Jewish Medieval and Renaissance Studies*, ed. A. Altmann (Cambridge: Harvard University Press, 1967), 190ff. See too Solomon Schechter, *Aspects of Rabbinic Theology* (New York: Schocken, 1961), chap. 13.; Harry A. Wolfson, *Philo: Foundations of Religious Philosophy in Judaism, Christianity and Islam*, 3rd ed. (Cambridge: Harvard University Press, 1962), II.194–96.; David S. Shapiro, "The Doctrine of the Image of God and *Imitatio Dei*," *Judaism* (Winter 1963), 69 ff.

be seen that there are two supplementary notions, or moments, in this concept. The first connotes an irreducible, ontically real, and finished quality: man's worth and dignity and separateness from the rest of creation derive from his spiritual nature – whether "spiritual" be defined as Power, Reason, or Freedom – which in turn derives from the Divine Source of all spirituality. The value-generating Image is a *character indelibilis* in man; it is irrevocable and uniform and cannot be manipulated by any utilitarian calculus. All men, without distinction, are created in this Image. Hence, murder – no matter of whom, no matter what his moral disposition – is punishable by death (*Bereshit* 9:6).[4]

The second moment is the capacity for spiritual growth, the infinite potential of man for self-transcendence and moral improvement. The first is indicative, it speaks of a gift. The second is imperative and speaks not only of a Divine gift but of a human duty: God is not only the prototype *from* whence I derive, but that *to* which I am bound to go, the model to which I must conform. We may distinguish between the two by referring to the first element as "*tzelem*," "Image," and to the second as "*demut*," "Likeness." Image is ontological, Likeness is teleological.

It is noteworthy that Ben Azzai, in the passage mentioned above, was discriminating in the particular verse he chose to counterpose his "greater principle" to R. Akiva's "great principle" of neighborly love. He did *not* cite any of the various verses referring to *tzelem*, "image," in chapter 1 of *Bereshit*, but selected, rather, chapter 5:1: "in the *likeness* of God made He him." Likeness, or *demut*, the companion concept of Image, or *tzelem*, more pronouncedly implies similitude (and the consequent imperative to realize it). "Image" suggests a grant of value as an impersonal gift. "Likeness" immediately connotes shared qualities, something in which both participate in common, a potentiality waiting to be actualized.[5]

---

4   See Maimonides *Guide for the Perplexed* 1:1, and cf. Commentary of Abarbanel, *ad. loc.*, who suggests the absolute, uniform nature of Imagehood.

5   Interestingly, the recently discovered *Targum Yerushalmi*, a pre-Christian Aramaic translation of the Pentateuch, renders "*tzelem*" itself as "*demut*" or "*demu*." Similarly, *Targum Pseudo-Jonathan b. Uziel* translates *tzelem*, "Image," as *deyokna*,

Image and Likeness each symbolizes another *type* of man.[6] Yet

---

"Likeness" (see Altmann, *loc. cit.*). See too *Mechilta de–R. Simeon bar Yohai*, cited and expanded upon by R. Ya'akov Zvi Meklenburg, *HaKetav v'HaKaballah* to *Bereshit* 1:26. In terms of practical morality, *demut* is more significant than *tzelem*.

The distinction here made between Image and Likeness was apparently antici- pated by the second-century Irenaeus, bishop of Lyons. His theme has been echoed by other Eastern Church Fathers, and in various forms has been repeated by modern theologians, such as (the Protestant) Friedrich Schleiermacher, and (the Orthodox) N. Berdyaev and P. Bratsiotis, and in our own day has been appropriated by John Hick in his *Evil and the God of Love*. However, there are significant differences between the Irenaen exegesis and the one I am here suggesting. For Irenaeus and those who fol- low him, the distinction serves the purpose of an eschatological anthropology, as an alternative to the Augustinian doctrine of the Fall. Image, for them, represents man's present spiritual value as a rational and free being, while Likeness, or similitude, re- fers to man's longing and striving for God, which will be culminated in the eschaton. But here a typically christological element enters – the incarnation is held up as the eschatological fulfillment. Thus, Schleiermacher (who, although he does not quote Irenaeus in this respect, yet follows him in his thinking) speaks of "the first Adam" and "the second Adam," the first referring to the biblical Adam, who possessed the potentiality for full God-consciousness (equivalent to Image), and the second Adam, identified by Schleiermacher as Jesus, in whom these spiritual potentialities were sup- posedly actualized (equivalent to Likeness). This pattern is adopted by Hick, too (*op. cit.,* 290). However, the two terms "Image" and "Likeness" are being used here in a dif- ferent sense, and not only because, of course, no christological reference is intended. My point of departure is not anthropological and eschatological but personal, ethical, and immediate. The growth from Image to Likeness is charged to each individual, not to the race as a whole. It is the immediate source for each person's duty or duties, and cannot be accelerated or impeded by the intrusion of extraneous soteriological ele- ments. It therefore does not lend itself to any type of *heilsgeschichte* or any modified doctrine of the Fall or of fallenness, such as Hick has so brilliantly essayed.

6   These two moments of Image and Likeness may be read as corresponding to "Adam the first" and "Adam the second" in Rabbi Joseph B. Soloveitchik's great essay, "The Lonely Man of Faith," in *Tradition* (Summer 1965: vol. 7, no. 2). These two types derive from the two accounts of creation in *Bereshit*. Note that the first verse in the first account, telling of the creation of man (1:26), speaks of both Image and Likeness, but that immediately thereafter (1:27) we read only of *tzelem*, not *demut*. Adam the first reflects Image, the charismatic spiritual endowment, or "dignity," which raises him above the natural order only so as to permit him to confront it as controller and

existentially rather than typologically, Image and Likeness are in a reciprocal relation to each other. One implies the other. The meaning of each becomes clear in the existential human situation which calls for moral decisions. I confront my fellow man and have the options of either hurting him or doing him good. When I acknowledge that *he* is possessed of the Image of God, I will not hurt him. It is *his* Image which controls my behavior. His Imagehood imposes certain minimal restraints upon me. Simultaneous with this consideration of his objective metaphysical worth is my own subjective awareness that *I* am created in God's *Likeness*, that it is imperative for me to act in a certain manner towards him – with compassion and concern and forgiveness – in imitation of my Creator. The Image within my neighbor gives him, in my eyes, juridical protection against my overreaching and concupiscence. The Likeness of myself generates concern for his well-being, over and above the ethico-legal restraints that flow from his Image status: the *lifnim mi-shurat haDin*, supererogatory conduct. Furthermore, Image endows my neighbor with value in my eyes in terms of my relationship with him, urging upon me that course of action which will benefit him or, at least, not injure him. It is an act of *goodness* toward my neighbor, created in the Divine Image, and in this sense, it is subject to some of the same limitations that circumscribe neighborly love (a theme I have developed elsewhere). Likeness, however, with its corollary of Imitation, demands *rightness*, my emulation of God's moral attributes over and beyond those of relationship which can be subjected to the utilitarian criterion.

Unlike Image, which is constant and indelible, Likeness is fluid and dynamic and can, therefore, be consciously denied fulfillment and subverted.

---

manipulator; but he remains, as Rabbi Soloveitchik puts it, part of the "natural community." Adam the second reveals the Likeness (although *Bereshit* 2 speaks neither of *tzelem* nor of *demut*, its noetic content indeed refers to the latter, which term is used exclusively in the summary given in 5:1), aspiring to fellowship with God, to the redemptive order, thus forming a "covenantal community." The togetherness with God implied in Likeness must result in a normative ethico-moral message in which men open up to each other, even as God steps out of His forbidding transcendence and reveals Himself to man.

The Sages of the Talmud thus speak of guilt as issuing from the inversion of the Likeness (*demut deyokno*) through sins committed by man.[7]

How is the Likeness to be fulfilled and its frustration or abortion avoided? By "walking in His ways," the Imitation of God. Likeness leads to *imitatio Dei*, which is its fulfillment and realization. It is Imitation which actualizes the moral potential of Likeness, spelling out the plentitude of its significance.

Likeness strains for release, and Imitation, breaking the chains, leads Likeness to the adventure of moral and spiritual growth, urging man on to the unattainable goal of God-likeness. It points to the distant actuality, which man can only approach asymptotically.

The sixteenth-century Safed mystic, R. Moses Cordovero, hints at this process in the opening sentences of his immortal little volume of Kabbalistic ethics, *Tomer Deborah*:

> It is proper for man to imitate his Creator, thereby entering into the mystery of the supernal Form: the Image and the Likeness.

In other words: the Imitation of God achieves for man the fulfillment of the Likeness implanted in him *in potentia*. One thinks of the demented Ophelia who, in *Hamlet*, cries out, "Lord, we know what we are, but know not what we may be." *Imitatio Dei* is the process of actualization of the *imago Dei* of Likeness, "what we may be."

The motivation for this urge for Imitation is love. A Midrashic Rabbi explains it by saying that God is like a king who sanctifies (marries) a wife (Israel) and says to her, "Since you are my wife, my glory; therefore, be holy even as I am holy."[8]

---

7 *Mo'ed Katan* 15b. But it cannot be completely abrogated, as the Christian scholastics and, later, Reformers maintained. Insofar as *demut* is dependent upon *tzelem*, which as a *proprium* is undeniable and irreversible, it too cannot be lost or removed, but it may be defaced or "turned upside down" as the Rabbis declare (ibid.).

8 *Tanh.*, ed. Buber, *Vayikra* 37a. (Other metaphors are: a father and his children – *Vayikra R.* 24; as clothing that embraces a man's loins – *Tanh.*, *loc. cit.* 37b; as the retinue of a king and the king – *Sifra* to *Vayikra* 19:2).

What is meant by the Imitation of God? *Sifre*, one of the earliest
Rabbinic Midrashim, explains in a comment on the verse quoted above, "to
walk in all His ways" (*Devarim* 10:12):

> These are the "ways of the Lord": as it is written [*Shemot* 34:6–7], "The
> Lord, the Lord, God, merciful and gracious, long-suffering, and abundant
> in goodness and truth, keeping mercy unto the thousandth genera-
> tion, forgiving iniquity and transgression and sin . . ."[9]

The qualities here enumerated, revealed to Moses after the disaster of
the Golden Calf, are referred to in the Jewish tradition as the "Thirteen
Attributes of Mercy." To "go in all His ways" means, therefore, to emulate
Divine compassion and forgiveness and love, in all the forms made manifest
to Moses.

The same passage continues with an exegesis of the verse in *Yoel* (3:5),
"and it shall come to pass that whosoever shall call on the Name of the Lord
shall be saved." Here the *Sifre* focuses on the word "Name," and reads the
verse, by repointing one word, as "whosoever shall be called by the Name
of the Lord."[10] It attempts to demonstrate that the imitable attributes are
aspects of Divine conduct and not His essence, an endeavor which anticipates the doctrine of Divine attributes popularized and developed by
Maimonides. Yet at the same time that the biblical description of the Divine
character is declared nonidentical with His essence, we find an implication
of the enormous significance of this description for man, for all we can
really know of Him is His Name – and a name, for the Semitic mind, is
far more than a conventional appellation; it points to a Reality behind the
name. Thus:

Is it, then, possible for a man to be called by the Name of the Holy One?
But

---

9  For other references to *imitatio Dei*, see S. Schechter, *Aspects of Rabbinic
Theology*, 119 ff., and Shapiro, *op. cit.*, 57–72.

10  Actually, the *Sifre*'s thought is intelligible without the change in pronunciation
from *yikra* to the passive *yikarei*. The substitution is for emphasis only.

this means: just as He is called "merciful and gracious," so must you be merciful and gracious, and give of your gifts freely to all; just as the Holy One is called "righteous" . . . so must you be righteous. The Holy One is called "loving," so must you be loving.

The definition of the relation between God's character and His essence is a theological one. Let us grant that He is only *called* merciful and gracious and loving. But man is called *by* His Name (the Image) by appropriating these traits as his own (Imitation).

In another passage, the Talmud specifies even more closely the kind of deeds that are part of *imitatio Dei.* Commenting on the verse, "After the Lord your God shall ye walk" (*Devarim* 13:5), R. Hama b. Hanina asks, in a manner similar to that of the *Sifre,* above,

> Is it, then, possible to "walk after" the Divine Presence? Has not Scripture already said, "for the Lord thy God is a devouring fire" [*Devarim* 4:24]? But it means, walk after the attributes of the Holy One. Even as He clothes the naked [clothing Adam and Eve with the garments of skins (*Bereshit* 3:21)] – so must you provide clothes for the naked. The Holy One visited the sick [appearing to Abraham after his circumcision (18:1)]; so must you visit the sick. The Holy One consoled the bereaved [blessing Isaac after Abraham's death (25:11)]; so must you console the bereaved. The Holy One buried the dead [interring Moses (*Devarim* 34:6)]; so must you bury the dead.[11]

It is instructive to note two further examples of how Jewish thinkers, centuries apart, formulated ethical doctrines as instances of *imitatio Dei,* or "walking in the ways of the Lord." The first is by the aforementioned R. Moses Cordovero, who begins with the verse in *Michah* (7:18), "Who is a God like unto thee?"

> This refers to the Holy One as an offended King Who patiently bears insult in a manner that surpasses understanding. For without doubt, there is nothing hidden from His providence. Furthermore, there is no moment when man is not nourished and does not exist by virtue of the Divine power which flows down upon him. It follows that no man ever sins against God without the Divine effluence pouring into him at that very moment,

---

11    *Sotah* 14a.

enabling him to exist and to move his limbs. Despite the fact that he uses it for sin, that power is not withheld from him in any way. But the Holy One bears this insult and continues to empower man to move his limbs even though he uses the power in that very moment for sin and perversity offending the Holy One, who, nonetheless, suffers it. Nor must you say that He cannot withhold that good, God forbid, for it is within His power in the moment it takes to utter the word "moment" to wither the sinner's hand or foot, as He did to Yerovam [*Melachim* 1:13:4]. Nevertheless, though it lies in His power to arrest the Divine flow, and He might have said, "If you sin against Me do so under your own power, not with Mine," yet He does not, on this account, withhold His goodness from man but bears the insult, pouring out His power and bestowing of His goodness. This is an instance of tolerance and the willingness to bear insult beyond words. This is why the ministering angels refer to the Holy One as the "patient King." And this is the meaning of the prophet's words: "Who is a *God* like unto Thee?" He means: "Thou, the good and merciful, art *God*, signifying the power to avenge and claim His debt, yet Thou art patient and bearest insult until man repents."

This is a virtue man should make his own, namely, to be patient and allow himself to be insulted even to this extent and yet not deny his goodness to the recipients.[12]

In these remarks, couched in an idiom from another era, we feel the remarkable ethical sensitivity that follows from the biblical ideal of "walking in the ways of the Lord."

The second illustration comes from a modern author, a distinguished Chassidic master of a century ago, R. Tzvi Elimelech Shapiro of Dinov. Here the Imitation is formulated more theologically. He treats first the classical problem of human free will versus Divine prescience: If God can foresee all the future, does that not deny man his freedom to act morally or immorally? He answers that we are dealing with a genuine paradox, which cannot be explicated by reason and can be accepted only by faith: God both knows and does not know. In truth, He knows all; yet He restricts His

---

12  Based upon the translation into English by Louis Jacobs, *The Palm Tree of Deborah* (London: Vallentine, Mitchell, 1960).

knowledge and prevents it from interfering in the flow of events and thus robbing man of his ethical freedom, so that He acts as if He does not know.

Whatever the theological merit of his argument, the significant step follows: just as God both knows and does not know, so must man, in "walking in His ways," both know and not know. This is what the Sages of the Mishnah meant when they counseled us to "judge every man on the scale of merit,"[13] i.e., to give every man the benefit of the doubt. Now, argues the Rabbi of Dinov, each of us knows full well that man, despite his reason, is full of abominations, his heart evil and corrupt, his instincts foul – a pre-Freudian anticipation of the contemporary disesteem into which we have fallen. How, then, can we be asked to judge man for the good and assume the best of him? His answer[14] is that man, in imitation of God, must both "know and not know!" We know that man, more often than not, is a beast. Yet in the absence of any incontrovertible supporting evidence, we must "not know" his propensity for evil and assume that he does right. It is this purposeful restraint of knowledge, this transcendental ignorance, which, in imitation of the Creator, makes civilized living possible for His human creatures.

It is God, then, who sets the norms for man's character and conduct, not only by direct command, but by exemplification. Man's response to God is not the impersonal obedience of a subservient vassal to his distant and absolute master, but the intimate implementation by a student of the lessons taught him by his teacher.

"And all thy children shall be taught of the Lord" (*Yeshayahu* 54:13). We are not only creatures of God the Creator, not only subjects of God the King, not only children of God the Father, but also disciples of God the Teacher.[15]

---

13   *Avot* 1:6.

14   At the end of his *B'nai Yisaschar*.

15   Expanding on this idea, the famous Chassidic teacher R. Moshe Hayim Ephraim, author of *Degel Machaneh Ephraim* (to *Re'eh*) invokes the Talmudic statement (*Ta'anit* 7a) of a teacher who said, "I have learned much from my teachers, more from my colleagues, and most of all from my students." In that case, says our author

Moreover, the doctrine of imitation was broadened, in the Jewish tradition, to include more than what is commonly understood as moral or ethical attributes. Thus, Judaism considers the study of Torah – the intellectual exercise *per se* – as one of the highest values, if not the highest.[16] But this is more than a commandment; it is an act of imitation. God Himself occupies Himself in the study of Torah.[17] Furthermore, even etiquette and courtesy are imitable Divine qualities. Man, say the Rabbis, should learn from God, who, though He knew that there were no righteous men in Sodom, did not interrupt Abraham in his plea of intercession, but waited till he finished.[18]

It is important, at this point, to note the limitations of *imitatio Dei*, the commandment to "walk in His ways." All the illustrations cited above call for the emulation by man of those Divine attributes which men acknowledge as moral and beneficent: love, patience, forgiveness, graciousness, feeding the hungry, etc. Yet these attributes do not exhaust the description of the Divine personality. For instance:

> O Lord, Thou God to Whom vengeance belongeth, Thou God to Whom vengeance belongeth, shine forth. Lift up Thyself, Thou Judge of the earth; render to the proud their recompense                    (*Tehillim* 94:1–2).

---

in characteristically quaint Chassidic logic, God the Teacher learns from man the student! What he apparently had in mind is that God acts toward man in the same measure that man succeeds in imitating the Divine character. If man is mean and ungenerous and unforgiving to his fellow man, then God "learns" from him and acts toward him in a manner that may be described by the same adjectives. This is reminiscent of the Rabbinic interpretation of *Eheyeh asher eheyeh* ("I am that I am" – *Shemot* 3:14) as "I shall be to you as you are to me." It should by no means be taken as an assertion of *imitatio hominis* by God, which Schechter (*op. cit.*, 37) has purported to find in Talmudic literature. See Shapiro, *op. cit.*, n. 65.

16   *Pe'ah* 1:1, and throughout the literature. For a summary, see my *Torah Lishmah: Torah for Torah's Sake in the Works of Rabbi Hayyim of Volozhin and His Contemporaries* (Hoboken, N.J.: KTAV, 1989), 102.

17   See, for instance, *Avodah Zarah* 3b, *Ber.* 8a, *Men.* 29b and elsewhere. Cf. Simon Ravidowicz, "Of Interpretation," *Proceedings of the American Academy for Jewish Research* 26 (19) (1957), 93–95.

18   *Derech Eretz*, chap. 5; *Bereshit. R.* 8:8; *Sukkah* 30a.

Yet this Divine attribute of vengeance is clearly *not* meant to be imitated by man: "Thou shalt not avenge, nor bear any grudge against the children of thy people" (*Vayikra* 19:18).[19]

Obviously, therefore, the Imitation of God is restricted to the "Attributes of Mercy" and must not include other attributes, such as jealousy or vengeance.

Thus, a Tannaitic Midrash relates: "Rabbi says: a God above jealousy – I rule over jealousy, but jealousy has no power over Me; I rule over slumber, but slumber has no power over Me."[20] What Rabbi apparently means is that whereas the Attributes of Mercy (*middot haRachamim*) are *characteristic* of God in that they in some way reflect the Divine personality, these other, sterner qualities (the *middot haDin*, or Attributes of Judgment) are *instruments* which He uses to advance His purposes in the world. It is only the former which may be described as the "ways" of God "after" which man is bidden to walk.[21] When man presumes to imitate those Divine

---

19   Here the King James version of the whole verse is particularly felicitous and far superior to the newest JPS translation (*The Torah*), which breaks up the one Hebrew verse into two sentences and eliminates the conjunction altogether. King James reads: "Thou shalt not avenge ... thy people, *but* thou shalt love thy neighbor as thyself: I am the Lord." The translation of the *vav* as "but" instead of "*and* thou shalt love," yields the meaning that the principle of neighborly love is meant to contradict the idea that *imitatio Dei* includes all the Divine attributes, including vengeance. We might add that the concluding phrase, "I am the Lord," follows the *etnahta*, and thus refers back to the whole of what precedes it; thus: do not take vengeance or bear a grudge, but instead, love thy neighbor, for only I am the Lord and have the right to take vengeance or bear a grudge.

20   *Mechilta* to *Shemot* 20:5. Cf. also *Midrash haGadol*, ed. S. Schechter, 549, that God used as His instruments four qualities which should not be imitated by man: jealousy, revenge, deviousness, and exaltation. See the illuminating commentary of Rabbi A. I. Kook to the opening passage of *Sh. A., O.H.* in *Mitzvot Re'iyah* (Jerusalem: Mossad Harav Kook, 1970).

21   Alternatively, we may interpret the statement to mean that whereas God is, in His Essence, always beyond and in control of these (actional) attributes, whether of Mercy or Judgment, man is possessed by the more severe attributes and has no power over them once he has submitted to them (cf. Samuel Belkin, *In His Image* [New York:

characteristics forbidden to him, he encroaches upon the Divine preroga-
tives: "I have placed in [men] the likeness of My similitude, and by means
of their sins they have overturned it."[22] By overreaching, man's wrongful
emulation of God brings into disrepute the fundamental reality upon which
Imitation is predicated: the Image and Likeness in which man was created.

These reservations point to the possibilities of abuse inherent in the companion concepts of Image-Likeness and Imitation. The grant of "dignity"
implicit in the creation of man in the Image contains within itself the seeds
of misuse and usurpation: man, created to be *like* God, imagines himself
to *be* God; he mistakes the reflection ("image") for the reality. The Image
grants man his dignity – his "honor" or "glory" (*kavod*): "Thou hast made
him but little lower than angels, and hast crowned him with glory [*kavod*]
and honor" (*Tehillim* 8:6). But man forgets the Source of this dignity and
lusts for *kavod* of his own in place of the *kavod* given him by his Creator.[23]
It is this latter *kavod*, divorced from its Source, that becomes a rampant
monster ultimately driving man out of his world, and against which he must
guard himself.[24] Instead of *imitating* God, man begins to *impersonate* Him,
and man declares his independence and proceeds on the road to self-apo-
theosis. The creature aspires to dethrone the Creator and rule by himself.
Religious man becomes secularist man.

There are unavoidable risks inherent in the concepts of Image and
Imitation. When they are no longer acknowledged as the spur to "walk *after*
the Lord thy God," the moral life becomes impossible. When they retain
their theistic base, man is directed toward the unfolding of a noble moral
career.

---

Abelard Schuman, 1960], 29f.). The Commandment to imitate God would therefore
not apply to qualities such as jealousy or vengeance or anger, because they contradict
man's freedom.

22   *Mo'ed Katan* 15b.
23   *Yoma* 38a; *Bemidbar R.* 4.
24   *Avot* 4:2; *Derech Eretz* 1.

Rabbi Francis Nataf

# Command, Coercion and Modernity[1]

## INTRODUCTION

In the last few years, several important Jewish thinkers have suggested looking into the halachic category of *eino metsuveh ve'oseh* (a person who is allowed to choose whether or not to do a commandment) as an avenue to make traditional Judaism more relevant to Western Jews. This suggestion is based on the premises that a widening gap exists between the assumptions of classical Judaism and those of contemporary Western society, and that this gap is counterproductive to the well-being of the Jewish people and to the goals of Judaism itself.

Simply put, Orthodoxy's demand that the individual categorically submit to halachah is at odds with the very basic principle of personal autonomy, which serves as a cornerstone of the democratic societies in which we live.[2] Though some might try, it would be intellectually dishonest to say that,

---

1   I would like to express my appreciation to Rabbi Dr. Yehuda Schnall for his very thorough and helpful review of this article.

2   See Moshe Sokol's preface to *Rabbinic Authority and Personal Autonomy* (Northvale: Jason Aaronson, 1992).

as traditionally understood, Judaism allows the individual Jew to choose whether or not to follow the laws of the Torah. On the contrary, classical Judaism asserts that the commandments of the Torah are legally binding upon every Jew, regardless of the individual's personal opinions or beliefs.

Not only is classical Orthodoxy at odds with the principle of personal autonomy, it also greatly limits the range of individual expression and creativity, values that have become particularly salient in the last few decades.

The intention of this article is to explore how commandedness has been understood in traditional Jewish literature and, via this exploration, to suggest various directions that would recognize the legitimate impact of modernity on how Jews relate to being commanded.

To be sure, were we to conclude that the gap between Western values and Judaism is unbridgeable, we would have to assert the primacy of the Jewish tradition. In this particular instance, however, it appears that such is not the case.

## Two Models

In several recent public talks, Rabbi Nathan Lopes Cardozo has suggested that we look to pre-halachic Judaism as a model to be used in presenting Orthodox Judaism to the non-halachic community. He proposes that, instead of trying to get non-religious Jews to keep halachah, it would be much more reasonable to get them to appreciate and act in accordance with the notions that inform halachah. To illustrate this idea, one doesn't have to keep all the prohibitions of Shabbat in order to see the beauty of a day in which, in the words of Alexis de Toqueville, "The solemn calm of meditation succeeds the turmoil of the week, and the soul resumes possession and contemplation of itself."[3]

In evoking the development of the Israelites before and leading up to their receiving the Torah, Rabbi Cardozo creates a model of *religious transformation,* which involves a gradual transition from a situation where

---

3   *Democracy in America* (Ware: Wordsworth Editions Ltd., 1998), Vol. II, Book II, Chap. 13, 242.

inspiration is the main source of the religious act, to a situation where law is its main source. According to this elegant model, one *cannot* reach the second stage of development without going through the first stage. Rabbi Cardozo posits this as the most logical approach to present to a non-religious Jew, who can only truly reach the stage of commitment to hala-chah by first appreciating the values behind it. Not only is such a position expected to hold greater favor with Jews who do not observe halachah, it also brings with it a compelling logic.

Such a suggestion's creativity and appeal notwithstanding, it leaves at least two issues that should be addressed: (1) It would appear that from a legal perspective, the model of pre-halachic Judaism has no bearing on a contemporary Jew's status. At best, a non-religious Jew would still only be equated with a Jewish captive taken away from his nation at birth,[4] a status which only serves to exonerate him from blame for his behavior. Nonetheless, such a status does not remove the fact that he remains legally commanded, and so cannot be considered as someone with a choice as to whether or not to follow the halachah. (2) The suggested two-tiered ap-proach to Judaism may well only encourage the condescension and paternal-ism already present among many of the Orthodox in their approach to the non-Orthodox, something that Rabbi Cardozo would certainly not want to do.

Rabbanit Chana Henkin also has recently suggested that we look to the realm of the *eino metsuveh ve'oseh* to find a model that will foster greater relevance for traditional Judaism.[5] As opposed to Rabbi Cardozo's sugges-tion of looking to the past, she looks to the present, pointing to the status of the Jewish woman today as an *operative* paradigm of *eino metsuveh ve'oseh.* Even though women are commanded in general, there are many areas where Jewish tradition has always considered them to be *eino metsuveh ve'oseh* – areas of Jewish law where their performance of commandments has

---

4    This is the well-known position of the Chazon Ish (see *Chazon Ish, Yoreh Deah* 2, especially the last paragraph).

5    From a lecture given on June 9, 2003 in Jerusalem for the David Cardozo Academy, entitled *Post-Modernism and Women's Avodat Hashem.*

been guided by their own personal inspiration and not by any legal obligation. For example, though women are not commanded to shake a *lulav* on Sukkot, many women *choose* to do so regardless.

Significantly, Rabbanit Henkin suggests the possibility of extending this womanly prerogative beyond whether or not a woman chooses to do an optional commandment to the question of how she will do it, and then even further to areas where there is no normative halachah at all. An example of the latter is the creation of a ritual that would celebrate a woman's birth experience. Rabbanit Henkin suggests that perhaps even such an innovative act as this be viewed as fitting under the traditional rubric of *eino metsuveh ve'oseh*.[6]

In this case, the argument would be that normative Judaism allows for a great deal of personal autonomy and creativity even in its current form. In other words, the problem is not classical Judaism but rather the narrow focus with which we approach it. Thus, it is only our choice of focus that has prevented us from taking advantage of the opportunities for autonomy and creativity that normative Judaism could authentically afford us. Rabbanit Henkin's model comes with an implicit recommendation that we expand our horizons to encourage optional religious acts, both in adopting existing ritual when it is not mandatory as well as creating new ritual where it does not exist.

Beyond the obvious advantages of this paradigm, it too runs into certain issues. Even if we are willing to define experimental practices as legitimate religious acts of an *eino metsuveh ve'oseh*, these acts are still peripheral to the major area of Jewish religious expression, which remains firmly in the sphere of legal obligation. As with Rabbi Cardozo's approach, Rabbanit Henkin's suggestion also creates an awkward combination of two conflicting models (i.e., normative halachah and religious experimentation) that must somehow coexist. While in this case it could be argued that the example of

---

6   This suggestion cannot be taken for granted, since it appears to contradict the statement made in the Talmud Yerushalmi, *Shabbat* 1:2, that someone should not follow a precept where no command exists at all (see *Chiddushei haRitva* on *Kiddushin* 31a).

contemporary women shows that such coexistence is entirely unproblematic, creating an expanded role for the *eino metsuveh ve'oseh* would necessarily complicate Jewish religious expression in ways that may have unpredictable consequences. If nothing else, one wonders to what extent there would be a devaluation of normative halachah in view of the new excitement that would be found in the realm of legitimate religious experimentation.

Having raised certain issues with the models examined thus far, it is now worthwhile to see whether there is not room for a bolder paradigm that could be applied to the Jewish people as a whole, a paradigm which would not only be operative at the margins of Jewish religious experience, but also at its center. In this vein, we will try to see whether we can expand the paradigm of the *eino metsuveh ve'oseh* to the totality of halachah for all of contemporary Jewry.

In order to see whether it is possible to redefine the legal status of *all* Jews as essentially being *eino metsuveh ve'oseh*, it will be necessary to analyze the nature of such a status through examination of the traditional literature on this topic.

### The Nature of Commandedness

The Talmud seems to take for granted that commandedness is simply the result of God mandating a certain law for a given population. The subsequent commentary about the superiority of one who fulfills a commanded mitzvah (*metsuveh ve'oseh*) over one who fulfills an optional mitzvah (*eino metsuveh ve'oseh*),[7] however, shows that the nature of commandedness is less clear than first meets the eye. In explaining this superiority, one notices different explanations as to what being commanded is all about.[8]

A major issue that distinguishes the various ways of looking at command-

---

7  *Kiddushin* 31a and *Avodah Zarah* 3a.

8  While the context of this particular discussion is the search for the critical variable that makes the *eino metsuveh ve'oseh* inferior to the *metsuveh ve'oseh*, via this search the various commentators are, in fact, defining the significance of commandedness.

edness is whether its superiority is qualitative or quantitative[9] – that is to say, whereas according to some commentators the *compulsory* nature of an obligatory mitzvah transforms the act into something completely different, according to others what distinguishes it from an optional mitzvah is merely the added value brought about by God's demand. According to this latter approach, however, the act itself remains the same.

### The Quantitative Approach

The quantitative approach appears most clearly in the writings of the Netziv,[10] who writes that while both the commanded and the non-commanded individual are doing an act that is good for themselves, the commanded individual is *also* doing what God wants. In other words, the Netziv is telling us that a Divine command is an intrinsically productive act, regardless of who is performing it. This being the case, the act *itself* can be viewed as equally valuable for the individual who is not commanded as it is for the one who is commanded. What distinguishes the latter from the former, however, is that the one who is commanded simultaneously does what God has demanded from him. As such, the distinction is quantitative, in that what makes the *metsuveh ve'oseh* superior to the *eino metsuveh ve'oseh* is the added value brought about by being commanded, and not through any difference in the act itself.

In his seminal commentary on the Torah, the Netziv elaborates on his approach by way of an analogy, comparing commandments to a doctor's prescription: whether or not the doctor can command the patient to take the medicine does not change its benefit for the patient. Yet there is a difference if the prescription is for the doctor's son, as the doctor can command his son to take the medicine. In addition, the doctor also has a personal vested interest in the patient's listening to him. As a result, continues the Netziv, the father would likely give his son an additional extraneous reward if his son

---

9   See *Etz Yosef* on *Shemot Rabbah* 39 who makes a similar distinction in a related discussion.

10   *Ha'amek Davar, Vayikra* 26:3, and *Meromei Sadeh* on *Kiddushin* 31a.

heeds his prescription. But as for the medicine itself, there is nothing that the doctor can do to make it more effective for his son than for anyone else.[11]

## The Qualitative Approach

The qualitative approach is most clearly expressed by the Maharal, who posits that the nature of the act *itself* is determined by whether it is Divinely commanded or not. To elucidate his point, Maharal gives us a very down-to-earth example: A battle in which a king commands his soldiers to fight is certainly more important *to him* than a battle in which he leaves it up to the soldiers whether or not to fight.[12] In other words, the importance of the battle (i.e., the act) is revealed to us by whether or not the king commands it.

It is significant that Maharal compares the situation to two completely different battles (i.e., acts) when in fact, a more precise analogy would have been for these same two groups of soldiers to have been involved *in the same battle*. In such a case, the battle itself has the same intrinsic importance to the king no matter who fights it, the only question being who is essential to the battle and who is not. By not drawing such an analogy, Maharal is telling us that he sees what is ostensibly the same act (for example, a man shaking a *lulav* and a woman shaking a *lulav*) as two completely different acts. (Such an approach reminds us of Ramban's mystical explanation of the performance of *mitzvot* outside of Israel. The act of performing a mitzvah outside of Israel may be exactly the same as the act of performing it in Israel, but its nature is radically different.)[13]

An important distinction between the approach of the Netziv and that of the Maharal is whether the focus is on the individual's benefit or, so to speak, God's. If the focus is on the latter, then doing the will of God is the only thing that truly matters, the intrinsic content of the commandment being only of secondary concern.

---

11   *Ha'amek Davar*, ibid.
12   *Chiddushei Aggadot, Avodah Zarah* 3a.
13   Ramban, *Vayikra* 18:25.

## Commandedness and Motivation

According to the Maharal's approach, there could well be a major difference in motivation between an individual who is commanded and one
who is not. After all, since the content of the act itself is not the central issue, a person will mostly be motivated by how important the act is to the
Commander. From this perspective, were we to put ourselves in the category
of *eino metsuveh ve'oseh*, we would likely undermine our motivation to do
mitzvot.

According to the approach of the Netziv, however, the primary motivation for fulfilling the command is self-interest. Going back to his illustration, no matter how great a gift the son hopes to receive from his father, the
doctor, the main reason we would expect the son to take the medicine is the
same as that for any other patient – to save his life. Making his father happy
and getting an extraneous prize are secondary benefits that only serve to
reinforce the patient's motivation.

It is perhaps worth noting that the textual source brought for the reward
given to non-Jews for doing commandments that are optional for them but
compulsory for Jews is, appropriately, "A man should do these (commandments) and *live* through them."[14] The implication is that Divine commands,
even when not required, lead to life. This would seem to lend additional
support to the Netziv's approach that the main motivation for anyone to
perform the commandments is *vital* self-interest. Thus, according to this
approach, were we to find ourselves in the category of *eino metsuveh ve'oseh*,
it would not likely threaten our observance, so long as we were aware of the
critical benefits of the mitzvot themselves. (We will discuss to what extent
awareness of these benefits can exist today later in the article.)[15]

Lest we get carried away with theory, it is worthwhile to remind ourselves
that the practical option of not doing mitzvot is always present, regardless

---

14   *Vayikra* 18:5 (quoted in *Avodah Zarah* 3a – the inference is from the fact that
the word "man" is used and not "Israelite," indicating the universal applicability of
this verse).

15   See the section entitled "Adaptation to a New Focus."

of legal categories and regardless of how one understands commandedness. After all, most laws in any legal system can be broken. On that level, we almost always have *some* choice as to whether we observe Divine or human law. Likewise, clear self-interest will also not always motivate people to act accordingly. To expand the Netziv's analogy, just as people often choose to do what they know is bad for them medically – as the success of the tobacco industry shows us most graphically – they may also choose to do what is bad for them spiritually.

### WHAT DETERMINES COMMANDEDNESS?

As mentioned earlier, one could understand commandedness as the situation that results from the giving of a command by a sovereign to those subservient to him. Still, one could ask whether it is that simple. For example, if the commander decides to move to another country or if he chooses not to enforce the command, will that have no impact on the nature of the commanded person's status? Likewise, if the subject doesn't perceive himself to be commanded, does that also not bear on his status at all?

From one perspective, a commander's interest in a particular law or his enforcement of that law may not be relevant; if there is an agreement between two parties, its enforcement does not make it any more or any less binding. Indeed, one can find many sources in Jewish literature that emphasize the notion that the Jews' agreement to follow the Torah is not subject to renegotiation.

### Command and Societal Consciousness

According to many philosophers of law, however, the actual validity of law is dependent on much more than its promulgation by an authority. Many versions of Legal Positivism, for example, also focus on the extent to which a law is actually obeyed. There are, in fact, variations of this approach, from the classical formulations of Jeremy Bentham and John Austin, which stress the enforcement of law, to the more modern presentations of H. L. A. Hart and Joseph Raz, which put more emphasis on social norms. Yet, what is common to all of them is the view that a law cannot be considered valid if it is not widely accepted.[16]

From this vantage point, commandedness can be a question of societal consciousness. This is because a person's obedience to the law is less influenced by the simple existence of a law in the books than by a given society's attitude towards it. For example, there are many places where the common practice is to walk across the street even when a red traffic light is on. Such a practice is formally against the law, and most people doing it are aware that it is "illegal." Still, if one were to ask those people whether they felt obligated by the state not to cross the street at a red light, they would likely hesitate. This hesitation would emanate from two factors: (1) the law is generally disobeyed and, obviously related, (2) the law is not usually enforced.

This distinction could be made clearer by describing the positivist perspective on legal validity as one that emphasizes *de facto* over *de jure* validity, the latter being the theoretical status of something based on its merits, and the former being a practical (or one might say positivist) definition of status that is largely unrelated to its merits.

The above distinction is a very real one that can also be found in the Jewish tradition. When the prophet Zechariah declares that in the future God will be king over the entire world, one could well wonder why he limits God's kingship only to the future. Is it not clear that God is and always has been the king over all His creation?[17] The intention of the prophet is that from the point of view of human consciousness, God is only king (perhaps here in the sense of a sovereign that is respected and obeyed) among the nations that recognize and respect His sovereignty. Even though He is always

---

16   Basing himself largely on Hart, Harvard Law professor Richard A. Fallen Jr. illustrates this condition very succinctly in applying it to the U. S. Constitution: The Constitution is law not because it was lawfully ratified, as it may not have been, but because it is accepted as authoritative. ("Legitimacy and the Constitution," *Harvard Law Review* [April 2005], 1805).

17   The Talmud, *Pesachim* 50a, asks the same question on the second half of the verse which states that on "that day God will be one" (*Zachariah* 14:9). The Talmud asks, is He not one right now also?

king over all the nations on a *de jure* level, He will not be king on a *de facto* level until all the nations of the world are conscious of his sovereignty.

In applying to Jewish law the same criteria used above to question the validity of laws pertaining to red lights, it is obvious that Jewish law is not obeyed by most Jews today. That this majority is made up of Jews who do not identify with Orthodoxy may not be so relevant[18] – the point is that we are all exposed to the flagrant violation of halachah by those we believe to be commanded.

As far as enforcement is concerned, the picture is somewhat less clear. Given traditional Judaism's assertion that Jewish law is not only meant to be enforced in this world, but also via otherworldly reward and punishment, it makes it difficult to say that it is less enforced today than it was in the past. Nonetheless, there are two major differences between enforcement in the past and today: First of all, the religious community, with only minor exceptions, no longer has the power to enforce Jewish law via human means. That is to say, religious authorities are no longer able to deliver corporal punishment or to impose any other credible sanctions. Such coercive powers were most strongly felt when the ancient nation of Israel was independent. Subsequently, these powers have slowly withered in the lands of our exile, taking a particular beating in modern states that have centralized law and its enforcement in the hands of the secular state. Ironically, due to its primarily secular nature, the State of Israel has only served to reinforce this trend away from the enforcement of halachah, even when the Jewish nation has regained its independence. Secondly, according to our tradition, God Himself has severely limited His intervention in human affairs, making His own presence in the world less apparent. This situation, known as "*hester*

---

18    One could actually make a case for the validity of Jewish law exclusively within the Orthodox community, inasmuch as it is largely practiced by the Orthodox. Such an argument would give support to Rabbi Cardozo's implicit suggestion that we only treat the Orthodox as bound by halachah. The validity of this proposition would depend on to what extent one is prepared to define the Orthodox community as socially and religiously distinct from the general Jewish community.

*panim*" (God's hiding His face), has been operative for over two millennia.[19] In short, on a supernatural as well as societal level, Jewish law is significantly less enforced than it once was.

Thus, in view of the widespread violation of Jewish law and its severely weakened enforcement, one can conclude that Legal Positivists such as Austin and Hart would likely have denied the validity of Jewish law today.

Societal consciousness is not only critical to creating legal validity among Legal Positivists, however. It is also critical to a major approach to the issue of *metsuveh ve'oseh* not yet discussed. According to the Ba'alei Tosafot, the superiority of the commanded individual over one who is not commanded rests upon the greater emotional pressure that comes with the knowledge that one is *obligated* to do something.[20] As formulated by others, this position is an application of the Talmudic dictum *lefum tsa'ara agra*, which could be translated loosely as "No pain, no gain."[21] One could suggest that such pressure is primarily the result of clear and present awareness of obligation, and that today such awareness is missing for the reasons cited above – namely that these obligations are flouted by others and that they are not blatantly enforced. While there still may be a certain amount of pressure that results from a personal sense of one's legal and theological obligation, it is likely that most people feel a greater amount of pressure when there are clear tangible consequences if they fail to meet their obligations. This is not to say that our sense of legal and theological obligation will not *motivate* us at all, but rather that these factors are less likely to make us feel *pressure* than tangible law enforcement or even social expectations.[22]

---

19   See *Chazon Ish, Yoreh Deah* 2:16, who makes a similar point in a slightly different context.

20   Tosafot, *Kiddushin* 31a.

21   See *Chiddushei ha-Ritva* on *Kiddushin* 31a. Parenthetically, the Maharal emphatically rejects this approach, saying that it would undermine the categorical nature of the Talmud's statement, since there could be situations where a non-Jew would also feel pain doing a commandment (though not as a result of the pressure of being obligated), in which case his action would ostensibly be just as valuable as that of the Jew.

22   It is interesting to note that for Hart, a law's validity is also subject to its reinforcement by serious pressure to conform. See H. L. A. Hart, *The Concept of Law,* 2nd

## Command and Personal Cognition

There is still another possible variable brought to bear by the modern collective consciousness upon our status as being *metsuveh ve'oseh*: the Maharal points out that if God gives someone the option to do something or not, the source of the resultant decision is human. When, however, God does not give an option, the source of the decision is Divine. The Maharal sees this as another dimension of the superiority of an obligatory command over an optional command.[23]

In view of the critical weight that the Maharal places on whether the decision is made by God or man, today it is certainly relevant to ask to what extent we can truly say that our decision to do *mitzvot* is Divine. Beyond the societal issues raised in the previous subsection, the agnosticism that pervades modern culture may also impact on how contemporary Orthodox Jews perceive their fulfillment of the mitzvot. In an agnostic society (i.e., one undecided about the existence of God), belief in God is deemed optional. In contrast, belief in the existence of a rock is not seen as optional. In other words, while pre-modern society would take God's existence as just as – and perhaps even more – objective and certain than that of a rock, contemporary Western society does not. We could describe this as the difference between faith and knowledge. While God has not changed, our cognition of Him has been weakened by contemporary Western attitudes towards theological knowledge. Such an intellectual climate puts a Jew in the position where he must constantly reaccept the very premises that God exists, that he can command us and that He has specifically done so in the case of mitzvot. As such, man becomes much more involved in the decision to accept even obligatory commandments.

The upshot is that here too, our attitude to performance of the commandments may have changed in a critical way. Since, according to Maharal, an essential component of being commanded is that it comes from a Divine decision, if we no longer approach it from such a perspective, our being

---

ed. (Oxford: Clarendon Press, 1994), 85–88.

23    *Chiddushei Aggadot, Avodah Zarah* 3a.

commanded is of much less consequence. The fact that we are commanded would remain a technical fact, the significance of which would be rather secondary when looking to the value of commandedness.

ADAPTATION TO A NEW FOCUS

The above discussion highlights the impact of various historical factors on our status as *metsuveh ve'oseh*. While the discussion is not conclusive, there are many reasons to propose that even if contemporary Jews formally remain commanded, the essence of their status is basically the same as that of the *eino metsuveh ve'oseh*. We have already discussed the possible weakening of motivation that could result in essentially placing all of contemporary Jewry in the category of *eino metsuveh ve'oseh*, and pointed out that such a weakening would largely depend on which approach we are taking. At this point, however, we will discuss the possible benefits of generally invoking such a status today.

The greatest benefit of the suggestion that we are primarily *eino metsuveh ve'oseh* is that it forces us to seek greater understanding of the halachah, both in its particulars and as a whole. In other words, if we see ourselves as people who are choosing to do *mitzvot*, we have a greater need to understand what it is we are doing and why we are doing it. Not only will a self-perception of being *eino metsuveh ve'oseh* carry more weight with those Jews who don't feel themselves bound by halachah (both as a relevant attitude and in response to more attractive and profound understandings of *mitzvot*, likely to be formulated as a result), it will probably also assure greater continuity within the observant community: In a society where a command is *de facto* not present, appeal to the command's *de jure* existence is less likely to be effective than an explanation of why it is worth doing the act in question regardless. Going back to our example of people who cross streets at red lights, telling them that it is against the law may not be sufficient to prevent them from breaking the law. If, however, one would explain all the reasons why one should not cross at red lights, he may well be more successful at gaining adherence.

Certainly, such an approach should not be seen as a panacea that will magically do away with all Jews' reservations concerning the fulfillment of halachah. Once the reasons for the laws are subject to examination, one leaves open the possibility that their rationale may seem wanting. There are areas of halachah that are difficult to explain even in relation to the general contours of Torah morality, not to speak of how they would be viewed by Jews that hold Western values more dearly than traditional Jewish values.[24] Thus, some may say that the search for greater understanding of why we do what we do may actually open a Pandora's Box that will undermine the commitment of many Jews to halachah.

The argument just put forward, of course, is only worth considering if there is an alternative. Our analysis so far, however, suggests that the alternative of emphasizing the authoritative nature of mitzvot (i.e., that we must do them whether we think they are right or not) may not really be present at all.

Nonetheless, it is our contention that the net result of a reevaluation of the legal status of the contemporary Jew will be overwhelmingly positive.[25] For a Jew already sympathetic to halachah, the approach of the *eino metsuveh ve'oseh* does not require that every halachah be explained to the satisfaction of the individual before he would accept it. To such a Jew, halachah presents itself as a system. As such, one need not agree with, or even understand, every law to realize that halachah will not retain its systemic integrity if it is reduced to a giant menu from which to pick and choose. For such a person, it remains sufficient that enough of the mitzvot have enough value that abiding by the system as a whole has more value than not abid-

---

24    See R. Aaron Lichtenstein, *Leaves of Faith* (Jersey City: Ktav 2003), 184–85.

25    This contention has admittedly much to do with my personal outlook on the mitzvot and Torah morality. Still, I doubt highly that I am an exception among Orthodox Jews. In my many discussions with other religious Jews, I only remember one curious case of a highly observant Jew who felt trapped by a system that he believed to be very unpleasant but true. I am not suggesting that my personal experience on this matter is conclusive and that it can take the place of proper systematic research, but I am convinced that the vast majority of seriously observant Jews today find great value in the halachic system as a whole.

ing by the system as a whole (i.e., picking and choosing within the system).²⁶ Moreover, when such a Jew believes that God is the author of such a system, it certainly gives the system a tremendous amount of weight, even though he may feel that he is ultimately making a choice to do the *mitzvot*.

For Jews that are not overly concerned with halachah, one loses nothing by dropping the contention that they are commanded. With this group, in any case, the notion that they are commanded is not a motivational factor to begin with. If a reorientation of Jewish legal status forces us to drop our formal demand that such Jews keep all the commandments and to validate their choice to only keep that which they endorse personally, on a practical level, it is a step forward and not a step backwards. Liberated from an attitude he sees as irrelevant, the non-halachic Jew would feel freer to pursue his interest in Judaism without a sense of debilitating coercion.

In addition, once a person sees the value of some of the mitzvot, he is more likely to see the value of the system as a whole. The more one sees that so many commandments are, not only rational, but even brilliant, the more one is willing to trust the halachah on those *mitzvot* that he is not able to understand.²⁷

Ultimately, however, the benefit of considering ourselves *eino metsuveh ve'oseh* should not be seen as ulterior: It is not a question of, "Since it will work better, let's say we are *eino metsuveh ve'oseh*." Rather, it will work better because it is closer to the truth. In other words, the reason that applying *eino metsuveh ve'oseh* status to ourselves will be more effective is that it is a reflection of our true communal self-perception. As such, more than a

---

26  When we speak about systemic observance as opposed to picking and choosing, there is obviously *some* picking and choosing that takes place among almost all Jews. Some commandments are always more in vogue than others. The critical difference is that among most Orthodox Jews, it is usually more a question of social trends determining the stringency with which certain *mitzvot* are observed than it is a question of conscious flaunting of the halachic system.

27  In fact, at least for observant and non-observant Jews who identify Jewish law with God, this very trust is beneficial to the Jew's relationship with God. From this perspective, it can even be argued that there is something beneficial to the existence of some laws that have no specific reason or that are actually contrary to our judgment.

policy decision, what we are writing about is a communal acknowledgment
of an attitude towards Jewish law that is already latently prevalent. An honest appraisal of the contemporary situation will lead us to admit that, in the
terms of the earlier analogy, we are more motivated by understanding why
the doctor wants us to take the medicine than to know that he is our father
and that he really has commanded it.

## ON THE SUPERIORITY OF COMMANDEDNESS

As a final point, getting back to the Talmud's discussion of the superiority
of one who fulfills an obligatory command over one who fulfills an optional
command, it should be pointed out that the Talmud does not present this
superiority as a foregone conclusion. Whereas all of the explanations examined earlier discuss the normative conclusion that the *metsuveh ve'oseh* is superior to the *eino metsuveh ve'oseh*, it is worth our while to briefly ponder the
other side of the argument (i.e., the possible superiority of one who fulfills
an optional command over one who fulfills an obligatory command).

The Talmud tells us that before Rav Yosef heard that an earlier authority
had already concluded that the obligatory command is superior to the optional command, he thought that the opposite was true[28] (*Kiddushin* 31a).
That is to say, Rav Yosef saw intuitive logic in saying that an *eino metsuveh
ve'oseh* is actually superior to a *metsuveh ve'oseh*. The commentators are silent
about Rav Yosef's rationale, either because it is obvious or because it is not
operative. For our purposes, however, it is important to note that while Rav
Yosef's position was not operative in the time of the Talmud, it doesn't follow that it will never be operative. In other words, the Talmud's conclusion
that Rav Yosef was wrong doesn't necessarily mean that he would be wrong
under all circumstances. Rather, it means that he was wrong under the conditions within which the discussion took place.

We can suggest a situation that would be significantly different from that
of the Talmud by examining another elaboration of this topic by the Netziv.
In his commentary on the Talmud, the Netziv again takes the quantitative

28   *Kiddushin* 31a.

approach to the superiority of the obligatory command over the optional one. Yet here he approaches the topic from a slightly different angle, saying that the essence of fulfilling an optional command is doing that which is "straight and good" (*hayashar ve'hatov*), whereas the fulfillment of an obligatory command not only accomplishes this purpose but also pleases God.[29] According to this approach in particular, and the quantitative approach in general, one needs to examine whether there could be a situation in which the obligatory command is only pleasing God without fulfilling "the straight and the good" – in which case we would then need to reevaluate which purpose is superior.

To illustrate one such scenario, if a religious Jew were fulfilling a command with complete lack of concern as to whether he was also doing that which is "straight and good," perhaps he would, as some philosophers have suggested, disqualify himself from being considered to have *done* that which is "straight and good."

If that is the case, the comparison might be as follows: Is it better to do what God deems to be correct (i.e., "the straight and the good"), or is it better to do what God determines is obligatory? Another way to put this is whether it is better to endorse the wisdom of God by choosing to follow it, or to accept the will of God by subordinating oneself to it. While such a question is somewhat speculative, one could certainly make a case that the former would be a greater sanctification of God than the latter: The voluntary endorsement of the wisdom of God shows that we acknowledge that wisdom, whereas doing God's will out of compulsion doesn't accomplish this important goal. While it is true that performing *mitzvot* out of compulsion would reinforce God's authority in a way that could not be accomplished by the *eino metsuveh ve'oseh*, it could be argued that such a value is not as critical in bringing about human awareness of God.[30]

---

29    *Meromei Sadeh* on *Kiddushin* 31a.

30    One could say the two values at stake are appreciation of God's omniscience and appreciation of God's omnipotence. The *eino metsuveh ve'oseh* is obeying the command out of a sense of God's omniscience, whereas the *metsuveh ve'oseh* is obeying the command out of a sense of God's omnipotence.

### CONCLUSION

Our starting question was whether modernity has affected the status of Jews as *metsuveh ve'oseh*. The question was raised in response to suggestions that there is a need to invoke the paradigms of the *eino metsuveh ve'oseh* in our times. These suggestions seemed to assume that even if we invoke such paradigms, the dominant paradigms in Jewish religious life would still be those of the *metsuveh ve'oseh*. The intention of this article was to examine this assumption and suggest various reasons why this may not, in fact, be the case.

Most of the study focused on the Talmud's discussion of the superiority of the *metsuveh ve'oseh* over the *eino metsuveh ve'oseh*. It was shown that the various approaches to this discussion show different possibilities about the significance of commandedness – according to some approaches, the *eino metsuveh ve'oseh* needs not be any less motivated to do *mitzvot* than the *metsuveh ve'oseh*. Once this was determined, we discussed the role of consciousness and cognition in the definition of commandedness, concluding that these two factors may well determine whether one is commanded *de facto* even if it doesn't determine whether one is commanded *de jure*. We then argued that the latter consideration is of much less consequence than the former. Moreover, it was suggested that the reason we should focus on our *de facto* status as eino *metsuveh ve'oseh* as opposed to our *de jure* status as *metsuveh ve'oseh*, is that it is truer to contemporary reality. As a result, such a focus would provide a more adaptive motivational framework for the contemporary Jew, regardless of whether he is observant or not. The last part of our discussion pointed out that even if we do shift our focus, it doesn't necessarily mean a *demotion* in status. This, as the Talmud does not present the issue as closed under all circumstances.

Lest the reader err, it should be clear that I am not suggesting a radical theological reformulation of Judaism. God remains the same, as does our technical and moral obligation to heed His word. What may have changed is not so much whether or not we are commanded, but rather the significance of being commanded. According to several approaches outlined above, the significance of commandedness may have been undermined by historical factors largely outside of our control. If we recognize that this is the case, we have much to gain by working within the paradigm of the *eino metsuveh ve'oseh*.

To be sure, it was not my intention to prove conclusively that contemporary Jewry can view itself as *eino metsuveh ve'oseh*. Rather, I hope that I have shown that we can no longer be sure that the category of *metsuveh ve'oseh* describes us adequately. It is my hope that such a reevaluation will have a positive impact on our ultimate adherence to the will of God as well as to His wisdom.

Rabbi Yitzchok Adlerstein

# The Middle Way:[1] The Maharal on *Hashgachah*

IT IS VIRTUALLY impossible to overstate the importance of *bitachon* – firmly trusting Hashem's providential oversight of our lives. *Bitachon* is both a mitzvah and one of the most important ingredients in every individual's personal relationship with his or her Creator. Rav Hirsch Michel Shapiro of nineteenth-century Jerusalem found extraordinary significance in the Rama's prescription for pursuing a livelihood.[2] A person should "work each day according to his subsistence if he lacks what to eat." Rav Hirsch Michel found these words to be nothing less than definitional. They are, he said, "the very foundation of Jewish life." In other words, people should choose to order their lives in such a way that they must place their immediate survival upon Hashem's doorstep each and every day. This is *bitachon* applied and lived the way it should be.

No one claims that it is easy to get to such a place practically, and it is no easier to come to grips with *bitachon* as an abstract concept. This all-important area is a minefield of competing understandings and claims.

---

1   Offered in tribute and appreciation to Rabbi Nathan Lopes Cardozo, who is not only a good friend, but a master of finding the middle way between extremes.

2   *Yoreh Deah* 246:21. Cf. *Sotah* 48b. "*Kol me she-yesh lo pas be-salo ve-omer mah ochal le-machar eino elah mi-ketanei amanah.*"

Who is entitled to trust in Hashem to the fullest? Everyone? Even those who know themselves to be evil?[3] Does the seeming regularity of phenomena that we call the "law of Nature" have any real importance? Or is it nothing more than a Potemkin village, masking nothing but a succession of instances of special Divine decisions? What place is there for human effort? Is it a smokescreen for the inevitable accomplishment of the Divine Will, or does it actually accomplish something? Can a person get to a level of *bitachon* where he is no longer required to make any effort at all?[4] Can the *bote'ach* depend on a particular desired result[5] or that the result will at least be what he considers to be good? Or should he think of Hashem firmly guiding him through stormy seas, without the traveler knowing anything of the destination?[6] Is *bitachon* effective even in the face of the free will that human beings have to harm themselves?[7] Does Divine Providence extend to

---

3  See *HaEmunah v'haBitachon* by the (student of the) Ramban. On the other hand, see *Haggadat Yeriot Shlomo* (R. Shlomo Kluger) s.v. *matzah zo.*

4  Customary wisdom has it that the Ramban (*Vayikra* 26:11) is the proponent of the more "extreme" view, that the mark of true *bitachon* is rising to the level that one makes do with no human intervention at all, trusting fully in God. Rabbenu Bachya (*Chovot haLevavot, Sha'ar Ha-bitachon,* chap. 4) seems to take the more "moderate" view – that *hishtadlut* (human effort) is always required of us. See, however, *Emet L'Ya'akov* (R. Ya'akov Kamenetsky) on *Vayikra* (ibid.), in which he argues the opposite. Rabbenu Bachya indeed demands *hishtadlut* of all people – but not because human effort has any real value. *Hishtadlut* really gets us nowhere. It is a mitzvah for our own good, however, lest we have too much time on our hands and slip into satisfying our growing passions. Changing occupations will never increase a person's bottom line, since he fulfills his obligation of *hishtadlut* by toiling at any job. Ramban, on the other hand, holds that *hishtadlut* can make all the difference in the world to anyone who has not attained the summit of perfect *bitachon.* The unsuccessful physician might very well think of becoming a plumber, unless he can become a *Tzaddik* first.

5  See *Sha'arei Teshuvah* 3:31–32: "If a person sees [the possibility of] tragedy approaching, he should keep Hashem's salvation at heart *and trust in it.*" See, however, *Kehilat Ya'akov* (R. Ya'akov Kanievsky), *Sotah,* no. 6 who points out that this cannot be taken at face value, since the verses addressed by the *Sha'arei Teshuvah*– proscribing fear to soldiers in battle – spell out the very possibility that some will die.

6  The approach of the Chazon Ish in *Emunah u'Bitachon.*

7  Much of the discussion focuses on the words of the *Ohr haChaim* to *Bereshit*

all phenomena without exception[8], or just to humans[9] – and then only to some, according to their level?[10]

Considering the permutations and combinations of positions maintained by great authorities, radically different pictures of the universe emerge. Roughly, one might point to two poles. On the one hand, it is Jewishly possible to conceive of a universe in which God micromanages each and every detail, without exception. Human, infra-human, living and inanimate – all are overseen by Providence. Human activity may make no difference at all. What is ordained to occur will occur with or without human assistance. God has His ways of getting things done.

On the other hand, there are Torah conceptions in which human activity means a great deal and shapes the real outcome of events. God does not intervene against Man's free will, or at least is less likely to do so than to step in against the activity of animals, for example. Neither will He intervene against the laws of Nature that He created – at least not for anything less important than a human being.

The Maharal seems[11] to steer a middle course between these extremes.

---

37:21 and its source in the *Zohar*. The sense of the *Ohr haChaim* is very much in dispute, as is its acceptance by other authorities. See *Ha'amek Davar* of the Netziv to *Bereshit* 37:13 (n. 2 in *Harchev Davar*), and the wealth of material in *Siftei Chaim* (R. Chaim Friedlander), *Emunah v'Hashgachah* vol. 1, pp. 390–399.

8   This is the default position of the Chassidic world. See *Minchat Elazar* 1:50, who considers any other position to be so wrong as to be "forbidden to read." Chabad circles attribute this widespread belief to its innovation by the Besht. Interestingly, the Gra, in *Sifra D'Tzneuta* chap. 5 s.v. *vehaclal* (cited in *Siftei Chaim*, loc. cit. p. 87) also seems to uphold a providential system in which every individual member, including those of the animal world, are dealt with individually.

9   Rambam, *Guide* 3:17.

10   *Seforno*, unexpurgated edition, *Vayikra* 13. See also *Chatam Sofer* to *Niddah* 52a s.v. *Eyov*.

11   Disagreement reigns supreme regarding most matters concerning *bitachon*, the law of Nature, etc. Some sources point to apparent differences and see antipodal positions; others see only difference in focus, and assume complete agreement. Some see in Ramban (*Shemot* 13:16) a repudiation of Rambam's acceptance of the law of Nature; others do not see this at all. (Rav Ya'akov Weinberg *zt"l* once told me that it

Providence is not an all-or-nothing proposition, but varies from person to person. The laws of Nature and undisturbed human free will are real phenomena. We should not be asking whether they or Divine Providence, are the "usual," or default configuration factors. Rather, we can picture two systems, each contributing to a final outcome. His is a view that has not seen much discussion in print, and yet is intriguing for its elegance and attractiveness to many who have studied it.

One of the classic loci for both discussion and confusion is the Talmud's description[12] of the three books that are opened on Rosh Hashanah. If everything is indeed sealed on Yom Kippur, what good does it do to pray for Divine assistance at a later point in the calendar? If the evil are decreed to die, why do so many apparently evil people live long lives? The classic commentators have much to say about this passage. The Maharal[13] begins with a consideration of this last question. He considers some alternatives and then presents the view that is so engaging. I present a free translation:

> "Life" in this passage does not refer to that which is determined by the *ma'arechet*.[14] Rather, it deals with life that is sustained by Hashem, Himself.

---

is "impossible" that there is any real disagreement between them.) I therefore hedge when I say that the Maharal *seems* to take an intermediate position. Perhaps all the positions syncretically merge into one. If there is genuine disagreement, Maharal might not be so different from one of them – particularly Rambam. Different people I have consulted have felt differently about this. On the face of things, however, the Maharal does chart a course that incorporates elements of the two possible extremes, and still comes up with something that looks different from either, as explained in the body of this article.

12   *Rosh Hashanah* 16b.

13   *Chiddushei Aggadot, Rosh Hashanah, loc. cit.*

14   Lit., the array. It refers to the heavenly bodies and their positions relative to each other. To those who attributed significance to astrological factors, this array essentially meant the host of variables that have a strong impact on a person's life and deal so differently with different people. (See especially the discussion of *mazal* in Abarbanel, *Devarim* 4:19.) Why are some people born smarter, or richer? What impact will a person's place and century of birth have on the quality of his life, as well as his "natural" longevity? What talents and traits are part of his make-up from childhood and before? All of these influences not only vary greatly from individual

Similarly, the "death" here of the evil does not mean death that results from the *ma'arechet*, but to death ordained by God.

The death decree [in the Book of the Evil on Rosh Hashanah] does not mean that the evil one will die in the coming year. Whatever life was ordained for him when he was born is not taken away by this decree.[15] Rather, he is inscribed for death that proceeds from Hashem.

The *ma'arechet* may give a person a certain expected number of years. If God removes the life that he enjoys as a result of God Himself, there are many accusers that will rise against him. Minimally, there will be times when the *ma'arechet* will not protect him.[16] There are times that will, in general, be good for him according to the *ma'arechet*, and times that will not. At these latter times, the decree of evil will prevail against him and he will die.

This is what is meant by "the evil are inscribed for death." It does not say that the evil are inscribed *that they will die*. Rather, they are decreed to a Godly death; He ordains them to death. There is no set day or time that this death is decreed to be a certainty. The judgment is that he will die. It is actualized at some appropriate moment.

Similarly, the righteous are inscribed for life. This means that God assigns them life coming from Him.[17] If they experience a time of bad *mazal*[18] or weakness, the life given to him by Hashem Himself will sustain him to whatever extent is possible.

The Maharal not only seems to find a middle position between the extremes, but he blends the two schemas of looking at reality, effectively harmonizing them. He attributes much power to the law of Nature – the

---

to individual, but they are distributed seemingly randomly between the righteous and the guilty. Despite the astrological implications of the word, *ma'arechet* essentially means the complement of natural causes and factors that would lead to more or less predictable results if not disturbed by influences outside of Nature.

15    I.e., the *ma'arechet* values assigned to him at the time of his creation.

16    I.e., natural factors and strengths will not prevail over the dangers of the hour, and he would succumb, without the special intervention by God that the Maharal sees as a second source of life – that which results from His special protection and intervention.

17    I.e., not from *ma'arechet*-law.

18    I.e., weak *ma'arechet* protection.

*maʾarechet.* Even those doomed to death by their inscription into the Book of the Evil are not ordained to die at a particular moment, but are left to fend for themselves in a world fraught with dangers and perils. One of them eventually will catch up with the evil-doer. At the same time, God deals with each individual with varying amounts of closeness and Divine assistance, offering life where the law of Nature would not. This assistance seamlessly works with the general context of *maʾarechet*-law, and stretches the parameters of an individual's life according to his desserts. The law of Nature is real; Providential law is real. Together they shape the events around us.

Professor Yehuda Gellman

# Rabbi Nachman × 2: The Unreflexive Self

## THE PARABLE OF THE *HINDIK*

R ABBI NACHMAN OF Breslav told this story:

Once the son of the king fell into a madness (craziness) that he was a fowl called a "*hindik*," a turkey, and that he must sit naked under the table and gather crumbs of bread and bones like a *hindik*. All the physicians despaired of helping him and curing him, and the king suffered greatly from this. Until a wise man came and said, "I accept upon myself the [task] of curing him," and took off his own clothes and sat under the table beside the son of the king, and also gathered crumbs and bones. The son of the king asked him, "Who are you and what are you doing here?" and he [the wise man] answered him, "And what are *you* doing here?" The son of the king answered, "I am a *hindik*." So the wise man replied, "I too am a *hindik*!" So the two of them sat together until they got used to one another. Then the wise man gestured and they threw him a shirt. The *hindik*-wise-man said to the son of the king, "You think a *hindik* cannot wear a shirt? One can wear a shirt and still be a *hindik*!" So they both put on shirts. Some time later, he gestured and they threw them trousers. And he said to him as before, "Do you think that without trousers one cannot be a *hindik*? Etc." Until they dressed in the trousers, and similarly for other clothing. Afterward he gestured and they threw them human food from the table, and he said to him, "Do you think that if one eats good food that one is no longer a *hindik*? One can eat [such food] and also be a *hindik*!" So they ate. Afterward he said to him, "Do you think a *hindik* must be only under the table? One can be a *hindik* and be [sitting] at the table." And so he treated him until he cured him completely. The moral is clear to those who understand.

A standard interpretation of this story explains that Rabbi Nachman has come to teach us an educational methodology: All the previous wise men tried to talk the king's son out of his belief that he was a *hindik*. None of them began in the place where the son himself was, namely, respecting his self-perception, that he was a *hindik*. So, naturally, they all failed. The wise man who ultimately succeeded understood that he had to begin where the son himself was in order to gain his confidence and grant him respect, before gradually moving the son of the king away from his madness. So too, all educators should take heart from this story to come down to the level of the person being addressed in order to raise him up.

What, then, are we to understand by the statement at the end of the story that the wise man treated the son of the king "until he cured him completely?" If the son of the king no longer believed he was a *hindik*, just what was it that the wise man did to rid the prince of that mad impression? It's hard to see what that could have been. Could not the prince have continued to think he was a *hindik* all the while behaving – as *we* would put it – as a normal human being?

Perhaps the affirmation of a total cure is meant as irony. Perhaps the prince continued to believe with all his heart and all his soul that he was a *hindik*. Yet, in Rabbi Nachman's eyes he was cured, as long as he acted for all practical purposes as a normal human being. The idea then would be something like this: People have all kinds of crazy ideas about who they are and what they can accomplish. This, however, should not concern us, as long as those people act normally. Self-images, as distinct from actual behavior, are toothless wheels turning without engaging with anything else. Here I am reminded of John Paul Sartre's idea that a person is the sum of his or her actions, and that one's self-definition is irrelevant to what one *is*. In his *Existentialism is a Humanism*, Sartre gives the example of the person who thinks of himself as a poet, though he has hardly written a poetic line in his life. He *is* a non-poet, no matter what he says about himself to himself. Just so, the son of the king might *think* of himself as a *hindik*, but he is not, and by the end does not act like it. However, unlike Rabbi Nachman, Sartre was all in favor of bringing our "transcendent" self-image into alignment with our actual reality. Anything short of that would be what Sartre called "bad faith." Here, though, Rabbi Nachman would be allowing a rupture between our self-image and our reality as lived.

So understood, however, there is some disparity or at least a lack of connection between the alleged educational message in the story and the irony of the conclusion. In what follows I wish to advance an entirely different account of Rabbi Nachman's story, based on careful attention to Rabbi Nachman's language, one that also provides a smooth transition from the body of the story to the conclusion that the son of the king was completely cured.

I cannot help thinking that the key to the entire story lays at its very beginning. Let's look again at the beginning of the story:

> Once the son of the king fell into a madness that he was a fowl called a "*hindik*," and that he must sit naked under the table and gather crumbs of bread and bones like a *hindik*.

In accordance with the understanding of the story given above, the madness was that the son of the king thought he was a *hindik*. However, notice that the son of the king, thinking he is a *hindik*, does not simply and *unreflexively* get under the table and start to peck for crumbs. Rather, having thought he was a *hindik* he now decided that since he is a *hindik* he "must" get under the table and peck for crumbs. So what happened was this: The son of the king got an *idea* of himself, an *image* of himself, *as a hindik*. He then asked himself, as it were, "Now that I am a *hindik*, what should I do?" He concluded "that he must sit naked under the table and gather crumbs of bread and bones like a *hindik*." His subsequent behavior, getting under the table and eating crumbs, was, therefore, not a natural outflow from his changed self. It was a conclusion, an inference, from his *idea* of what a *hindik* should be doing.

Suppose one morning the son of the king had awoken to find that he had metamorphosed, Kafka-like, into a *hindik*. Then his condition would not have been one of madness at all. He would have been a freak *hindik*, but a *hindik*. And then he would have gone down under the table not because he *thought* he was a *hindik*, but because he had *become* one.

The deep madness of the son of the king is this: if you think you are a *hindik*, then if you were really a *hindik* you would act like one without any calculations. It is pure madness to act like a *hindik if your acting like one results from a calculation to the effect that you should act in such-and-such a way because you are a hindik*. If you were a *hindik*, you would just be one without calculations. If you are a *hindik*, calculations are madness. It is this (let us call it) "reflexive-generation" of the *hindik*-behavior on the part of the son of the king that is the key to the rest of the story. Here's why: The first wise ones who tried to cure the poor boy failed miserably. They failed to understand that the source of the problem was a madness that was generated by the self-image of a *hindik* and inferred behavior thought by the prince to be required by that self-image. Whatever they did failed to dislodge him from that self-image. The wise one who finally cured him understood this, and that's why he could cure him. Here is what he did: He told the son of the king that he was wrong in thinking that because he was a *hindik* he had to be without clothes. The wise man convinced him that he could be a *hindik* – that is keep the image he had of himself – and also wear clothes. The wise man interfered in the prince's inference from, "I am a *hindik*," to "I should be without clothes." "You can be a *hindik* and still wear clothes" attacks the validity of the prince's inference to the necessity of being without clothes. The wise man did the same for the rest, like eating *hindik* food and staying under the table. Had the prince *really* turned into a *hindik*, and not merely had the crazy idea that he had and that he *must* therefore act like a *hindik*, no attack on his inference structure would have succeeded in weaning him from his *hindik*-like behavior. For in that case, the prince would have been without clothes, for example, because that was simply what he did, having become a *hindik*. Only the last wise man understood all of this.

"And the prince was cured." How could he have been cured if he still "thought" he was a *hindik*? The answer is that when he realized that he had merely the *image* of a *hindik* without any of the *behavior* of the *hindik*, he realized the madness of acting from an *image* he had of himself. The last wise man had undercut the efficacy of basing one's actions on an image, for an image could always be manipulated and one's behavior deflected away from its target. Thus cured, the son of the king discards his thinking of himself as a *hindik*, and returns to being himself.

The moral of this story, then, is that when we assume a stance in a self-reflective way rather than being naturally what we are, then we are always in danger of easily losing the effects of that self-reflective stance. When we are naturally what we are, we simply are. In that case, no wise person could talk us out of it.

## WHEN A PERSON HAS A HEART

In his work *Likutei Moharan*, it is recorded that Rabbi Nachman said the following:

> When a person has a heart, there is no idea of "place" for that person at all; on the contrary, that person is the place of the world. For Divinity is in the heart, as it is written (*Tehillim* 73) "My heart is the rock [i.e., God]." Regarding the Blessed One [God] it is written (*Shemot* 33): "Behold place is with me," – for the Blessed One is the place of the world, and the world is not the place of the Blessed One [*Bereshit Rabbah*, Section 68]. Therefore, it is not fitting for one who has a heart of Israel to say that "This place is uncomfortable for me," for there is no idea of place for such a one. On the contrary, such a person is the place of the world, and the world not the place of the person.

To Rabbi Nachman, "Israel" denoted the highest spiritual being, so he is really talking about the life of a spiritually enlightened one. In this passage, we receive a new interpretation of the old idea of *imitatio Dei*, that one is to imitate God in one's life. Rabbi Nachman is saying that just as God is "the place of the world," so are we to be "the place of the world."

What does it mean that God "is the place of the world?" After God creates the world, God gazes at the fullness of the world that God has created (*Bereshit* 1:31) and declares it to be very good. By God's encompassing the world in the Divine consciousness in this way, the world comes to rest in God. When God then rests from creating, God rests in God's own self: "And God rested on the seventh day *from* all his work which he had made" (*Bereshit* 2:2). God's well-being does not depend upon God's finding a place to rest in the world. The well-being of the world, its being "very good," depends upon its finding a place to rest in God.

God invites the world to rest in God: If something evil happens in the world, it is absorbed into God's being along with the good. If something good happens in the world, God rejoices, not because in the good God has finally found a place to dwell, but because the good is deserving of celebration. Were the world God's place, God would need to find a place to rest in the world; God's very being would be threatened by evil, and would need to be affirmed by good.

God is the *place* of the world. In truth, between God and the world there is no subject-object relationship. Rather, the relationship is one of place and that which is in the place, of ground and content. God is the ground of being in which everything has its life. Hence, there is a natural pull to pantheism: God and the world are not separate, but are the encompassing border and the fullness therein.

What does it mean, now, for *me* to be "the place of the world?" To see this, consider a quite ordinary occurrence: I cut my finger. It is bleeding, and is painful. What is to be the ultimate ground of this experience? That is, must I find my place in the painfulness and bleeding of the finger, or must they somehow find their place in me? If the cut finger is to be the ground of the experience, then it becomes the riveting focus of my attention and I must be able to rest in *it*. But I cannot rest in it! How can I? The finger hurts! Look! It's bleeding! "This place is uncomfortable for me!" When the world is my place, I must find my place in *it*. This finds me seeking and hoping, alternately frustrated and elated. There is no rest.

When *I am the place of the world,* on the other hand, the world rests in me. Return to my bleeding, painful finger. When I am the place of the world, the ultimate ground of the event is not the bleeding finger. The ground is I. The painful finger finds its place in me. It is absorbed into its ground, with the bleeding and all, and takes its place there alongside the fullness of my world, the good and the bad, the painful and the pleasurable, alike. I rest in myself, not in the world.

But what is "the world" that rests in me? And what am "I" that the world rests in? Here we can be helped by Buddhist teachings. The Buddha taught that "the world" exists not just outside of my body, but includes my body as well as my inner experiences and thoughts. Everything I can possibly be aware of is, for me, "the world."

Here is a profoundly significant aspect of Buddhist sutras like the *Satipatthana Sutra* and the *Anapanasati Sutra*. In the *Satipatthana Sutra* we read:

> A practitioner remains established in the observation of the body in the body .... He remains established in the observation of the feelings in the feelings .... He remains established in the observation of the mind in the mind .... He remains established in the observation of the objects of mind in the objects of mind.[1]

And in the *Anapanasati Sutra*:

> He trains himself to breathe in sensitive to the entire body, and to breathe out sensitive to the entire body .... He trains himself to breathe in sensitive to mental processes, and to breathe out sensitive to mental processes .... He trains himself to breathe in sensitive to the mind, and to breathe out sensitive to the mind .... He trains himself to breathe in sensitive to the entire body, and to breathe out sensitive to the entire body ....[2]

In these and several other sutras, the idea is to be aware of the body and of our entire mental goings-on. These are to be objects of my awareness just as much as are the mountains and the streams. Ordinarily my experience is structured in such a way that my body, sensations, and thoughts are, as it were, on *this* side of a line dividing me as subject from the objects of my experience, on the one hand, and what is outside my body and mind is the

---

1   Thich Nhat Hanh, trans., *Transformation and Healing, The Sutra on the Four Establishments of Mindfulness* (Berkeley: Parallax Press, 1990), 3–4.

2   Thanissaro Bikkhu, trans., http://dharma.ncf.ca.

object of my experience, on the other hand. Thus, my body and my mental goings-on become the fixed background, the very location in which my life takes place. I, then, must find my place in the variegated goings-on in my body and mind, which serve as the *ground* in which I seek my comfort. Because I must find my place in the body and in my mental goings-on, only sometimes have I a place. Most often I am a wanderer, looking for an oasis. However, when *everything* is an object of my awareness, including my body and all mental goings-on, then ultimately *everything* comes to rest in me.

What, then, is the "I" in which the body and the mental goings-on rest? What is left of *me* when all of that is subtracted? In the first instance, what is left is only the bare awareness itself. The awareness itself becomes the boundary containing the fullness of my world. This awareness encompasses "the world" within it, without seeking to rest in it.

In the first instance, then, I am the sheer awareness that takes everything as object. In the second instance, though, if we follow the Zen master, Dogen Zenji (1200–1253), in his *Shobogenzo*, the sheer awareness fades from reflexive consciousness, and all that is left is the content of the awareness, the "world" itself. There is no longer subject and object, because there is no reflexive awareness *of* the awareness. Here arises a pull to the analogue of "pantheism," wherein what exists rests in itself, within its own non-reflexive boundary conditions. Here is the enlightenment of action, where the self disappears into the non-reflexive *tathata* or *thisness* of existence. In non-reflexive being, the world is not my place. The "I" disappears as a separate, reflexive reality, and, like God, becomes the place of the world.

"When a person has a heart," said Rabbi Nachman, "there is no idea of 'place' for that person at all." A person who is the place of the world is a person who has a heart, because "divinity is in the heart."

"Just as God lives from God's own non-reflexive nature, so shall you live from your own non-reflexive nature."

Just so, Rabbi Nachman ubiquitously praises the unreflective service of God of *emunah peshutah*, of simple faith, and inveighs against self-conscious philosophical religiosity. I can do no better than to end with the following quotation from Rabbi Abraham Isaac Kook:

Whatever is set in one's nature does not require hearing and study. The bee builds the compartments of her hive with perfect arithmetical precision, without having heard lectures in engineering. For it is already set in her nature . . . . And we, at Mount Sinai . . . we reached this high level, and became natural, pure Jews, in accordance with the firm nature of our pure souls. Therefore we first said "We will do," and only after, "We will hear."[3]

---

3 Rabbi Abraham Isaac Kook, *Ma'amarei Ha-Ra'ayah* (Jerusalem: N.P., 1984/5), 171–172.

## Rabbi Dr. Alon Goshen-Gottstein

# Eretz Yisrael in the Thought of Rabbi Nachman of Breslav

I WOULD LIKE TO open the discussion of the significance of Eretz Yisrael in Rabbi Nachman's thought with a quote from one of his teachings. An examination of this teaching will help us understand the thematics that are characteristic of his discussion of the topic.

He who knows of Eretz Yisrael, who has tasted in truth the taste of Eretz Yisrael, he can recognize if someone was with a Tzaddik on Rosh HaShanah or not ... because the taste of Eretz Yisrael can be described to someone who knows the taste of the mind ... Whoever knows of reasoning, like Talmudic students who learn and feel a bit of the taste of reason in discussing the plain meanings and arguments, as Talmudic students do, or the wise people who study other wisdoms and who feel the taste of reason, they can understand the taste of Eretz Yisrael, because the air of Eretz Yisrael makes wise (*Bava Batra* 158, *Zohar Pinchas* 245b, and *Tikkun* 22). And the taste of wisdom and reason is certainly very precious. But the essential quality of the holiness of Eretz Yisrael is only through Divine providence. And since God always watches over Eretz Yisrael, as it is written (*Devarim* 11) "The eyes of the Lord your God are always upon it, from the beginning of the year to the year's end," thereby Eretz Yisrael is sanctified and its air makes wise. Because eyes refer to wisdom, because the opening up of wisdom is called an aspect of eyes, as it is written (*Bereshit* 3) "And their eyes were opened," which Rashi interprets: "This is said as an expression of wisdom." And since God's eyes are upon Eretz Yisrael, for He is watching it always, thereby the air of Eretz Yisrael makes wise. But wherefrom is this aspect of eyes, the providence mentioned above, drawn and awoken in God? This is achieved by means of the souls of Israel, in whom God exalts, as it is written (*Yeshayahu* 49) "Israel in whom I shall be exalted." And through this exaltation the aspect of *tefillin*, which are called "glory" (*Sukkah* 25) is made. And the *tefillin* are an aspect of *mochin*,[1] and they enter and penetrate the eyes, and from this God's providence is made, through which the holiness of Eretz Yisrael is made, the aspect of air of Eretz Yisrael which makes wise, as shown above. And on account of this it is called "Eretz Yisrael," for it receives its holiness from the aspect of "Israel in whom I shall be exalted."

But whoever can see this exaltation, that God exalts in His people Israel, he receives an aspect of glory and *mochin* from this exaltation that he sees. And in him also an aspect of *tefillin* is formed, and they enter, as stated above, and penetrate the eyes, as stated above. And then, his eyes too become an aspect of God's eyes, and then wherever he looks becomes also an aspect of the air of Eretz Yisrael which makes wise. Because the essence of the holiness of Eretz Yisrael is only through the aspect of eyes, as stated above. But who could see God, blessed be He, so that he would be able to see His exaltation? However, whoever sees the true Tzaddik, who brings people close to the service of God, and who is the mainstay of bringing Israel closer to their Father in heaven, so that he himself (the Tzaddik) is the exaltation that God exalts in his people, because through him is the coming closer and the exaltation, so whoever looks at him, and the foremost time is the time of the gathering when all the crowd who comes to listen to God's word gathers around him, and especially on Rosh HaShanah when the great gathering takes place . . . so whoever really looks at this true Tzaddik, he also receives from this exaltation, and the aspect of *tefillin*, mind, is formed in him as well, as stated above. And then his eyes too become the aspect of God's eyes, and then wherever he looks becomes an aspect of Eretz Yisrael, an aspect of the air of Eretz Yisrael which makes wise, because he makes the

---

1  *Mind or consciousness.*

air wise by looking with the eyes of which we spoke ... We thus conclude
that whoever has a desire and a longing for Eretz Yisrael, especially he who
has tasted the real taste of Eretz Yisrael, when he meets and comes together
with someone who was on Rosh HaShanah with a true Tzaddik, he must
then feel the taste of Eretz Yisrael, because through this person also this air
has been transformed into the aspect of Eretz Yisrael, as shown above, and
it is proper that longing and yearning for Eretz Yisrael should awaken in
him now, in everyone according to his aspect.[2]

Before I attempt to explain the meaning of this teaching I would like to
point out the structural and conceptual parallel between the Tzaddik and
Eretz Yisrael.[3] The process described in this teaching takes place in several
dimensions. In the spatial dimension, it takes place in Eretz Yisrael, but it
also occurs wherever God exalts in Israel, i.e., in the Tzaddik, and even in
any person who sees the Tzaddik and who is close to him, especially on
Rosh Hashanah. Concerning the relation between Eretz Yisrael and the
Tzaddik we learn also in Torah 81: "The general principle is that the words
of a Tzaddik, which he utters when expounding the Torah or in prayer, are
called Eretz Yisrael." Eretz Yisrael plays an important part in this set of
parallels, because the different processes described in Torah 40, create the
aspect of Eretz Yisrael in different contexts. It is also clear that by Eretz
Yisrael is not meant only the actual physical land. Rabbi Nachman uses the
expression "an aspect of Eretz Yisrael." This allows him to address the spiritual aspect which it represents.[4] This twofold perspective, conveyed by the

---

2   *Likutei Moharan*, Part 2, 40.

3   On the transference of the geographic dimension to the inner processes in man,
especially the Tzaddik, see also Moshe Idel, "On the Land of Israel in Medieval Jewish
Mysticism," *The Land of Israel in Medieval Jewish Thought*, ed. M. Hallamish and A.
Ravitzky (Jerusalem: Yad Yitzhak ben Zvi, 1988), 213 [Hebrew]. See also Yochanan
Silman, "The Earthliness of the Land of Israel in the Kuzari," ibid., 81 [Hebrew]. In
light of the sources brought by Idel in his article, it is important to emphasize the concreteness of Eretz Yisrael in Rabbi Nachman's teachings. See also Schweid's position,
noted below, n. 8.

4   A good example of the application of this principle of equivalence in different
dimensions, including the relation to Eretz Yisrael, can be found in the second part of

expression, *"an aspect of* Eretz Yisrael," is essential to the structure of Rabbi Nachman's thought that weaves a thick net of associations between different concepts. In this weave, every concept represents not only itself but also its spiritual aspect. Rabbi Nachman said about his system of thought: "All my teaching is in aspects."[5]

## ERETZ YISRAEL – PHYSICAL AND SPIRITUAL REALITY

The question of the relationship between Eretz Yisrael as a geographical domain, and spiritual dimensions to which it is related, has already been raised by several scholars.[6] As soon as Eretz Yisrael is understood as a spiritual entity, there arises the question of the relation between the physical Eretz Yisrael and the spiritual reality that it expresses. In this context, it is important to highlight a fundamental distinction concerning the possible ties between the physical Eretz Yisrael and the broader aspect of Eretz Yisrael. In principle, one might consider the various expanded or metaphorical references to Eretz Yisrael as substitutes for the actual physical land. The physical distance from Eretz Yisrael alongside the need to maintain the conceptual vitality of the land, lead to searching for equally valued substitutes for Eretz Yisrael.[7] This does not seem to be the case before us. We do not encounter here an endeavor, certainly not a conscious endeavor, to find a substitute for the physical land of Israel. It seems that in the thought of Rabbi Nachman, Eretz Yisrael and the aspects of Eretz Yisrael exist si-

---

*Likutei Moharan*, Torah 8. Among others, this Torah presents an equivalence between place (Eretz Yisrael), time (Rosh Hashanah) and man (a rabbi and his disciples; the lung in the body).

   5  *Shivchei Moharan*, His Teachings and His Holy Books, 11.

   6  See n. 3 above.

   7  So it is, for example, in Talmudic literature. The transferal of the spiritual center from Eretz Yisrael to other Torah centers is the result of an attempt to compensate for a lack. See *Ketuvot* 111a. But there also is not a conscious attempt to deal with the question of a substitute for Eretz Yisrael. A case of a conscious suggestion of a substitute can be found in the epistle of Rabbi Ezra, see Gershom Scholem, *Teudah Chadashah l'Cheker Reshit haKabbalah* (Tel Aviv: Bialik, 1934), 162.

multaneously. The effort is not to find a substitute but to establish spiritual equivalents. As we can see in the passage we read, this effort is based on a parallel occurrence that takes place on different levels. The equivalence of values is based on equivalence of processes. I will attempt to clarify this process farther along. At this point I would like to dwell some more upon the question of the relation between the physical land and the more broadly understood aspect of Eretz Yisrael.

In his discussion of the place of Eretz Yisrael in Rabbi Nachman's thought, Eliezer Schweid sees Rabbi Nachman's great novelty in his emphasizing the literal meaning of the actual physical land.[8] "This Eretz Yisrael – simply – with these houses and flats."[9] "Eretz Yisrael is literally in this world."[10] This emphasis on the physicality of Eretz Yisrael is, according to Schweid, original in its historical and ideological context and it conveys the main aspect of Eretz Yisrael's significance in the teachings of Rabbi Nachman. The meaning of Rabbi Nachman's visit to Israel is related to this contact with the physical and concrete.

In light of the above quote, however, I cannot accept this characterization of Rabbi Nachman's view of Eretz Yisrael as the only one. As we saw, a Tzaddik is an equivalent of Eretz Yisrael. Even the eyes of someone who is near a Tzaddik are changed into the aspect of God's eyes, and wherever he looks is transformed into the aspect of Eretz Yisrael. Undoubtedly, the land does not lose its concrete significance. Eretz Yisrael is the primary means of expression of a spiritual reality, and only on account of this primacy, is there a meaning to an expanded sense of Eretz Yisrael.[11] Eretz Yisrael's primacy is

---

8   Eliezer Schweid, *Homeland and a Land of Promise* (Tel Aviv: Am Oved, 1979) 93–105 [Hebrew].

9   *Chayei Moharan*, Sayings about his Teachings, section 15.

10   *Likutei Moharan*, Part 2, Torah 116.

11   It should be noted here, that there is one context in which I was unable to find a source that reflects the centrality of Eretz Yisrael in Rabbi Nachman's thought. I refer to the place of music in Rabbi Nachman's teaching. I did not find any explicit saying of Rabbi Nachman that addresses the *niggun* in relation to Eretz Yisrael. The statements of I. K. Miklishenski, *Eretz Yisrael b'Mishnat Moharan miBreslav*, an off-print from *HaChassidut v'Zion* (Jerusalem: Mossad Harav Kook, 1963), 246–256,

due to the revelation of a particular spiritual quality, in space, which we shall discuss below. However, its manifestation in space is not its only manifestation.

In discussions of Rabbi Nachman's view of Eretz Yisrael, the significance and centrality of the land are usually presupposed. When examining the teachings of Rabbi Nachman with the question "What does Rabbi Nachman say about Eretz Yisrael?"[12] it is likely that we will find in his teachings important sayings that highlight the significance of Eretz Yisrael. However, in light of our discussion thus far, the question posed to Rabbi Nachman's teachings, ought to be framed differently: "What is the position of Eretz Yisrael in the economy of Rabbi Nachman's teachings?" Such a formulation will allow for a more nuanced appreciation of Rabbi Nachman's teachings. The claim that Eretz Yisrael occupies a central position in Rabbi Nachman's thought certainly remains valid.[13] However, the primacy and

concerning the value of the song of Eretz Yisrael, are based on secondary adaptations of Rabbi Nachman's words and not on his own statements.

12   Posing the question in such a manner is characteristic of most of the discussions of this topic. These discussions are obviously influenced by contemporary Zionist concerns. See Miklishenski in the previous note. See also Yitzchak Werfel, *HaChassidut v'Eretz Yisrael* (Jerusalem: Hotzeat HaSefarim HaEretzYisraelit, 1940), 107–118; Martin Buber, *Bein Am l'Artzo* (Jerusalem: Schocken, 1945) 99ff.

13   Yehuda Liebes, "R. Nahman of Bratslav's *ha-Tikkun ha-Kelali* and his Attitude towards Sabbateanism," *Zion* 45 (1980): 209, n. 32, noted that in contrast with Eretz Yisrael, Jerusalem does not play a central role in the teachings of Rabbi Nachman. It should be added that nor does the Temple carry similar value. This differs from the emphases that characterize older writings, where we can see that the decline in the conceptual centrality of Eretz Yisrael leads to an emphasis upon Jerusalem and the Temple. See Moshe Weinfeld, "Inheritance of the Land – Privilege versus Obligation," *Zion* 49 (1984): 126ff. In the teaching of Rabbi Nachman we seem to witness an opposite process that places Eretz Yisrael in the center.

It seems that the reason for this does not stem from ideological considerations, but is a product of the way in which Rabbi Nachman's thought took shape. Rabbi Nachman wove a web of associations around a spiritual and conceptual structure that will be described below. The values and concepts that are central to Rabbi Nachman's thought derive from his personal experience and not from an abstract theoretical framework. The biographical element is therefore very important in understanding centrality of Eretz Yisrael should be understood not only in relation to the actual physical land. The centrality of Eretz Yisrael can be understood only through an appreciation of the complex between the spiritual reality that manifests in Eretz Yisrael and the physical concreteness of the land.[14]

The dual perspective in light of which Eretz Yisrael can be viewed stands at the core of many sayings that speak of the manifestation of Eretz Yisrael in contemporary spiritual life. In Rabbi Nachman's thought these sayings are a topos, the purpose of which is to extend Eretz Yisrael beyond its physical boundaries. "Through clapping hands one dwells in the air of Eretz Yisrael." "By giving *tzedakah* (charity) to Eretz Yisrael one is incorporated in Eretz Yisrael."[15] This inclusion in the holy air of Eretz Yisrael is part of a two way process. *Tzedakah* on behalf of Eretz Yisrael links a person to Eretz Yisrael, and by being included in the air of Eretz Yisrael one draws the wisdom of Torah.[16] But we must remember again that the expansion of the aspect of Eretz Yisrael is not accomplished only by actions that form a direct or indirect link with the physical land. The equivalence that exists between a Tzaddik and Eretz Yisrael enables a different extension of the reality of Eretz Yisrael. "The true Tzaddikim inherit Eretz Yisrael, for they merit that the site of their grave is holy in the holiness of Eretz Yisrael, in the literal sense."[17]

The topos of the expansion of the holiness of Eretz Yisrael is a part of the eschatological vision. We find several sayings from which we learn that not

---

Rabbi Nachman's teachings. The Breslav tradition rightly pays close attention to the circumstances under which sayings were delivered, as part of the key to their understanding. It is therefore reasonable to assume that the prominence of Eretz Yisrael in Rabbi Nachman's teachings stems from his visit to the land and from his own acknowledgment of the importance of this visit to his spiritual formation.

14   The only one to have noticed the complexity of the physical and spiritual dimensions in Rabbi Nachman's perception of Eretz Yisrael is Yehuda Liebes in *Zion* 45 (1980): 209. As to the essence of Eretz Yisrael, I do not share Liebes's understanding. See also n. 52 below.

15   Ibid. See also *Likutei Moharan*, Part 2, 71.

16   *Likutei Moharan* 37.

17   *Likutei Moharan*, Part 2, 109.

only is it possible to expand the aspect of Eretz Yisrael beyond its borders, but also that in the future the aspect of Eretz Yisrael will be revealed in the whole world.[18] "And in the future God will renew the whole world in this aspect of Eretz Yisrael, for then it will be revealed that God created everything, and then He will renew the whole world in the aspect of Eretz Yisrael."[19] However, this expansion of Eretz Yisrael is not only a vision for the future.[20] The spiritual processes taking place at present anticipate the future state. The famous verse concerning the giving of Eretz Yisrael to the people of Israel – "He has declared to His people the power of His works, that He may give them the heritage of the nations"[21] – is expounded by Rabbi Nachman not in the context of the inheritance of Eretz Yisrael, but in the context of the expansion of the holiness of Eretz Yisrael to the lands of the nations, i.e., outside of the land. Broadening of the concept is based on recognition of the relation between the whole creation and the Creator. The entire creation is the handiwork of the Creator, and the twenty-eight letters of the alphabet,[22] which are the source of Divine vitality in creation, are found in every part of creation.

> [God] told that all worlds are His handiwork, and to whomever God wishes to give, He gives ... and all the things are called the power (כח) of His deeds, corresponding to the 28 (כח) letters through which the world was created ... and it is known that the air of the lands of the nations is unclean, and the air of Eretz Yisrael is holy and pure, because God took it out of their hands and gave it to us. But the land of the nations that is outside the land, there the air is unclean. And when we clap hands, thereby the 28

---

18   For previous occurrences of this topos, see the article by Idel, above n. 3, 200ff.

19   *Likutei Moharan*, Part 2, 109.

20   It is interesting to note the manner in which the processes related in Part 2, Torah 8, are formulated. The processes and actions that take place are described in the present tense as if they were happening here and now, in the arena of the spiritual life described by Rabbi Nachman. These spiritual processes are equivalents of the future renovation of the world, which is indeed described in the future tense. The spiritual present is equivalent to the eschatological future.

21   *Tehillim* 111: 6.

22   28 = כח (strength), the key term in the prooftext.

letters of creation are awoken, the power of His works. The consequence of this is that He has the capacity to give us the heritage of the nations, because everything is God's, and thereby we have the power in our hands to purify the air of the lands of the nations, because the land of the nations returns under God's dominion, and it is in His power to give it to whomever he wants, as it is said "to give them the heritage of the nations," and then the air of the place in which a man of Israel is praying becomes purified and he draws the holy air as in Eretz Yisrael.[23]

Conceptually, what enables the spreading of the holiness of Eretz Yisrael is the recognition that the whole world belongs to God and that He is omnipresent, by means of the letters.

But what is the meaning of this conquest and what is the significance of this expansion? The answer to this question will determine the relationship of physical and spiritual reality in understanding Rabbi Nachman's teaching concerning Eretz Yisrael. It is obvious that Rabbi Nachman does not intend territorial expansion. Furthermore, Rabbi Nachman does not speak about a supernal and lower Eretz Yisrael, as can be found in writings of other kabbalists.[24] Any recognition of the tension between reality and symbol, between physical and spiritual reality, is absent from his writings. It seems to me that in order to capture Rabbi Nachman's intention we should resort to a term that was not at his disposal, but which will greatly help us to understand many sayings in the mystical literature,[25] including the complex writ-

---

23   *Likutei Moharan* 44. It is important to notice the different formulations of the idea. The more common expression teaches that by clapping hands in prayer a person enters into the air of Eretz Yisrael. But in the last words in the above quotation we might hear a different nuance: "And he draws in the holy air as in Eretz Yisrael." It is possible that there is not a substantial difference between these two formulations. But it is also possible that the latter wording teaches of the equivalence of the expansion of the holy atmosphere, as opposed to the direct drawing from the air of Eretz Yisrael.

24   See Haviva Pedaya, "The Spiritual vs. the Concrete Land of Israel in the Geronese School of Kabbalah," *The Land of Israel in Medieval* etc., (above n. 3), 238ff. [Hebrew].

25   The terms used in the classical literature are varied, e.g. vitality, spirituality, power of abundance etc. This is not the context for a discussion of the energetic aspect

ings of Rabbi Nachman. It can be said that Eretz Yisrael is a spiritual "energy." We will discuss the characteristics and definition of this energy later. At this stage I would like to simply introduce the term into our discussion. This energy is anchored in the physical Eretz Yisrael, hence the importance of the physical and concrete dimension of the land. But as an energy, it can also break beyond the geographical borders of the land.[26] Hence the discussions of how to expand the scope of the energy: *tzedakah*, clapping hands, etc. Herein lays the key to the equivalence between the Tzaddik and Eretz Yisrael. The Tzaddik is the one who attains the energy, which is identified in and of itself, and in its territorial expression, with Eretz Yisrael.

The importance of the physical Eretz Yisrael is reflected in the fact that the energy finds expression in the fruits of Eretz Yisrael. Moreover, Eretz Yisrael endows other lands with their physical power. "Because all lands receive from the essence of Eretz Yisrael."[27] But also this physical dimension, which is bound to the fruits of the land, can be transferred outside the geographical boundaries of Eretz Yisrael. "Because when the air is sanctified in the aspect of the air of Eretz Yisrael, then all the fruits and crops that grow there, from which one is nurtured, and from which comes the semen, everything is in the aspects of Eretz Yisrael. And from there the body is formed, in the aspect 'I was formed in the depths of the land,' which is the

---

of Jewish mystical literature. See M. Idel, "Perceptions of Kabbalah in the Second Half of the 18th Century," *Journal of Jewish Thought and Philosophy*, vol. 1, 68ff.

26   See, for example, *Likutei Moharan* 37:4. The air of Eretz Yisrael is an aspect of holy sinless breath. Such identification facilitates the transferal of Eretz Yisrael from the geographical domain. Every breath without sin is *ipso facto* an aspect of Eretz Yisrael.

27   *Likutei Moharan* 277. From the context it is clear that what is meant is the physical influence of Eretz Yisrael on all other lands. One should point to the parallel between the discussion in this Torah and in Torah 71 in the second part of *Likutei Moharan*. In both teachings, Eretz Yisrael influences other countries. In Torah 277 the emphasis is on the physical abundance, while in Torah 71 it is on spiritual effects and the domain of consciousness. In both cases one notices the equation according to which the aspect of Eretz Yisrael is related to peace, and argument is identified with the aspect of outside the land, which impairs the aspect of Eretz Yisrael.

aspect of Eretz Yisrael, and then the body is in the aspect of the fruit of the land."[28] We will not be able to understand such a saying if we simply understand the expanded sense of Eretz Yisrael as symbolic. It seems to me that by understanding the expansion of Eretz Yisrael in terms of energy, we can understand also the physical influence of this energy on the physical fruits outside the land.

## ERETZ YISRAEL AND OTHER LANDS

These descriptions of expansion and spreading bring us to reflect on the meaning of the holiness of Eretz Yisrael and its relationship to other lands. In many classical sources the holiness is based on the principal of separation, isolation and lack of contiguity. The non-contiguous nature of the land can be illustrated by means of the famous saying that all other lands are ruled by ministers or angels, while Eretz Yisrael is governed by God Himself.[29] Such an understanding demonstrates the rupture that exists between Eretz Yisrael and other lands. I want to point out that I did not find any evidence of this conception in the writings of Rabbi Nachman.[30] It seems that the

---

28   *Likutei Moharan* 61:3.

29   An ancient witness to this conception can be found in the translation of the *Septuagint* to *Devarim* 32:8. It can also be found in rabbinic literature. See e.g. *Sifrei, Devarim*, section 38, 74. See also Moshe Hallamish, "Some Characteristics of the Land of Israel in the Kabbalistic Literature," *The Land of Israel in Medieval etc.*, (n. 3 above), 215 [Hebrew]. See also James Kugel, "The Holiness of Israel and the Land in Second Temple Times," *Texts, Temples and Traditions, a Tribute to Menachem Haran*, ed. M. Fox et al. (Winona Lake: Eisenbrauns, 1996), 21–32.

30   This, despite the claims of Buber, *Bein Am l'Artzo*, 115. The issue of contiguity and non-contiguity is also reflected in Rabbi Nachman's understanding of the people of Israel. Against the background of far more radical statements that are made in his spiritual environment, Rabbi Nachman's sayings about non-Jews are read as moderate, and usually as lacking the tension that is born from a non-contiguous understanding of the relationship of Israel and other people. Hence Rabbi Nachman's unusually positive attitude to conversion, as finds expression in numerous teachings in *Likutei Moharan*. The idea of conversion is a structural equivalent of the idea of the spreading of Eretz Yisrael to other lands.

conception that describes the spreading of the aspect of Eretz Yisrael must rely on different basic assumptions concerning the meaning of holiness, and the relation between Eretz Yisrael and other countries. In this context I would like to raise several possibilities for understanding the potential continuity between Eretz Yisrael and other lands.

The first possibility that I would like to introduce here is that Eretz Yisrael is to be identified as a spiritual center, in accordance with the teaching of the *sefirot*. One of the schemes that serve the *sefirotic* system is the analogy to the body. The *sefirot* are organized according to the composition of the body. As I will suggest below, Rabbi Nachman identifies Eretz Yisrael with the higher *sefirot*, and maybe even with the highest in the system of *sefirot*. The identification of Eretz Yisrael with the higher *sefirot* contrasts with the more common identification of Eretz Yisrael with the *sefirah* of *Malchut*,[31] and it enables us to think of a model according to which Eretz Yisrael is the center, from which other countries spread out. This model assumes that there exists a continuity between Eretz Yisrael and other countries, similar to the continuity that exists in the *sefirotic* body. The identification of Eretz Yisrael with the *sefirah* of *Malchut*, as is found in the writings of the kabbalists, accords with the non-contiguous presentation of Eretz Yisrael's relations to other lands. The ontological break in the territorial realm corresponds to the ontological shift between the *sefirah* of *Malchut* and the spiritual reality that is below it, which is not part of the *sefirotic* order.[32] According to this understanding of Rabbi Nachman's teaching, the expansion of Eretz Yisrael into other countries can be understood as the expansion of the higher energy to other parts of the body of earth. This model has a great explanatory force. This explanation is helpful in clarifying the relations between Eretz Yisrael and other countries. "The whole world is nurtured from the abundance of Eretz Yisrael."[33] Its main flaw, however,

---

31   See below. Even those kabbalists who identified Eretz Yisrael with the higher *sefirot* did not draw conclusions that presented Eretz Yisrael as contiguous with other lands.

32   See Hallamish, 216.

33   *Likutei Moharan* 47. This teaching is available to us in two versions, one

is that it is imported into Rabbi Nachman's teachings, but is not formulated there explicitly. In my opinion, there is nothing in the teachings of Rabbi Nachman that would contradict this possibility, yet neither is there a saying that would support it. Our model can function as a hermeneutic framework that provides meaning to Rabbi Nachman's teaching, even though we cannot base it upon his own words.

Even if we are unable to document a conception according to which lands are organized in the structure of a body, it is important to appreciate the meaning of spatial contiguity in light of the monistic outlook that underlies Rabbi Nachman's teaching. In this context it is important to point to a fundamental conceptual tension between the idea of the holiness of Eretz Yisrael and the fact of God's omnipresence. The pantheistic element in religious thought undermines the meaning of concentrating holiness within geographical borders. We already saw above that the power of the letters of the creation can be found everywhere. That is, the Divine is present everywhere. This presence makes possible the manifestation of the aspect of Eretz Yisrael anywhere. The holiness of Eretz Yisrael is thus evaluated in light of God's omnipresence. In another rendition:

> The essence of the power of Eretz Yisrael lies in the aspect of the Ten Utterances, in which the world was created, which are in the aspect of the strength of His works, that through them were Israel able to go and conquer Eretz Yisrael. And also here outside the land this aspect can be found. For the holy nation of Israel comes sometimes to places that were very very far from the holiness of Eretz Yisrael, e.g., to a place that from the beginning belonged to the nations and even now it is in the possession of someone who is distant from the holiness of Israel, and Israel come there, and conquer the place, and sanctify it that it should become a place of Israel, which is also an aspect of Eretz Yisrael. And the nations might say "You are thieves

of Rabbi Nachman, the other of Rabbi Nathan. The above quotation is taken from Rabbi Nathan's version. The subject of the discussion is food, which supports the physical meaning of the abundance of Eretz Yisrael. From Rabbi Nachman's rendition, however, we hear of the abundance that is drawn to the people of Israel, and not the abundance that is drawn to other lands. The wording of Torah 277 also emphasizes the influence of Eretz Yisrael upon other lands.

because you conquered a place that does not belong to you," but through the strength of His works, which is an aspect of the Ten Utterances, thereby we have permission to conquer the whole world and sanctify it in the holiness of Israel, because He, blessed be He, created it and in His will gave it to us.[34]

Creation thus enables the expansion of the holiness of Eretz Yisrael.

In a system in which God's presence can be found in everything, the significance of all oppositions and divisions is only temporary. The ultimate truth is the truth of the revelation of the one Divine unity, which abolishes all levels and distinctions. From this follows that underlying the pantheistic perception of the presence of God in everything is to be found the monistic concept of the unity of all. From these conceptual assumptions it is obvious that territorial holiness cannot remain bound within geographical boundaries. The idea of the expansion of the boundaries of holiness actually anticipates the future in which all divisions will be abolished and one unity will be revealed. This conception is formulated in Rabbi Nachman's teachings as the revelation of the Torah of *Atiqa*, the ancient one, through which all the opposites that exist in the world will be annihilated, and the unity of reality will be revealed.[35] The monistic conception is thus a conscious principle in Rabbi Nachman's system, in light of which we should also examine the issue of the relation between the physical Eretz Yisrael and the expanded sense of the land. However, I was unable to locate a discussion in which the subject of the teaching of *Atiqa* is related to the expansion of the holiness of Eretz Yisrael.

The expansion of the energy of Eretz Yisrael beyond its borders is made possible by virtue of the web of relations that exists between Eretz Yisrael and the people of Israel on the one hand, and the Torah on the other hand. We saw already in the quotation that opened our presentation, how the holiness of Eretz Yisrael is formed by virtue of the souls of Israel, and that Eretz Yisrael is identified with the aspect of wisdom, "The air of Eretz Yisrael makes wise." Neither the Torah, nor the people of Israel are

---

34  *Likutei Moharan*, Part 2, 78.
35  See *Likutei Moharan* 33:5 and 51.

restricted by geographical borders. They are, nevertheless, essentially tied to Eretz Yisrael. We will presently turn to an examination of the conceptual ties between Eretz Yisrael and the Torah and the people of Israel, as this is presented by Rabbi Nachman. Let us begin with a discussion of the relation between Eretz Yisrael and the people of Israel.

## ERETZ YISRAEL, THE PEOPLE OF ISRAEL AND THE TORAH

The first question I wish to introduce in this context is whether there is a natural tie between the people of Israel and Eretz Yisrael. Differently put: we tend to assume that certain religious conceptions, especially those that incline towards religious realism,[36] i.e., towards emphasizing the essentialist and ontological dimensions that underlie spiritual ideas, would portray a sharing of essence between people and land. The religious outlook of the book of *Kuzari* is a typical example of a realistic religious outlook.[37] The being of the people is linked to the nature of the land, and vice versa. The statement of *Sefer Haredim*: "As a man without his wife is considered half bodied (i.e., incomplete), so Israel when they are not in Eretz Yisrael, are also only half a body" gives a concise expression to such an understanding.[38] In Rabbi Nachman's teachings we cannot find such formulations. It seems to me that the organic and natural relationship of people and land is not part of the conceptual web he spins. It seems to me that seeing the land as anchoring and emanating energy allows for a different emphasis in his teaching.[39] The emphasis is on the land as a source of energy. This empha-

---

36   I use the term "realism," in opposition to "nominalism," following the discussion of Yochanan Silman, "Halachic Determinations of a Nominalistic and Realistic Nature: Legal and Philosophical Considerations," *Din Israel* 12 (1984/5): 249–266.

37   See Yochanan Silman, ibid., 85.

38   This text is quoted in Mordechai Pachter, "The Land of Israel in the Homiletic Literature of Sixteenth Century Safed," in *The Land of Israel in Medieval* etc. (n. 3 above), 316 [Hebrew].

39   Moreover, it seems to me that it is difficult to describe the essential qualities of Eretz Yisrael, as Rabbi Nachman sees them. He does not resort to climatological or other conditions in order to explain the uniqueness of Eretz Yisrael. Its uniqueness is

sis weakens the possible meaning of the natural bond that exists between people and land. Of course, the assertion that the energy of Eretz Yisrael is the energy that is natural to the people of Israel will certainly fit the patterns of Rabbi Nachman's thinking. It follows from the presentation, in our opening quote, of the sanctity of the land as rooted in the souls of Israel. The following saying further illustrates the meaning of the association of people and land: "Everyone of Israel has a portion in Eretz Yisrael, and everyone according to his portion that he has in Eretz Yisrael, receives from the consciousness of Eretz Yisrael."[40] In a particular sense, a natural relationship between every individual and the land is here established. But the meaning of this bond does not relate to the collective existence, nor to the individual. Rather, it relates to the possibility of expanding the consciousness of Eretz Yisrael beyond its borders. Once Eretz Yisrael is appreciated in terms of energy, something of its territorial reality is lost. The theory that sees the relation of people to land as an organic one, assumes that there is no spiritual perfection outside Eretz Yisrael.[41] In the teaching of Rabbi Nachman, and it seems this is the case also in the teaching of Chassidism as a whole,[42] spiritual perfection is possible even at present, outside the boundaries of the land.[43] The emphasis upon the spiritual realization of the individual and the emphasis upon Eretz Yisrael as a source of energy turn the physical bond between the people and the land into a relative one, and reduce the quality of the natural bond that exists between the people and the land.[44]

---

an obvious result of his religious outlook.

40   *Likutei Moharan*, Part 2, 71.

41   So, for example, according to *Sefer Kuzari*, prophecy is not possible outside of Eretz Yisrael. See *The Kuzari*, Part 2, Paragraph 9ff.

42   See the article of Idel, n. 3 above.

43   As an interesting illustration of this claim, it is worth pointing to the relation of prophecy and Eretz Yisrael in Torah 8 in *Likutei Moharan*, Part 2. The causal chain described by Rabbi Nachman puts the renewal of prophecy prior to attaining the aspect of Eretz Yisrael (compare also *Likutei Moharan*, Part 2, 1:8, and compare Part 1, 7:1). This seems to contradict the opinion of Rabbi Yehudah HaLevi in the *Sefer Kuzari*, mentioned above, n. 40.

44   The *sefirotic* identification of Eretz Yisrael, which we discuss below, raises the

Nonetheless, as we learn from the last quote, one should not underplay the importance of Eretz Yisrael in the spiritual processes that are Rabbi Nachman's primary concern. Spiritual realization and religious worship are related to Eretz Yisrael. Hence the need to connect to the reality of Eretz Yisrael, and to expand it beyond its territorial boundaries. The two primary foci of spiritual life, prayer and Torah, are connected to Eretz Yisrael. We learn that "There [in Eretz Yisrael] is the centerpoint of the ascent of prayers, as it is written 'And this is the gate of heaven.'"[45] The connection of prayer to Eretz Yisrael explains the need to draw the presence of Eretz Yisrael at the time of prayer. Hence the need to clap hands during prayer. Clapping hands at the time of prayer draws the presence of Eretz Yisrael.[46]

It is important to clarify that the influence of Eretz Yisrael is not dependent on the concrete state of the land. The national and historical circumstances, destruction of the Temple, Diaspora etc., are not described as diminishing the potential and the influence of Eretz Yisrael. In this sense, Eretz Yisrael is autonomous from the historical fate of the people. Only in one teaching, and there too in a marginal context, Rabbi Nachman relates to Eretz Yisrael from the collective national perspective in the context of the question of the right to return to the land.[47] One should not account for the scarcity of attention to the current historical dimension through the strong emphasis on the spirituality of the individual that we find in his teachings. Expansion of the energy of Eretz Yisrael beyond its borders is not only a matter for the individual and his religious activity. We already

---

question whether one can describe the relations of people and land in terms of the *sefirotic* structure. For the time being, I do not have a clear answer to this question, and I am not sure if we can assume a clear identification in the writings of Rabbi Nachman.

45   *Likutei Moharan* 7:1.

46   *Likutei Moharan* 44.

47   See the end of *Likutei Moharan* 11: "Because of this we cannot arrive at and return to Eretz Yisrael, i.e., because of pursuit of greatness and honor." In a spiritual context in which it is possible to attain the consciousness of Eretz Yisrael also outside of the land, it is obvious that the question of the return of the whole nation becomes a less burning question. Hence the scarcity of reference to this side of the bond to Eretz Yisrael.

saw that when the people of Israel come to a certain place they sanctify it
in the holiness of Eretz Yisrael Also the next quote relates to the continued
presence of Eretz Yisrael in the life of the whole nation: "And we, the children of Israel, receive the abundance via Eretz Yisrael, and the abundance
of Eretz Yisrael is the radiance of the countenance of Ya'akov, the radiance
of *tefillin*."[48] This drawing forth of abundance applies to the entire people.
This quotation is especially interesting in the context of our discussion. We
encounter again the association of Eretz Yisrael and *tefillin*, which we found
in the opening Torah, and to which we will later return. For the time being, let us simply consider the radiance of *tefillin* as a spiritual energy. And
Rabbi Nachman continues: "And when we eat the true abundance that
comes via Eretz Yisrael, and with this force we then recite God's praises,
then a new heaven and earth are made ... because the new heaven is made
by the radiance of the countenance of Ya'akov, and the new earth is made
through Eretz Yisrael, because the abundance passes through Eretz Yisrael."
From these words we learn how physical the bond to Eretz Yisrael is. The
abundance that we receive from Eretz Yisrael is a physical abundance. The
spiritual energy is contained in the food we eat. The doubling of heaven and
earth is the doubling of the physical reality of Eretz Yisrael and the spiritual
illumination that is related to it. Receiving abundance through Eretz Yisrael
relates to the physical land. The spiritual abundance, in our wording, the
spiritual energy, passes through the physical land. However, despite the double perspective from which the land is viewed, this teaching is concerned
with the possibility of expansion of the energy that has a physical form to
the children of Israel, wherever they may be.

The paradigm for understanding the relations between people and land
here is that the people are a channel that draws forth the spiritual reality
of Eretz Yisrael.[49] It seems this paradigm is valid also when the meaning of

---

48  *Likutei Moharan* 47.

49  One of the interesting emphases in Rabbi Nachman's teachings about Eretz
Yisrael is related to the status of the forefathers and their relation to the land. As I
noted in my "The Covenant with the Fathers and the Inheritance of the Land – between Biblical Theology and Rabbinic Thought," *Da'at* 35 (1995): 5–28, the Biblical

this drawing is the engendering of Eretz Yisrael.[50] As we saw, wherever Israel come, that place is sanctified with the holiness of Eretz Yisrael. In this context, Israel constitute the aspect of Eretz Yisrael.[51] But the meaning of such constitution is not the subordination of the territorial dimension to the national dimension. This statement does not indicate that the existence of the people of Israel is the main thing, and that every place where Israel live becomes automatically an aspect of Eretz Yisrael. Rather, Israel, by virtue of their spiritual labors, draw the spiritual presence of Eretz Yisrael beyond its

---

concept that the inheritance of the land comes to us by virtue of our forefathers undergoes transformations in rabbinic literature, and is not significantly echoed there. It seems that following rabbinic literature, later Jewish literature also does not place this idea in the forefront of ideas relating to Eretz Yisrael. One cannot say Rabbi Nachman deviates from this tendency. However, the adaptation of several Zoharic sources introduces this conceptual note in the ensemble of his teachings on Eretz Yisrael. The use of this motif reflects the *sefirotic* understanding of the forefathers, as is common in kabbalistic literature. See *Likutei Moharan* 55:2. The Zoharic expressions identify Eretz Yisrael with the *sefirah* of *Malchut*. In the rendition of Rabbi Nachman, it seems we encounter a vertical adaptation, according to which the spiritual level of Eretz Yisrael is attained through a process of ascent that passes through the forefathers on its way to Eretz Yisrael. See also *Likutei Moharan* 37:4, which seems to describe the opposite direction of influence. On the aspiration "that the forefathers will be revealed in the world by you," see *Chayei Moharan*, New Stories, 12.

50   As will be argued further in our presentation, it is possible to describe Israel as a stage in the drawing of the spiritual reality in a vertical and a horizontal manner. The description of the abundance that is drawn to the children of Israel resorts to a horizontal model. The sources that describe the constitution of the holiness of Eretz Yisrael by virtue of the people of Israel, especially the teaching that opened our presentation, use the same relationship, vertically. The people of Israel mediate the possibility of the drawing and formation of Eretz Yisrael, according to the stages of the ascent of the *Shechinah*, as I shall suggest below.

51   The assumption that man establishes spiritual reality is most important as a background to understanding these issues. For extreme cases of this assumption see Moshe Idel, *Kabbalah: New Perspectives* (New Haven: Yale University Press, 1988), 185. See also Charles Mopsik, *Les grands Textes de la Cabale, Les Rites qui Fait Dieu* (Paris: Lagrasse, 1993).

geographical boundaries.[52] The people of Israel form an intermediary step in the expansion of the spiritual presence of Eretz Yisrael. In this light, we can reexamine the text with which we opened our discussion. As we read there: "And therefore it is called Eretz Yisrael, for it receives its holiness from the aspect of "Israel in whom I shall be exalted." Here too we are dealing with the establishment of the holiness of Eretz Yisrael. It does not flow from Israel's national existence. It is a product of the exaltation that is a consequence of Israel's worship of God. This means: Israel through their spiritual service create the quality that finds expression in the being of the land.

As we suggested above, the Torah also has an important function in relation to Eretz Yisrael. The identification of Eretz Yisrael with the aspect of *Chochmah*, wisdom, leads to the near identification of Eretz Yisrael with the Torah.[53] There is a circular, or a two-way, tie between Eretz Yisrael and

---

52   It is worth noting that it is possible to present two different models that account for how existence outside of Eretz Yisrael receives its spiritual being. The one model is the drawing from Eretz Yisrael. The other is the discovery of divinity that is omnipresent, outside the boundaries of Eretz Yisrael. This aspect may be identified with the aspect of Eretz Yisrael from the spiritual point of view, but it does not necessarily rely upon drawing from the territorial expanse of Eretz Yisrael. I think one can discern these different emphases in Torah 78 in the second part of *Likutei Moharan* and in Torah 47 in the first part. Torah 78 does not resort to the principle of drawing in, but to the principle of the revelation of the Ten Utterances of creation. It is Israel who reveal the force of the Ten Utterances, and what is being thereby revealed is the aspect of Eretz Yisrael. Spiritual reality is thus established by means of Israel. This does not mean, however, that a land is sanctified as an extension of the holiness or the being of the people of Israel. Also the territorial understanding of the expansion of the holiness of Eretz Yisrael, as found in Torah 47, resorts to the people of Israel as conveyors of holiness, but holiness itself does not stem from them. The possible contradiction between these two models is not so sharp from the point of view of Rabbi Nachman, because what is revealed through the Ten Utterances that are in all of Creation, is the aspect of Eretz Yisrael, which is drawn from its territorial boundaries.

53   See *Likutei Moharan*, Part 2, 78. From Rabbi Nachman's discussion, we learn of the identity or equivalence of Torah and Eretz Yisrael. The journey to Eretz Yisrael parallels the state of the world prior to receiving the Torah. Hence the equivalence of Eretz Yisrael and the Torah.

the Torah. The more common conceptual context in the teachings of Rabbi Nachman focuses on the Torah, which is appreciated in the light of Eretz Yisrael and which is attained through it. "All *mochin* are in the aspect of the *mochin* of Eretz Yisrael, because they all receive from there, because there in Eretz Yisrael is the center point of *mochin* and wisdom."[54] *Tzedakah* for Eretz Yisrael forms the link to the land, and by its virtue the wisdom of Torah is drawn forth.[55] On the other hand, engaging in the Torah is a preparation for Eretz Yisrael. Engaging in the Torah is drawing forth the illumination of Eretz Yisrael. "According to the novel interpretation of the Torah that one makes, the illumination of the holiness of Eretz Yisrael is drawn to him."[56] This saying emphasizes the illumination of Eretz Yisrael as the goal, and engagement in the Torah as the means of attaining this illumination. This saying stresses the spiritual illumination of Eretz Yisrael in relation to the Torah. In other contexts, spiritual reality forms the basis for a renewed

---

54   *Likutei Moharan*, part 2, 78. This and similar sayings present, in my opinion, a definite refutation of the suggestion of Yehuda Liebes, ibid., 215, concerning the essence of Eretz Yisrael in Rabbi Nachman's teachings. Eretz Yisrael is an aspect of *mochin*, consciousness, and an aspect of spiritual attainment, and not an aspect of lack of knowledge. The absence of knowledge is characteristic of the *journey* to Eretz Yisrael, while Eretz Yisrael itself is an aspect of *mochin*. Liebes does not offer even one source to support his identification of the aspect of Eretz Yisrael itself with the aspect of simplicity, as used by Rabbi Nachman. Contrary to an impression one might receive from Liebes, Rabbi Nachman does not contrast his own entry into Eretz Yisrael with Moshe's not entering the land. Consequently, any theoretical comparison between Moshe and Rabbi Nachman is irrelevant in the present context. Therefore we have only the sayings of Rabbi Nachman himself, and these emphasize precisely knowledge and wisdom as the characteristics of Eretz Yisrael. See also the double formulation in *Sichot HaRan*, section 153. It seems that the significant formulation is the one used in *Likutei Moharan*, Part 2, 78: "How one invigorates himself, from the simplicity of the journey to Eretz Yisrael."

55   *Likutei Moharan*, end 37.

56   *Sefer HaMiddot*, Eretz Yisrael, 2.

bond to physical reality.[57] "By virtue of the Torah that one draws, one merits Eretz Yisrael."[58]

## ERETZ YISRAEL AND THE RAISING OF THE *SHECHINAH*

But what is the meaning of this identification of Eretz Yisrael and the Torah? What is the meaning of the constitution of the holiness of Eretz Yisrael through the religious activity of the people of Israel? What is the meaning of the equivalence of Tzaddik, Torah and Eretz Yisrael? Let us have a look at the combination of motives that was used in the teaching that opened our presentation. In it we found a tie between wisdom, providence, eyes and *tefillin*. These terms recur in many of Rabbi Nachman's teachings that refer to Eretz Yisrael.[59] Another important context in which Eretz Yisrael is discussed is that of faith and prayer, which are related in other teachings to this cluster of motives.[60] An exposition of the meaning of these terms brings us to the fundamental issue of the manner of understanding Rabbi Nachman's teachings, and especially the structure of the teachings in *Likutei Moharan*. Whoever examines the book will easily notice the oddness of Rabbi Nachman's expressions. His teachings are complex and unclear, full of allusions and aspects, and they are usually incomprehensible. His unique way of expression is a part of his charm, as it makes possible a variety of readings of his teachings, and allows for finding different emphases in his teachings, at times suiting the fancy of the individual scholar. As Yehuda Liebes noted,[61] we have to adopt specific criteria when we interpret

---

57    See the words of Rabbi Nachman at the end of *Likutei Moharan* 11 concerning the question of when Israel can return to their land. The rectification of spiritual reality is a condition for attaining the physical reality of Eretz Yisrael.

58    *Likutei Moharan* 20:5.

59    See for example *Likutei Moharan*, Part 2, 8:10. Regarding the renovation of the world, compare 35:2, where we learn that the renovation of *Ma'asei Bereshit* is a renovation of wisdom. This combination reinforces the identity of Eretz Yisrael with the aspect of wisdom, as follows from our discussion.

60    See *Likutei Moharan* 9:5 and 7:1.

61    Yehuda Liebes, "Tendencies in the Research of Bratzlav Hassidism: A Reply to

Rabbi Nachman's thought. The interpreter's endeavor has to be aimed at finding a key that will decipher the code in which his teaching is encoded. Therefore, the study of *Likutei Moharan* cannot simply take as its frame of reference the teaching of any particular teaching. Rather, it must rely upon a conception that addresses the meaning of the book and its teachings. The ability of presenting a complete and comprehensive picture that would elucidate the book, is in itself the test of plausibility for any proposed interpretation of *Likutei Moharan*. The present study is not the fitting context in which to present and document comprehensively the reading of *Likutei Moharan* that will be presented in what follows. In this framework, I can only present in a general manner my reading of the book. Our concern here is with the implications of this reading to the understanding of Eretz Yisrael in Rabbi Nachman's thought.

At the base of *Likutei Moharan* stands a structure that is both a conceptual structure and a structure of religious experience. The conceptual structure is the structure of the *sefirot*. Rabbi Nachman is an interpreter and expositor of the Kabbalistic tradition, according to his own particular understanding.[62] From the kabbalistic tradition, we learn of the ascent of the *Shechinah* from the base of the *sefirotic* tree, and of its union with the highest levels of the *sefirotic* tree. From this perspective, it seems there is no great innovation in the works of Rabbi Nachman. It seems to me that the meaning underlying the book is to be found in the significance Rabbi Nachman imparts to this process. As I understand Rabbi Nachman, this process is a process of personal experience that takes place within a person.[63] The basic

Y. Mondshine," *Zion* 47 (1982): 225.

62   Concerning the special relationship of Rabbi Nachman to Rabbi Shimon bar Yochai and the importance of the *Zohar* in his works, see M. Peikaz, *Chassidut Breslav* (Jerusalem: Mossad Bialik, 1972), 13ff.

63   For an earlier kabbalistic understanding of the personal, perhaps even bodily, characteristics of the processes that take place in the *sefirotic* tree, see Moshe Idel, "An Anonymous Kabbalistic Commentary on *Shir HaYichud*," *Mysticism, Magic and Kabbalah in Ashkenazi Judaism*, ed. K. E. Groezinger, J. Dan (Berlin: de Gruyter, 1995) 151ff. Expressions that ground these processes within a person can be found already in the Rabad's commentary to *Sefer Yetzirah*.

process of the spiritual life, according to this understanding, is the raising of
the energy of the *Shechinah* from the inferior state, via the spiritual centers
of the *sefirot*, and its unification with the higher spiritual centers. This is the
significance of *Tikkun HaBrit*, the rectification of the covenant, which is, in
my opinion, the key to understanding Rabbi Nachman's teachings.[64] *Tikkun
HaBrit* is the raising of the energy, that when not rectified is expressed as
sexual energy, to the head. This process opens a person spiritually to the
realization of the spiritual reality that is revealed through the opening
of the higher spiritual centers that are in the head. Moreover, this process
stands at the base of many sayings in *Likutei Moharan*, that relate to the
union of man and God.[65] Only in light of the centrality of this process will
we be able to understand the great emphasis upon sexual rectification, as
found in Rabbi Nachman's teachings, and the meaning of the transformation that Rabbi Nachman enjoins regarding the sexual force. This process
parallels the processes of spiritual transformation that are found in other
religious traditions.[66] This process stands at the base of the greater part of
*Likutei Moharan*. The various sets of interrelated aspects, presented by
Rabbi Nachman, allude to the various aspects and stages in the ascent of the
energy. The structure that holds together the series of associations presented
by Rabbi Nachman is the proposed structure, in light of which the book is
transformed from a strange riddle to a methodical and consistent description of the religious experience that underlies Rabbi Nachman's teaching.[67]

---

64   On the significance of *HaTikkun HaKlali* as a key to understanding Rabbi
Nachman's teaching, see also Yehuda Liebes, *Zion* 45, (1980): 201ff. My understanding of the meaning of *HaTikkun HaKlali* differs from that of Liebes.

65   For the principle of the union of man with God, see e.g., *Likutei Moharan*
22:10, and the last part of Torah 21.

66   See M. Eliade, *Yoga: Immortality and Freedom* (Princeton: Princeton
University Press, 1969), 245ff.

67   According to this suggestion, one should examine anew the issue of revealing
and concealing in the Breslav tradition. Is the manner in which ideas are presented
by Rabbi Nachman simply the fruit of an associative way of thinking, or did Rabbi
Nachman intend to reveal and conceal at one and the same time? On this issue, see Y.
Weiss, *Mechkarim b'Chassidut Breslav* (Jerusalem: Mossad Bialik, 1975), 181ff., and M.

The associative complex that accompanies Rabbi Nachman's discussion of Eretz Yisrael is related to this understanding of the raising of the energy. Eretz Yisrael is identified with a stage in the ascent of the *Shechinah*. This means that the energy of Eretz Yisrael is the energy that flows from the ascent of the *Shechinah* to a spiritual level, to a particular *sefirah*. Hence Eretz Yisrael is a place in which the ascent of *Shechinah* is possible, and it is the place where this energy is available. We may thus recap all that was said until now regarding the expansion of the energy of Eretz Yisrael beyond its territorial boundaries in terms of the drawing forth of the energy that is made available from the presence of the *Shechinah* in its highest form, in union with the higher *sefirot*.

## SEFIROTIC IDENTIFICATION OF ERETZ YISRAEL

At this point, it is proper to ask with which *sefirah* Rabbi Nachman identifies Eretz Yisrael. Before I try to answer this question, we have to be reminded that the spiritual enterprise of Rabbi Nachman carries the stamp of an original and creative personality. Rabbi Nachman made use of earlier traditions, which he adapted creatively, without being restricted to their original meaning. This fact is important as we come to identify the *sefirah* with which Eretz Yisrael is identified. Put differently: to what degree does the *Shechinah* ascend in Eretz Yisrael? Classical kabbalistic literature tended to identify Eretz Yisrael with the *sefirah* of *Malchut*, the lowest *sefirah* in the *sefirotic* tree.[68] This identification is not corroborated in Rabbi Nachman's teachings.[69] If the process of the spiritual life is the raising of the *Shechinah*,

Peikaz, *Chassidut Breslav*, (Jerusalem: Mossad Bialik, 1972) 10ff.

68   See Idel (n. 3 above), 194ff.; Hallamish, 215ff.

69   The only source in which Rabbi Nachman seems to identify Eretz Yisrael and *Malchut* is *Likutei Moharan* 48: "With the Lord, your God, this is the aspect of Eretz Yisrael," as the context indicates. Nonetheless, the identification with the aspect of *Sukkah* brings the discussion back to the aspect of *Binah*, as the opening of this teaching suggests. The well known association of these two *sefirot* facilitates this conceptual shift. It is thus possible that even the one occurrence that links Eretz Yisrael and the *sefirah* of *Malchut* cannot be sustained.

that is identified with, or dwells in the *sefirah* of *Malchut*, it is unlikely that the higher spiritual values will be identified with the lower *sefirot*. Rather we should expect an identification with the higher *sefirot*. There are indeed kabbalistic conceptions that identify Eretz Yisrael with the *sefirot* of *Chochmah* and *Binah*.[70] These conceptions are closer to my understanding of Rabbi Nachman. However, it is possible that Rabbi Nachman carried out a yet more radical move. At the end of this presentation, I will explore the possibility that Rabbi Nachman identifies Eretz Yisrael with the *sefirah* of *Keter*. Such an identification, that from the point of view of kabbalistic sources is probably unprecedented, is not so surprising when we consider that the spiritual process that underlies Rabbi Nachman's writings is that of raising the energy to the head. Focusing the energy in the head makes it difficult, at times, to distinguish between the different centers in the head, that is: *Keter* and *Chochmah*.[71] Indeed, it is possible that Rabbi Nachman intends to make no distinction between them and wants to deal with them as a unit. Nonetheless, as I will suggest below, the *sefirah* of *Keter* has an important function in the spiritual process described by Rabbi Nachman, and in several sources, one can find allusions to the relationship that exists between Eretz Yisrael and the ascent of the *Shechinah* to the *Keter*. In the next stage of the discussion, I will refer to the ascent of the energy to the head without distinguishing between the different centers, regardless of whether they form a unity, or whether Rabbi Nachman limits his intention in these contexts to the *sefirot* of *Chochmah* and *Binah*. At the conclusion of this discussion I will examine the possibility that Eretz Yisrael is identified with the *Keter*.

Following these introductions, let us turn our attention to a clarification of the meaning of the cluster of associations that are related to Eretz Yisrael.

---

70   See Haviva Pedaya, n. 3 above, 266ff.; Mordechai Pachter, ibid., 300.

71   One of the reasons that Rabbi Nachman offered for his journey to Eretz Yisrael was that he went in order to obtain the Higher *Chochmah*. In understanding the meaning of this term in Rabbi Nachman's words, one does not need to limit it to the *sefirah* of *Chochmah*. In *Likutei Moharan* 22:10, the Higher *Chochmah* is identified with the aspect of *Ein Sof*.

Before we turn to the specific motifs, I would like to introduce once more a term common in our language, and which might assist in elucidating Rabbi Nachman's intentions. The term is "consciousness." The energy discussed above creates a special state of consciousness. This state of consciousness is the key to the understanding of the significance of Eretz Yisrael. Eretz Yisrael is a state of consciousness. This is the meaning of Rabbi Nachman's reference to the "*mochin* of Eretz Yisrael."[72] This state of consciousness is a product of the revelation of the high energy that is characteristic of Eretz Yisrael. The revelation of this energy is the abundance of supernal bliss, as Rabbi Nachman describes the *mochin* of Eretz Yisrael.[73] This coupling of the high energy and the corresponding state of consciousness is critical in understanding Rabbi Nachman's sayings about Eretz Yisrael.[74]

What are the characteristics of the state of consciousness particular to Eretz Yisrael? The consciousness of Eretz Yisrael is characterized by the direct recognition of Divine being and wisdom. Hence the recognition of God's actions in everything.

> And those people who deny miracles, and say that everything follows the course of nature, and if they see a miracle they cover the miracle with the way of nature, saying this is the course of nature, in effect they impair prayer, for prayer is miraculous in that it changes nature, and they impair faith, because they do not believe in the providence of God, and they impair Eretz Yisrael, which is the place of the miracles.[75]

God's providence is thus revealed in Eretz Yisrael. Providence is used here in the sense of the revelation of the Divine presence in all of existence. The meaning of providence is rising above the consciousness of nature, and the

---

72    Likutei Moharan, Part 2, 71.

73    Ibid.

74    See also *Likutei Moharan*, end of Torah 9: "According to the impairment that one impairs in prayer, and in faith and in Eretz Yisrael, he has to descend to the depths of the Egyptian exile." The Egyptian exile is identified, in another context, with the exile of consciousness (דעת). See, among others places, *Likutei Moharan* 56:7.

75    Likutei Moharan 9:7.

realization of faith. Faith is the recognition of the presence and reality of God that are expressed in everything. Faith is thus a state of consciousness. In this state of consciousness the distinction between nature and miracle is abrogated, and true prayer becomes possible. Thus, God's providence is revealed. In the opening text, God's providence was identified with wisdom. Indeed, the revelation of the state of consciousness that characterizes Eretz Yisrael is truly wisdom, as it reveals Divine wisdom, and enables man to unite with it.

In order to understand the meaning of this union with wisdom, we must clarify the issue of *tefillin* that is found in this teaching. This issue is significant not only to the understanding of the meaning of Eretz Yisrael in Rabbi Nachman's thought, but to understanding his entire system of thought. As Rabbi Nathan testifies, in the notes at the end of Torah 38, "Know, that I heard from his holy lips that he contemplated several teachings. And he said that they all are about the secret meaning of *tefillin* . . . and additional lengthy teachings, the details of which I do not recall, he said that all of them are the secret meaning of *tefillin*, happy is he who attains them." I see in this note a hermeneutical key to the totality, or at least to the bulk of Rabbi Nachman's conceptual teachings. If indeed the secret of *tefillin* has such an important place in Rabbi Nachman's thought, we should not be surprised if also his teaching on Eretz Yisrael is structured in light of this secret.[76]

The relation between Eretz Yisrael and *tefillin* is spelled out in explicit

---

76   Mark Verman, "*Aliyah* and *Yeridah*: The Journeys of the Besht and Rabbi Nachman to Israel," *Approaches to Judaism in Medieval Times*, Vol. 3 (Atlanta: Scholars Press, 1988), 159–171, has already noted the importance of *tefillin* to the understanding of Eretz Yisrael. However, Verman interpreted the secret of *tefillin* as the union of *Tiferet* and *Malchut*. In my opinion, the place of *tefillin*, for Rabbi Nachman, is higher, and the *tefillin* of which he speaks are the *tefillin* of the head. Classical kabbalistic symbolism of *Tiferet* is applied by Rabbi Nachman also to higher *sefirot*. See e.g., *Likutei Moharan* 1, the identification of Ya'akov with the mind. Torah 47, upon which Verman bases himself, is extant in two versions. In Rabbi Nachman's version the issue of glory (פאר) is emphasized more than the issue of *Tiferet*. Note also the discussion of the face and its shades, which fits better the sense of *tefillin* I propose.

sayings of Rabbi Nachman. The following story is told concerning his visit
to Eretz Yisrael:[77]

> Once one of the prestigious people, who was very important in Eretz
> Yisrael, came to him ... And when he came to our master, of blessed mem-
> ory, Rabbi Nachman had all bystanders taken out, so that no one should
> be with them, as they got to know each other. And this man, who was with
> our master, of blessed memory, stayed there, and pleaded with him, and said
> to our master, of blessed memory, in the following expression: "We know
> that the honor of your Torah (i.e., Rabbi Nachman) did not come to Eretz
> Yisrael like the rest of the multitude, with a petty consciousness, with the
> intention of walking four cubits in the Land of Israel, so he may inherit the
> world to come, or other thoughts in the manner of simple folk. Obviously
> the honor of your Torah has come here with a great state of consciousness,
> to attain a great understanding in God's service. We therefore wish to know
> which aspect of Eretz Yisrael the honor of your Torah has entered in, and
> what you aspire to achieve here in the service of God, and I am ready to
> serve you, in my body, and in all aspects of my soul, etc." And our master
> replied: "My soul friend, do not distress me in this matter, for it is not
> a light matter to reveal to you, God forbid, what is this service, and why I
> have come here, and perhaps there is even a heavenly decree forbidding my
> sharing this, etc." And again the great rabbi implored him, and said: "Our
> request and demand is that at least our master teach us one of his delight-
> ful and pleasant novellae, which God has granted him ... And perhaps we
> will thereby also understand and attain some allusion of the previous mat-
> ter." Immediately, our master, of blessed memory, became aflame, with a
> heavenly fire, and his face became aflame like true torches, and on account
> of this excitement his hair stood on end, and he threw his upper hat off,
> and started to speak, saying: "Do you know the secret of *tefillin?*" This man
> replied, saying some of the mystical intentions. Rabbi Nachman said: "No.
> This is not the path of the secret of *tefillin*, and since you do not know the
> secret meaning of *tefillin*, you do not know the secret of the four directions
> of Eretz Yisrael. And now let me give you a slight clue thereof." And as he
> began to talk, blood came forth from his throat. And he said to this wise

---

77  *Shivchei HaRan*, 31.

man: "Now, see with your own eyes that from heaven above they do not agree to reveal anything to you."

From this story we learn not only about the importance of Eretz Yisrael in terms of *tefillin*, but also about the meaning of Rabbi Nachman's journey to Eretz Yisrael The sage from Eretz Yisrael entreats Rabbi Nachman that he should reveal to him a teaching from which he might glean what was Rabbi Nachman's purpose in coming to Eretz Yisrael. Rabbi Nachman begins to reveal to him the secret of *tefillin*, but is stopped from heaven. The association of *tefillin* and wisdom, in the Torah with which we opened our presentation, will also illuminate one of the explicit explanations that Rabbi Nachman himself offered for his journey to Eretz Yisrael. "I heard in his name that he said before he went to Eretz Yisrael, that he wants to travel in order to attain the high wisdom. Because there is a higher and lower wisdom, and he already has the lower wisdom, and he still has to attain the higher wisdom, and for this he travels to Eretz Yisrael."[78]

The time has come to uncover the secret of *tefillin*. According to my understanding, *tefillin* is the symbolical expression of the situation that occurs when the *Shechinah* ascends to the head. This is *Tikkun HaBrit,* the rectification of the covenant, that creates the unique state of consciousness, identified with Divine wisdom, with providence, and that is expressed by means of *tefillin*. The *tefillin* in Rabbi Nachman's discussion are the *tefillin* of the head.[79] It is worth noting that the *tefillin* are placed at the height of the head, the location of *Keter*, while the text of the Torah refers to "between your eyes,"[80] i.e., in the place of the eyes, which are identified in kabbalistic tradition as *Chochmah* and *Binah*. The *tefillin* are thus an external religious symbol, the meaning of which is the raising of the energy to the head. The

---

78  *Chayei Moharan*, His Journey to Eretz Yisrael, 6. See also Arthur Green, *Tormented Master*, (Alabama: University of Alabama Press, 1979), 78ff., where we learn that also another answer of Rabbi Nachman's, that the goal of his journey is to receive the light within vessels, has to do with the illumination of wisdom.

79  This emerges from the ensemble of associations, and from the contexts in which the *tefillin* are discussed. See the verse "God is *upon them*, they shall live," that is brought regarding *tefillin* in *Likutei Moharan* 47.

80  *Devarim* 6:8.

symbol can represent the ascent of the energy either to *Chochmah* or to the
*Keter*. Torah 40, which opened our discussion, discusses the identification
of *tefillin* and eyes: "The *tefillin* are in the aspect of *mochin*, they enter and
penetrate the eyes." Now we can understand what is intended by the constitution of the holiness of Eretz Yisrael, and the formation of an aspect of
Eretz Yisrael. The raising of the energy to the head is the aspect of Eretz
Yisrael. This aspect is not a given, but is attained through a spiritual process.
This spiritual process is what constitutes the spiritual reality that is identified with Eretz Yisrael and that is revealed in it.

Many sayings concerning Eretz Yisrael will be understood in light of
the above. The saying according to which "Eretz Yisrael is a great rectification to the impairment of the covenant"[81] is understood in this context.
*Tikkun HaBrit* is the raising of the energy to the head. Eretz Yisrael has a
vital role in this process.[82] Also the importance of prayer is understood in
this context. Prayer is the central value in Rabbi Nachman's teaching. Space
prevents me from documenting the following understanding in the present
context. Suffice it to state that in my reading of *Likutei Moharan*, prayer
is not only a process of saying fixed formulae, nor even a free outpouring
of the soul in prayer. The meaning of prayer is identified with the raising
of the *Shechinah*.[83] We even find the word "prayer" as a nickname for the
*Shechinah*.[84] We find a strong emphasis on the connection between prayer
and Eretz Yisrael. We already saw above how at the time of prayer, there
is an attempt to draw the aspect of Eretz Yisrael. The power of prayer, its
effectiveness, the awareness of God's presence, faith, which is the basis of
prayer – all these are dependent upon *Tikkun HaBrit*, the ascent of the
energy and its reaching the unique state of consciousness that enables the

---

81   *Likutei Moharan*, Part 2, 109.

82   See the end of Torah 44. Purification of the brain in the air of Eretz Yisrael
is connected to the rectification of the eternal covenant. See also Torah 20, 10, where
*Tikkun HaBrit*, the aspect of knowledge, and entering Eretz Yisrael are interrelated.
See also Torah 31, p. 46, column 2. Through *Tikkun HaBrit* one merits the aspect of
miracles, identified in teachings 7, 1 and 9, 5 with Eretz Yisrael.

83   Compare *Likutei Moharan*, Part 2, 84.

84   See, for example, *Likutei Moharan* 2:6.

fulfillment of prayer. Efficacy in prayer is a function of the acquisition of power, which in turn is a function of the raising of the energy. Only thus can a prayer that produces miracles transpire. The relationship between this understanding of prayer and Eretz Yisrael will be understood in light of the suggested conception of Eretz Yisrael, and the process of the ascent of energy. "And the essence of faith, the aspect of prayer, the aspect of miracles, is only in Eretz Yisrael ... and there is the centerpoint of the ascent of prayers, as it is written this is the gate of heaven."[85] I would like to suggest that the meaning of the ascent of prayers is not simply a description of the ascent of the prayers of each individual to God's dwelling place in heaven, but also the ascent of energy, which is the essence of prayer. This is how one might understand the meaning of the ascent from one level to another in the following source: "Whoever wants to be a true Israelite, i.e., that he will rise from level to level, this is impossible except by means of the holiness of Eretz Yisrael. Because all the ascents that one must ascend to holiness are possible only by means of Eretz Yisrael, and also all ascents of prayers are possible only in Eretz Yisrael."[86] The ascent of prayer itself and the rising of man from one level to another are both in the aspect of Eretz Yisrael.[87] According to this suggestion, both reflect the same spiritual process that is essentially connected to the reality of Eretz Yisrael. Eretz Yisrael is thus where the energy is found in its highest form. Eretz Yisrael is the place where the ascent of the *Shechinah* and the realization of Divine consciousness is possible. Were we to say that these processes take place only in man, because they are *an aspect* of Eretz Yisrael, we would be neutralizing the significance of Eretz Yisrael in its reality, and making of it simply a spiritual aspect. It seems Rabbi Nachman's position is more complex. The particular

---

85    *Likutei Moharan* 7:1.

86    Quote taken from *Likutei Etzot*, Eretz Yisrael, 3. I am unable to locate the reference as cited there.

87    In light of the above, we can understand also the meaning of his saying: "My place is only Eretz Yisrael. Wherever I go, I go only to Eretz Yisrael," in *Chayei Moharan*, His Journey to Novoritzs, section 6. The journey to Eretz Yisrael, according to this, is the constant rising from level to level, by virtue of Eretz Yisrael and within the state of consciousness particular to it.

energy is present in Eretz Yisrael and is expressed in space through it. The physical presence of the energy in Eretz Yisrael enables a person to induce a parallel process within himself.

It seems to me that in light of the above we will be able to understand better both the meaning of Rabbi Nachman's journey to Eretz Yisrael and his ability to leave it, and even his desire to return from it. Green already explained the meaning of Rabbi Nachman's journey to Eretz Yisrael as an important stage in his spiritual development, and as an entry into a new phase in his spiritual existence.[88] From the understanding of the meaning of Eretz Yisrael, according to the conceptual and existential structure we suggested underlies *Likutei Moharan*, we may now suggest more precisely the meaning of Rabbi Nachman's journey to Eretz Yisrael. If Eretz Yisrael is the place where the energy unites with the aspect of wisdom and consciousness, coming to Eretz Yisrael helps the individual to realize this process within himself. The very fact of physical presence in Eretz Yisrael enables the absorption of energy, and it is the catalyst that helps to raise the energy within a person. This is the meaning of the union of the lower wisdom – an attribute of the *Shechinah* – and the higher wisdom. Hence the immense importance that Rabbi Nachman attributed to his visit in Eretz Yisrael. Hence the sharp distinction made by Rabbi Nachman between the teachings that preceded his journey and the teachings that followed it, having attained the

---

88    Green, *Tormented Master*, 63–93. Our discussion might throw a new light on Green's conclusion, according to which the purpose of Rabbi Nachman's journey to Eretz Yisrael is related to a spiritual initiation. It seems that the suggested description of the ladder of spiritual development will help us to understand in what way his journey aided the development of his spiritual life. Unlike Green, who emphasizes the process of the journey to Eretz Yisrael itself, I would emphasize the presence in Eretz Yisrael as the decisive moment, as do also the classical descriptions of his journey. This emphasis does not deny the understanding that finds messianic significance in his journey, but rather explicates it. For the association between the suggested process and the messianic rectification, see among other sources *Likutei Moharan* 2. See also Verman's article, n. 74 above.

energy and consciousness typical of Eretz Yisrael.[89] Hence also his ability to leave the land once this process took place in him.

The tradition that narrates that after he walked four cubits in Eretz Yisrael he accomplished all he desired and was ready to go back[90] can be understood in light of Rabbi Nachman's explanation of the expression "The land that eats its inhabitants." "For it is a land that eats its inhabitants, for he who dwells there is devoured by it, and transformed into its holy essence, therefore even he who walks four cubits in Eretz Yisrael, the next world is promised to him."[91] The transformation into the essence of Eretz Yisrael implies the absorption of the energy in man and the assistance that the energy of Eretz Yisrael provides in this process of spiritual transformation. This process can take place even within a four-cubit long walk, as Rabbi Nachman testifies.[92]

We can now understand the place of the Tzaddik in the teaching of Rabbi Nachman, Rabbi Nachman's self-image, and the equivalence we found between the Tzaddik and Eretz Yisrael. A Tzaddik is he who succeeds in raising the energy to the head. Thus, it is clear why the Tzaddik is equivalent to Eretz Yisrael. A Tzaddik lives the spiritual meaning of Eretz Yisrael permanently in his being. The equivalence between the Tzaddik and Eretz Yisrael is, in this understanding, a fact. Both reveal the same aspect of energy, and can therefore fulfill the same spiritual function.

---

89    See *Shivchei Moharan*, His teachings and Holy Books, 18.

90    *Shivchei HaRan*, 2, 15. It is clear that according to this understanding, Rabbi Nachman's departure is not a result of failure, but rather of having attained his spiritual goal.

91    *Likutei Moharan* 129.

92    See also the story in *Sichot HaRan*, section 153. The mention of Eretz Yisrael and the drawing of vitality from there, reestablish Rabbi Nachman's lost state of consciousness, and take him out of his condition of non-knowing. It is interesting to note that immediately after this Rabbi Nachman commands to have the song *Azamer b'Shvachin* sung, which is usually sung only at a later stage in the meal. The subject of this song is the raising of the *Shechinah*. It is thus possible that the singing of this song reflects the process that Rabbi Nachman himself experiences by virtue of drawing from Eretz Yisrael.

ERETZ YISRAEL AND THE *KETER*

In defining the precise nature of the energy of Eretz Yisrael we touched above on the question of the identification of Eretz Yisrael within the *sefirotic* order. The recurring mention of the air of Eretz Yisrael making wise, and of the aspects of wisdom and eyes, facilitate seeing in Eretz Yisrael an expression of the *sefirah* of *Chochmah*.[93] However, it seems that in order to understand Rabbi Nachman's position we must also examine the possibility that Eretz Yisrael is identified with the *Keter*, and that the energy that emanates from it is the energy that flows from the ascent of the *Shechinah* to the *Keter*. Mark Verman has suggested that Rabbi Nachman saw himself in the aspect of *Keter*.[94] Beyond this, we must remember the proposed experiential structure that underlies Rabbi Nachman's teaching. This structure strives for union with God and incorporation in *Ein Sof*.[95] There is thus no reason in principal to limit the ascent of the energy to *Chochmah*. The inclination to the highest form of unity would lead to reference to the union of the *Shechinah* with *Keter*. In my opinion, the structure of unity to which the book aspires leads to this point, if not beyond. It is therefore reasonable that also the speculations regarding the level of Eretz Yisrael will assume this union of energy and will therefore identify Eretz Yisrael with the *Keter*. I have not found a saying that explicitly identifies Eretz Yisrael with the *Keter*. However, this lack is not surprising, since all of Rabbi Nachman's teaching is in allusions, and few are the things that are articulated explicitly. In order to corroborate the suggestion that Eretz Yisrael is identified with the *sefirah* of *Keter* we can add several allusions to make a strong suggestion.

In Torah 7, where we read of the importance of prayer and its ascent in Eretz Yisrael, we read: "Know, that exile is principally because of lack of faith, as it is written 'Come, look from the head (top) of *Amana*,' and faith is

---

93    See n. 70 above, where I suggested that wisdom, at least the higher wisdom, is not limited to the *sefirah* of *Chochmah*.

94    Ibid., especially the discussion from n. 14 onwards.

95    See n. 64 above.

the aspect of prayer."[96] In the continuation of this Torah, the aspect of faith is identified with the aspect of circles, on the basis of the verse "And your faith encircles you." In a discussion with parallel thematics,[97] Eretz Yisrael is called Cana'an according to the following etymological chain: "And therefore the land is called Cana'an, Cana'an in the sense of merchant, which is an aspect of faith, as it is written 'and your faith encircles you.'" The reference to the circle which we find in both texts suits the *sefirah* of *Keter*. Moreover, the emphasis on the *head* of faith in the verse concerning faith draws our attention to the head. All these sayings are brought in the context of discussions in which the status of Eretz Yisrael is addressed. Beyond these allusions, we must reflect on the meaning of Rabbi Nachman's placing faith and prayer at the top of the spiritual ladder, higher than Torah and higher than wisdom. The identification of faith and prayer with the aspect of the *Keter* will help us understand the high position they occupy in Rabbi Nachman's teaching.[98]

In this context we should also note several general sayings concerning the sanctity of Eretz Yisrael. Eretz Yisrael is called by Rabbi Nachman the greatness of greatness.[99] The following teaching is also significant in this context:

> In order that one should merit to be similar to Him, blessed be He, to distinguish between light and darkness as discussed above, this is achieved through providence, that is that one leaves nature, for this is the aspect of the totality of holiness. And this is attained through Eretz Yisrael, because Eretz Yisrael is the totality of holiness that is in all holinesses, because all the ten degrees of holinesses are there, and therefore it is said concerning Eretz Yisrael, 'God's eyes are always upon it,' because exclusive providence is there, the aspect of 'Look from Your holy abode,' and this is the meaning

96   Rabbi Nachman is playing upon the name *Amana*, as expressive of *emunah*, faith, in association with the raising of the energy to the head. Thus raising energy/prayer to the head is an aspect of faith.

97   *Likutei Moharan* 9:7.

98   By this is undermined by the characterization of faith in Breslav Chassidism as the opposite of mysticism, as suggested by Yosef Weiss. See Y. Weiss, *Mechkarim b'Chassidut Breslav* (Jerusalem: Mossad Bialik, 1975), 87ff.

99   *Chayei Moharan*, His Journey to Eretz Yisrael, 12.

of the verse: 'I have placed God always before me,' i.e., when I want to be compared and similar to God, blessed be He, as mentioned above, then always *before* me i.e., the aspect of Eretz Yisrael, as the Midrash says, the word *always* means Eretz Yisrael, as it is written God's eyes are *always* upon it.[100]

This Torah teaches that one can transcend one's natural condition. Not only is it possible to rise in prayer beyond the aspect of nature and attain the aspect of miracle, as we saw above. One can leave the confines of his natural being and attain a spiritual level of resemblance and similarity to God. This is a confirmation of the spiritual transformation discussed above. This resemblance is dependent on the aspect of Eretz Yisrael. Here it is said that Eretz Yisrael is the totality of the holiness that is in all holinesses. This generalization might allude to the aspiration to the highest level of holiness. This allusion is explained in the words that follow: "because all the ten holinesses are there." I would like to suggest that the mention of the ten holinesses is intended to point to the special aspect of Eretz Yisrael. The *Shechinah* has ascended there through all aspects of the ten holinesses, i.e., through all ten *sefirot*. The mention of ten is an indication of the totality of holiness, which is expressed in the attainment of the holiness of the *Keter*.

These words can serve us as a key to understanding the topos of ten in *Likutei Moharan*. That there are so many things that are an aspect of ten stems from the foundation of the book, according to which the purpose of the spiritual life is the raising of the energy through these ten aspects and their rectification. This principle is reflected in the different ways in which the number ten is expressed. If this is indeed so, then the appearance of the number ten can be taken as indication of the ascent of the *Shechinah* up to the tenth aspect, which is the *Keter*. The reference to the aspect of ten in connection to Eretz Yisrael in the following quotations will be used therefore as additional support to the understanding that the holiness of Eretz Yisrael is the holiness of the *Keter*. This suggestion will furthermore help us to understand the oddity of some of the following teachings. The drawing

---

100   *Likutei Moharan*, 234. The subject of the teaching are the stories told of Tzaddikim. Once again, we have here the equivalence of the Tzaddik and Eretz Yisrael.

of the air of Eretz Yisrael at the time of prayer, by clapping hands, is justified in the following way: "'You are standing today,' 'standing' always means 'praying,' 'before the Lord your God,' this is the aspect of Eretz Yisrael, as the Sages say: 'Whoever lives in Eretz Yisrael is considered to have a God,' that is, how will you merit that your prayer will be in the air of Eretz Yisrael? 'Your heads, your tribes' etc. and scripture details ten aspects, i.e., the aspect of clapping hands. Through clapping hands prayer takes place in the air of Eretz Yisrael."[101] The ten aspects lead to standing before God, and they parallel the structure of the body that is activated when clapping hands. When we decipher the symbolical structure that underlies this saying, it is easier to understand the associative flow of this teaching.[102]

In another context we read: "the essence of the force of Eretz Yisrael is from the aspect of the Ten Utterances by which the world was created."[103] In another context we learn that the ten levels of prophecy lead to faith, which is an aspect of Eretz Yisrael.[104] These allusions may add up to a complete understanding, according to which the level of Eretz Yisrael is the level of the *Keter*.

---

101   *Likutei Moharan*, 44.

102   Does Rabbi Nachman emphasize *your heads* as the beginning of the counting of ten, i.e., from the head?

103   *Likutei Moharan*, Part 2, 78. One should note that this structure of ten can be found throughout existence and not only in Eretz Yisrael. The system of ten *sefirot* is structured as a wheel within a wheel, and the aspect of Eretz Yisrael can be reflected also throughout creation, as we saw above. As I suggested above, Rabbi Nachman presents continuity, rather than discontinuity, between Eretz Yisrael and other lands. This continuity facilitates the discovery of the identical ten-fold structure in Eretz Yisrael and in other lands.

104   *Likutei Moharan*, Part 2, 8:7 and 8:10. See further, Part 1, end of Torah 9. The ninth aspect is the aspect of Eretz Yisrael. But it seems that this Torah was articulated as a commentary on a Zoharic saying, which is woven around the number nine, and one should not identify the nine *Tikkunim* mentioned there with the *sefirotic* system.

CONCLUSION

In presenting the place of Eretz Yisrael in Rabbi Nachman's thought I tried
to focus the discussion on three main aspects:

1. The relationship between the physical Eretz Yisrael and its ability to
spread and extend. Here I suggested that Eretz Yisrael is an energy which is
also expressed in space, in Eretz Yisrael, and hence the physical drawing of
the energy of Eretz Yisrael.

2. Identification of this energy on the basis of the processes that are central
to Rabbi Nachman's thought. I suggested that at the base of his teaching and
experience is the experience of the raising of the energy to the head. This
process brings about a fundamental spiritual transformation, and leads to
union with God. Recognition of this process is the key to understanding
*Likutei Moharan.* Against this background it is possible to understand the
significance that Rabbi Nachman attaches to Eretz Yisrael. Eretz Yisrael is
the place where the energy is found in its highest form. This presence aids
whoever turns to it with the proper intention to attain it in his own being.
Hence the meaning of Rabbi Nachman's journey to Eretz Yisrael. Eretz
Yisrael is internalized in a process that is fundamentally bound to its physical existence, and hence the ability to expand it beyond its geographical
boundaries.

3. A detailed examination of the nature of the energy that characterizes
Eretz Yisrael and of its relationship to the *sefirotic* system led me to suggest
that it is possible that Rabbi Nachman identifies the being of Eretz Yisrael
with the reality of the *Keter*.[105]

---

105   Heartfelt thanks to Moshe Idel, a friend and a teacher. As a teacher, he
helped me elucidate some of the matters discussed above. As a friend, he gave me the
courage to publish in this area of study. Shoshana Liessman labored on the English
translation that underlies the present text. I cherish both her labor and her friendship.

Rabbi Zvi Grumet

# Patriarch and King: Two Models of Repentance

A CHARISMATIC LEADER. SEXUAL impropriety. A woman named Tamar. A cover up, in which the innocent will die. When confronted, a dramatic acceptance of responsibility.

The generic elements outlined above could easily describe the story of Yehudah and Tamar. They could just as easily describe the story of David and Bat Sheva, with the epilogue of Amnon and Tamar. (David's son apparently learned too well from his father.) Not surprisingly, Yehudah is the patriarch of the tribe from which David emerges.

Despite the overt similarities, there are profound differences between the stories. And, as in any instance in which there are similarities, they are meant to draw our attention to the differences. Our focus in these pages is to understand the nature of the downfall of these two individuals, and, perhaps more importantly, to explore the nature of their repentance. Ultimately, we will argue that they present two different types of sin, and therefore, two distinct models of repentance.

## YEHUDAH – THE FALL

Let us briefly review the story of Yehudah and Tamar. Yehudah leaves his family to start his own. He marries the unnamed daughter of a Cana'anite man named Shua, and she bears him three sons – Er, Onan, and Shelah. Yehudah marries his eldest, Er, to a woman named Tamar, but Er dies soon afterwards, childless. The second son, Onan, is called upon to "uphold his brother's name" in some form of levirate marriage (this practice was wide-spread even before the Torah's explicit command), yet Onan, aware that the seed "will not be his," spills his seed on the ground. God, angry with Onan, kills him as well. Unprepared to have his last son suffer the fate of the first two, Yehudah tells Tamar to wait for Shelah to be old enough to fulfill his levirate duties while having no intention of allowing Tamar to marry him.

With the passage of time, Tamar realizes that she is in a bind – legally she is bound to Shelah and forbidden from marrying anyone else, yet she will never be given to Shelah. Dressing up as a prostitute, she positions herself strategically so that Yehudah sleeps with her without his being aware that it is Tamar sharing his bed.

When her pregnancy becomes apparent, Yehudah is informed. Still un-aware that it is his child she is carrying, he pronounces her infidelity and a death sentence. Quietly, Tamar sends a message to Yehudah with the signet ring and staff he had left with her (he apparently had no money to pay the prostitute, and left behind collateral), indicating that the owner of those items was the father of her child. Without hesitation, Yehudah announces her innocence and his guilt. The sentence is rescinded, Tamar is his, and she bears him two children.

Let us begin with two observations.

First, as Ibn Ezra has already noted, this story had to have taken place over the course of many years. There had to be enough time for Yehudah to marry, have three children of marriageable age, bear another pair of children with Tamar, and become a grandfather from one of those children – all before the descent of the family to Egypt. That descent took place twenty two years after the sale of Yosef – not nearly enough time for this entire saga to take place, even though the story is first told to us *after* the sale of Yosef! What is clear is that a significant part of this story happened earlier, and its juxtaposition to the sale of Yosef is thematic rather than chronological.

Second, Yehudah's departure from the family unit: וירד יהודה מאת אחיו. The language of the text is unambiguous; Yehudah leaves the family, he is not forced out. Why he leaves, one can only speculate. Yet it does appear that one goal of his leaving was to establish his own clan. Yehudah had separated himself from Ya'akov's clan and that of his brothers to begin his own dynasty. And so the only thing the text tells us is that he marries, and arranges for his children to marry.

Yehudah's marriage is dreadfully problematic, and emblematic of his breaking his ties with his clan. In Bereshit, marrying a Cana'anite woman is the pathway out of the blessed family. Avraham insists that his servant not allow Yitzchak to marry a Cana'anite. Rivkah insists that Ya'akov not marry a Cana'anite woman. Esav's marriage to Cana'anite women was a source of deep distress to his parents – which even he ultimately understood. Yehudah's breaking of that taboo signifies his purposefulness in leaving his clan.

How long Yehudah's abandonment of his ancestral family lasted is unknown, yet at some point he returns, so that the narrative places him as a central figure in the sale of Yosef. "What profit will come to us if he dies?" proclaims Yehudah, "let us sell him to the Yishmaelites so that our hands not bear responsibility." Yehudah has mastered the art of avoidance of responsibility. Let someone else do whatever dirty work there is to do, lest our hands be sullied.

This abdication of responsibility is perhaps his signature. He refuses to take responsibility to let Tamar know that she will not be permitted to marry, and refuses to do the responsible thing to let her marry Shelah. Not to mention the responsibility to his son – how long will he hide Shelah? How long will he not allow Shelah to marry?[1] In his irresponsible drive to save Shelah's life, he destines Shelah to never marry, burying the future of his dreams for establishing a new dynasty.[2]

---

1    Yehudah's denial of the marriage of Shelah to Tamar was predicated on Shelah's youth – "until the lad matures" he declares as the period Tamar must wait. Once Shelah becomes of age, Yehudah's pretense will become transparent. Once Shelah marries, Tamar is expected to rightfully demand her own redemption. The awareness of that will keep Yehudah from allowing Shelah to marry.

2    Ironically, the one area Yehudah is prepared to take responsibility for is his

It may even be that Onan learned well from his father. In refusing to allow his seed to become identified with his dead brother, he ensured that he
would have no future as well. And so God struck him down.

Returning to his ancestral clan, Yehudah, well-practiced in the art of
shirking responsibility, leads his brothers to do the same. Following the sale
of Yosef, the brothers (with their rejoined leader) refuse to take responsibility for their action vis-à-vis their father. "Do you recognize it; is this your
son's coat?" The feigned innocence can barely hide their cynical smiles, and
the inability to acknowledge their deed to Ya'akov leave him is a deep state
of despair with no possibility of comfort.

Ironically, in his ancestral clan, Yehudah may even have succeeded in
teaching his own father to act irresponsibly. When the brothers return the
first time from Egypt, they inform their father that the master of the land
[of Egypt] will not allow them to return without Binyamin. Ya'akov steadfastly refuses to allow Binyamin to go, even when the food stocks have been
completely depleted. In other words, Ya'akov is prepared to sacrifice his
entire family in order to ensure that Binyamin doesn't leave his side. An act
surely worthy of Yehudah.

The Torah's point, repeated at various stages, is that an individual or
group that is unprepared to take responsibility, with all the attendant risks
involved, is destined to have no future.

---

financial matters. Surely it is apparent in his suggestion that making Yosef disappear
can be profitable. It can also be observed in his dealings with the prostitute. Upon his
return from the sheep-shearing festival, Yehudah sends his trusted friend to ensure
that she gets paid. When his friend returns with the payment, unable to find the
rightful recipient, Yehudah is beside himself. Whether he is afraid of being exposed as
visiting the prostitute or of not paying his debts, Yehudah is distraught. In an interesting twist, he finds himself in a similar position when the brothers return from Egypt,
their bags filled with grain but their money still intact. The fear of being accused of
financial misdeed is terrifying to them all. This may be a carryover from their father's
albatross from the taking of the blessing – he was always afraid that he would be accused of dishonesty. Hence Ya'akov's preparedness to accept Lavan's shady dealings,
and his outrage at being accused of stealing Lavan's idols.

### Yehudah – the Rise

Yehudah's recovery/repentance is dramatic. Operating quietly, behind the scenes (like many biblical heroines), Tamar sends him a clandestine message. Yehudah has an easy way out – he can ignore the message and allow Tamar to be burned at the stake, burying all the evidence with her. Yehudah, however, chooses to acknowledge his role and his responsibility, despite his easier option.

The echo of Tamar's words is not lost on the careful reader. הכר נא she implores – acknowledge and recognize, to who do the staff and the signet ring belong? Immediately, the text records, ויכר – he recognized, and acknowledges his role and all that emanates from it. It was this same word which the brothers had used when presenting the bloody tunic to their father: הכר נא – recognize, is this your son's?[3] In recognizing his role vis-à-vis Tamar, Yehudah begins a process of personal transformation. He is now prepared to take personal responsibility, even at the cost of losing his reputation.

In the story of Tamar, the effects of that transformation are immediate. Whereas Tamar had previously been the prime mover in the story, the focus now shifts back to Yehudah. In the first half of the story, in his abandoning responsibility, Yehudah loses two children. In the latter events, when he stands up to take responsibility, Tamar bears him two children – from whom the rest of the historic leadership of Yehudah's clan will emerge.

The roots of what Yehudah addresses impact on his role in both of his clans – the one he once abandoned and the one he tried to start. His personal redemption in one opens the door to the redemption of the other. In contrast to his personal abdication of הכר נא regarding Yosef's tunic, the

---

3   This word, indeed, is one of the repeating theme words of the narrative. Beginning with Ya'akov's deception of his own father and down to Yosef's encounters with his brothers, the multigenerational chain of deceiving family members is regularly accompanied by the same verb.

In one twist, Yosef's deception of his brothers is described by the word ויתנכר – and he acted like a stranger (נכרי). The play on words must be intentional. The stranger is one from whom I distance myself, absolving myself of responsibility. להכיר – to recognize and acknowledge, is to take the reverse position.

rehabilitated Yehudah twice takes personal responsibility for Binyamin. First, when trying to convince Ya'akov to send Binyamin, Yehudah puts himself up as Binyamin's personal guarantor – if I don't fulfill my responsibility and return him to you then I will be a sinner to you for the rest of my days. Those words must have taken Ya'akov by surprise, who knew the old Yehudah well. Second, in his confrontation with Yosef (when Yosef wants Binyamin to remain behind for his "crime" of stealing the goblet), Yehudah offers himself in place of Binyamin – for I have placed myself as his personal guarantor. Yosef certainly knew the old Yehudah as well as Ya'akov did – the sounds of Yehudah's cavalier "let's sell him" must have rung in Yosef's ears for years afterward. Hearing the new Yehudah had to have had an impact on Yosef, just as it had on Ya'akov.

Yehudah's repentance was not for a single act, but was the beginning of a transformative process in which he made himself into something he was not before. It was that redeemed personality who would ultimately be able to bring both Ya'akov and Yosef, the other key players to their senses, and enable the reunification of the fractured family

### YEHUDAH – THE BLESSING

It is not just we readers of the text who were aware of Yehudah's powerful transformation, but Ya'akov addresses this directly in his death-bed blessings to his sons, in which even Yehudah's name takes on a new meaning. Named by his mother, the original etymology of his name emanates from a deep sense of gratitude – הפעם אודה את ה' – this time I will thank God. Yet the Hebrew להודות bears another meaning – an acknowledgement of the rectitude of the other. It was that sense of acknowledgement which was at the core of his redemptive moment with Tamar, and which Ya'akov recognizes in his blessing. יהודה, אתה יודוך אחיך – Yehudah, your brothers will both thank and acknowledge you. The acknowledgement, so fitting for the master of acknowledgement, comes in the wake of both Yehudah's departure from the family and his ultimate return.[4]

---

4  One may even notice a pattern in the patriarchal stories of a need to descend as

The ambiguity of the opening of the Ya'akov's blessing begins to fade as the blessing develops. מטרף בני עלית – you picked yourself up from the טרף – the tearing apart. The veiled reference to the story of Yosef's sale is apparent to anyone familiar with the text, as Ya'akov's initial reaction to the bloodied tunic is טרף טרף יוסף – surely Yosef has been torn apart. The meaning of Ya'akov's comment is apparent – you sank, with everyone else, in that despicable act, yet you picked yourself up and rehabilitated yourself. It is for that that your brothers must both thank and acknowledge you.

This same idea is carried in the continuation of the blessing. כרע רבץ כאריה וכלביא מי יקימנו – you crouched like a lion, and like a lioness: who can pick him up? Much of the language and imagery used here is strikingly similar to that found in the song of Devorah as she describes Yael's "conquest" and vanquishing of Sisera. That language is rife with sexual overtones, something that did not elude the Sages in their comments on Devorah's song. The implications for Yehudah's blessing are apparent – he, too, compromised himself in his sexual endeavor. But the blessing focuses not on the fall *per se*, but on that failing as a precursor to his eventual rise. The rhetorical question of מי יקימנו – who can pick him up, has the answer ready – only Yehudah can, and he did.

It is precisely because Yehudah demonstrated the inner strength to recognize and acknowledge his own failings, and be prepared to take the necessary steps afterward, that he earns the leadership. לא יסור שבט מיהודה – the staff [of leadership] shall never veer from Yehudah. Once again, images from his encounter with Tamar dominate the scene – did he not once lose his staff to Tamar, because he was not prepared to take responsibility? What more appropriate blessing could there be that, as long as Yehudah continues to rise to the challenge, he will never be without the staff of leadership.

The delightful pun in the continuation of that verse helps us to forget the

---

a pre-cursor to the rise. Avraham descends to Egypt, only to return stronger than he left. Ya'akov needs to discover his own source of inner strength in Haran before returning to confront his brother and father. Yosef's rise must come after a series of personal crises resulting from descents into pits and dungeons. And Yehudah must leave the clan to find an inner core prior to returning a position of leadership in his own family.

difficulties it posed for commentaries throughout the ages. On the surface, the phrase עד כי יבא שילה – till Shiloh comes – defies rational explanation, and has generated significant controversy in the classic Jewish-Christian debate. Yet the name Shiloh brings to mind the third son, Shelah, whom Yehudah was paradoxically prepared to sacrifice in his myopic effort to save him.

The final, cryptic lines of the blessing may also refer to events past, for which Yehudah must own up to his responsibility. כבס ביין לבושו ובדם ענבים סותה – he washed his clothing in wine and in the blood of grapes – is traditionally understood to refer to Yehudah's portion of the Land of Israel, which is blessed with grapes. Yet, it may also be a veiled reference to the past, particularly evident in the powerful image of "washing the cloak in blood of grapes." One cannot help but sensing that Ya'akov in invoking the image of the bloody cloak brought to him by Yehudah and his brothers, one which was dipped in the blood of the goat mentioned in the final line of Ya'akov's blessing.

In sum, while the poetic/prophetic sections of Tanach beg for multiple interpretations, one of those readings suggests that Ya'akov is both acknowledging to Yehudah where he brought himself as well as from where Yehudah came. Ya'akov's point is to highlight the power of personal transformation – so much so that, in Ya'akov's eyes, it earned Yehudah the uncontested and immutable leadership, as long as Yehudah continued the path he struggled to find.

### DAVID – A REPLAY OF YEHUDAH?

An initial look at the story of David suggests multiple parallels, almost to the extent of seeing Yehudah as the prototype patriarch and David as the "exemplar" scion. David falls into irresponsibility, taking a woman under morally problematic circumstances (like Yehudah, sleeping with a woman who is bound to another man by a covenant), and upon discovery of her pregnancy decides to cover it up through multiple methods (Yehudah tries to pay for Tamar's silence while David tries to arrange for Uriah to sleep with Bat Sheva to make it appear that the child was legitimately conceived by her husband), including the death of innocents (Yehudah is prepared to have Tamar burned at the stake, while David conveniently arranges for Uriah's death in battle). Natan the prophet confronts him, and David immediately takes responsibility for his actions, just as Yehudah owns up to his responsibility when confronted in secret by Tamar, launching himself into a process of contrition and repentance.

A closer reading of the story reveals even more parallels. The chapter opens with David's soldiers at battle while he is sitting comfortably in his palace, taking afternoon naps and watching a beautiful woman bathing from his rooftop perch. This focus on the fulfillment of his personal desires while the nation is at war parallels Yehudah's departure from the family in their time of need and his participation in the sheep shearing festival and fulfillment of his own sexual needs even as he denies Tamar and Shelah of theirs.

David's lack of responsibility and pursuit of personal pleasure can best be contrasted with the positions of Uriah, Bat Sheva's husband. In an attempt to cover up his own actions, David summons Uriah from the battlefield and encourages him to spend the night with his wife. Uriah steadfastly and repeatedly refuses, preferring to sleep in the street outside his home. "The ark, Israel and Yehudah are dwelling in tents, my master Yoav and his men are camped in the battlefield, and should I should go home to eat, drink and sleep with my wife? By my life and yours, I will not do such a thing!"[5]

David's encounter with Bat Sheva was not the product of a momentary weakness, but a premeditated act involving multiple stages of information gathering and planning. After seeing her on the rooftop,[6] David sends men to investigate who she is and sends men again to bring her to him. Her identity and status are well-known to him, and by now, to the small circle of people who have been doing his bidding regarding her. And just as Yehudah

---

5    Uriah's comment is reminiscent of an earlier chapter, in which David cannot justify his living in a palace while the ark of God dwells in a humble tent. That chapter, and its relevance to this story, will be discussed later. The implication is clear – David should have been the one to recognize that, as he did earlier. Yet; like Yehudah, David suffers from a form of myopia.

6    This is not the place to discuss the role Bat Sheva played in the incident.

is more concerned with how he will look in the eyes of others than with the essence of his own actions, David seems more concerned that she is "purifying herself from her impurity" than he is with the fact that she is a married woman. The sense of proportionality, of priorities, of justice, seems to have become distorted. And when David's attempts to cover up with Uriah fail, he digs his hole even deeper, preparing to sacrifice Uriah and other innocents in battle. And every attempt at hiding his actions brings even worse actions, and exposing himself even further to eventual discovery as increasing numbers of people become involved in the conspiracy.

The parallels between the stories are further accentuated in some of the details. Both Yehudah and David use proxies to carry out their trysts, thus endangering the very secrecy they sought. And, paradoxically, in both stories, the children born from the illicit unions take on positions of particular prominence – Yehudah's Peretz becomes the ancestor of the Davidic dynasty, and David's Shlomo carries that dynasty forth.

Despite the many parallels between the respective narratives of Yehudah and David, a closer reading reveals profound differences between them.[7] These differences emerge not from reading the structural and thematic elements which are common to the stories, but through a careful analysis of the unique features of David's saga.

GOD'S STRANGE RESPONSE

God's response to David's actions is bizarre, both in its content and its timing. Let us examine the parable of Natan the prophet. A rich man with lots of sheep and cattle decided that he wanted a delicious meal. Rather than using one of his own stock, he stole the one sheep of an impoverished shepherd – a sheep held so dearly that it ate from its master's plate, drank from his cup and slept in his bed.

The transparency of the parable, with its intimate description of the relationship between man and beast, is obvious to everyone except David! Yet

---

7  It may even be that the similarities are designed to evoke the search for the differences.

the parable is woefully inadequate; it addresses a simple theft, with the additional complication of sentimental value. How could such a parable even come close to David's situation, which involved adultery, deceit, abuse of the throne, manslaughter, and more?

Further, the timing of God's response (via Natan) is strange. One might have expected a visit from the prophet on the morning after the fateful encounter with Bat Sheva, or perhaps after summoning Uriah back from the battlefield. For sure the prophetic rebuke should have come, at least, upon the death of Uriah. Yet God is strangely silent throughout the story. It is only after Bat Sheva arises from her mourning, that David does what in the Bible is apparently the most honorable thing[8] – taking her into his home as his wife – does Natan appear. In fact, Natan's words seem to suggest that it is David's taking of Bat Sheva as a wife, rather than his taking her from her husband, which has found disfavor in God's eyes. And the closing verse of chapter 11, which describes the taking of Bat Sheva as a wife, is the very verse which says that David's actions were bad in God's eyes.

Perhaps the most bizarre twist is that, after the death of the child conceived on that fateful night, Bat Sheva again conceives a child with David. David calls him Shlomo, while God calls him Yedidyah, or friend of God. Assuming that David's relationship with this woman is born in sin, how could the product of that union be the blessed Yedidyah, beloved by God?

Interestingly, chapter 51 in Tehillim is explicitly dedicated to David's inner response to this affair. In that chapter, in which David begs for God's forgiveness, "in the vastness of Your mercy please erase my sin . . . cleanse me from my misdoing . . . make for me a pure heart," there is a surprising twist. David's notion of his sin is profoundly different from that of the narrative in the Book of Shmuel. The reader expects David to enumerate the variety of crimes he has committed – adultery, manslaughter, etc. – but none of that is

---

8    In the biblical world this was considered the honorable thing to do. Following a rape or a seduction of an unmarried woman, a man was expected to take the victim under his wings and was forbidden from divorcing her against her will. Indeed, is this not what Yehudah ultimately does upon acknowledging his own responsibility?

to be found. Instead, David makes the outrageous claim that "to you [God], alone, I have sinned; I did what was wrong in Your eyes."

The dissonance in David's words along with God's unexpected reactions in the narrative forces us to re-examine the entire story. Is it possible that there is another reading which will help to make sense of all this? Is it possible that God does not consider the relationship with Bat Sheva illicit? Is it possible that the death of Uriah can be glossed over? That David's abuse of power is not relevant?

### DAVID'S SIN – A BREACH OF RELATIONSHIP

A closer look at Natan's rebuke, as well as the broader context of the story, may help shed some light. Recounting God's words, Natan reports:

> I, the God of Israel, anointed you as king, and I saved you from Shaul. I gave you your master's house, and put his wives in your bosom and I gave you the house of Israel and Yehudah, and if that were not sufficient, I would have provided for you more of this and more of that. Why did you despise the word of God to do that which was evil in My eyes? – you slew Uriah the Hittite by sword and his wife you took for you as a wife and you had him killed by the sword of Ammon. Now, the sword shall not be removed from your house forever,[9] since you despised me and took Uriah's wife as your own.

There are a number of noteworthy observations to be made on this speech. First, there is no mention of the taking of Bat Sheva prior to the slaying of Uriah, only afterward. This brings up images of Avram's fear in Egypt – that they would kill him and take his wife. Apparently, this was not an uncommon practice among potentates in the biblical era. Second, the taking of Bat Sheva as a wife is mentioned twice, emphasizing that it, in itself, was problematic. Third, the repetition of the verb בזה – to

---

9   This is eerily reminiscent of Ya'akov's blessing to Yehudah, that the staff of leadership will never be removed from him. Even the same verb, לסור, is used in both contexts. Yehudah is granted leadership; David is told that his leadership will be stained with strife.

despise, describing God's perception of David's taking of Bat Sheva as a wife, stands out.

The background God provides in this speech is also interesting. Why is it relevant to mention that God gave him the house of Shaul, and his wives, and would have given him more, had only David asked?

The picture that seems to emerge from the above is that, for whatever reason, this story is not concerned with the adulterous relationship. It is concerned with the death of Uriah only because of its relationship to the subsequent taking of Bat Sheva as a wife. *Why* the text is not concerned with adultery is not clear.[10] But *that* the text is not concerned with it is clear. What, then, is God concerned with?

A close reading of Natan's speech suggests that it is the taking of Bat Sheva, without including God in the quest. Is that not what Natan says? "I gave you your master's house, and put his wives in your bosom ... and if that were not sufficient, I would have provided for you more ..." It is not the one-time act of sleeping with Bat Sheva that invokes God's ire, rather, it is the permanent taking of her as a wife. That is precisely why God first addresses David following the marriage and why Natan omits any mention of adultery. Why Natan's parable overlooks what one might think are the essential crimes. Why the explicit rebuke focuses on the fact of his taking Bat Sheva, and how God can sanction the relationship afterward, highlighting the fruit of that union as beloved.

The background for such a reading emerges, I believe, from a reading of the broader context of the Book of Shmuel. One thematic element which emerges repeatedly in the saga of David's rise to the throne is his regular and persistent acknowledgement of the role played by God in his success. It is, perhaps, one of the keys to reading David's story, and focuses the distinction between himself and Shaul. The climax of this story comes in Chapter 7 of

---

10 There are multiple explanations and justifications offered explaining the technical means through which David was able to take Bat Sheva. None of them are relevant in this context. For a comprehensive presentation of the range of opinions see Ya'akov Medan's *David and Bat Sheva: The Sin, the Punishment and the Rectification* (Alon Shevut: Yeshivat Har Etzion, 2002) [Hebrew].

Shmuel 2, an episode which can be titled "the love story of David and God." The chapter opens with David's desire to build a (literal) house for God, to which God replies that it is He who will build a (figurative) house for David, in the form of a royal dynastic family. Only once such a dynasty is established will God accede to having a house built for Him. That chapter is emblematic of the deep relationship between the two – each trying to do what is best for the other.

The following chapter continues the love story. David engages in a series of successful military campaigns, ostensibly with God's help. His immediate reaction is to gather the spoils of those battles and dedicate them to the construction of the Beit HaMikdash – a goal he will not personally witness to fruition but to which he has dedicated all his energies.

In sum, the story of David is punctuated by his intense inclusion of God in all his central decisions and his recognition of God's guiding hand. It is equally marked by the active role God has played in bringing him from behind the sheep to the ultimate position of national leadership. God provides all that David could dream for, and more. David, on his part, regularly consults with God and acknowledges His active hand.

With this as the background, happening only two chapters prior to the incident with Bat Sheva, God's (and Natan's) responses to David begin to come into focus. It was not the single act which God found problematic. Rather, it was David's machinations to arrange for the marriage to Bat Sheva (the one thing the reader would have thought was honorable!) without including his Divine benefactor. Had David asked, God would have found a way to make it happen. Instead, David's behavior is described twice as "despising God" – a term used regarding Esav to describe his relationship to the birthright after selling it to Ya'akov. The despised item is considered useless; the despised partner is one who is seen as equally useless.

This also explains David's strange proclamation in *Tehillim* 51, "to you, God, alone, have I sinned." Technically, David's formidable legal team would have found a way to extricate him from prosecution or conviction for the variety of apparent interpersonal or moral violations. Indeed, considerable Rabbinic literature is devoted precisely to that cause. Yet that is beside the point. It is not the legalities which are at the focus of the story, but David's violation of his partnership with God. "God, make for me a pure heart," he cries, "do not cast me out from being in Your presence and do not take Your holy spirit from me."[11] What David fears the most is the distance he currently feels from God, perhaps the most devastating experience for a human being. "Hide Your face from my sin," he pleads, but not from me.

## DAVID – THE EPILOGUE

The narratives which follow the incident with Bat Sheva all emanate from it organically – Amnon's rape of Tamar, Avshalom's avenging the despoiling of his sister, and his eventual rebellion against David. None of this is surprising, as it is a fulfillment of Natan's prophecy – "the sword shall not be removed from your house." What is striking is how deeply David internalized the lesson of this incident as he attempts to rebuild his relationship with God.

When Avshalom's design for the throne becomes apparent, David chooses to flee rather than fight. In one particularly poignant moment (*Shmuel* 2:15:25–26), he turns to Tzadok the high priest:

> If I find favor in God's eyes, then He will return me to show me Himself and His resting place. But should God say "I do not desire you," then here I am – let Him do to me as He pleases.

David's comment reflects a profound understanding that the events which have transpired are part of God's design, hence he will not fight it. Should God not desire him to be on the throne, then he has no right to be on the throne. He will only return should it become clear that such is the Divine will.

---

11 The theme of being before God – לפני ה' – is central to the Yom Kippur experience. It is only through achieving a state of being before God that atonement can be achieved – לפני ה' תטהרו. It is the theme of many biblical passages as well. One of the punishments described in *Devarim* is that we will serve wood and stones, and a key element of God's warning to the people is that in response to our sins He will hide His face from us – ואנכי הסתר אסתיר פני ביום ההוא.

David's comments reveal a deep internalization of a simple concept: the throne is only his should God be his partner. For David to have come to peace with that *after* having sat on the throne indicates a profound commitment to the idea, and it is that commitment which signals the beginning of his rehabilitation.

This reading may even provide an explanation of the befuddling rabbinic passage that anyone who says that David sinned is in error. There is no doubt that David sinned – the narrative says it, Natan says it, and David himself says it. What is unclear is what the nature of that sin was. Anyone who reads the story as a simple one of adultery, manslaughter and power play is missing the essential message of the story – that of the violation of the relationship with God and the need to repair that relationship.

## CONCLUSION

Although structurally and thematically, the narratives of Yehudah and David reveal many parallels, in truth they describe two profoundly different types of sin, hence, two different models of repentance.

Yehudah's failing was essentially an internal, ethical one, causing him to sin against his daughter-in-law, son, father, and even his own future. God was not part of his sin, nor was He part of the repentance. Repairing the ethical flaw brought about a personal transformation which impacted beyond the specific event that had sparked it. In the process, Yehudah redeems not only himself, but all those against whom he had sinned earlier. Ultimately, as Ya'akov recognizes, Yehudah's personal self-redemption set the tone for his progeny to take the reigns of leadership and take center stage in the ultimate redemption of the clan and nation he had once abandoned.

In contrast, David's sin was primarily not toward others, but toward God. He had violated the intensity and intimacy of that relationship, and must now see to restoring it, regardless of the personal cost. The impact on people was not unimportant, but plays a secondary role to the primary focus of the incident.

Are the parallels between the stories designed just to highlight the

differences between them, or do they reflect some sense of coherence
nonetheless? Indeed, it could be argued that these two have nothing in
common other than familial relationship and literary similarities. Certainly,
one meaningful parallel between the two is that repentance carries a price;
one must be prepared to sacrifice. Yet repentance carries a reward as well.
The model of Yehudah presents the reward as a personal transformation,
one which affects the way in which we interact with everyone. The model
of David presents the reward as the restoration of our relationship to being
"before God." In fact, the elements they have in common are too important
to be glossed over in a comment which allows them to be presented as two
models of repentance.

The most profound common thread is the ability to acknowledge wrongdoing and be prepared to suffer the consequences.[12] The strength of both
Yehudah and David was their ready admittance of wrongdoing and responsibility, with all the attendant consequences. It could even be argued that
this preparedness is not only a laudable personal trait, but also a necessary
one for carrying the mantle of leadership.

One could imagine the argument that the story of David is built upon
that of Yehudah – that responsibility before God is predicated upon responsibility before people. Indeed, that would make a neat argument, if only it
were true in this case. While David's sin was primarily in breach of a trust
relationship with God, quite a number of individuals paid with their lives
for that. And whereas the text points to the death of Uriah multiple times,
David seems to have brushed it off without mention.

Still, the stories beg for further exploration of the relationship between
them. That exploration is complicated by the fact that, whereas Yehudah is
acting primarily as an individual, David's status as king creates an entirely
different set of circumstances. It is not unusual for kings to take personal
liberties, even with the lives of their subjects. And while I make no attempt
to whitewash or justify such behavior, it is perhaps inherent in the position.[13]

---

12   Martin Luther King, Jr., argued that what makes civil disobedience a moral
act is the preparedness of the players to suffer the legal consequences of their actions.

13   This is not the time for an exploration of the morality of government. It is

As such, what is left for the king is the reminder that he is not the ultimate authority. It is not for naught that, in its discussion of Jewish kings, *Devarim* presents only their obligations toward God and the people, not their rights. And one of those responsibilities is to consult regularly with a personalized version of the Torah, as if to remind them that they are answerable as well.

In that case, what makes David's repentance extraordinary is not that he remembers his ultimate accountability to God as authority. What stands out in David's repentance is his personalization of the relationship with God. That even as king, his crime vis-à-vis God is a violation of that personal relationship, not just a violation of rules or even of special rules pertaining to national leaders. In doing so, he not only set the bar for the behavior of kings, but erased the distinction between the behavior of kings and that of the ordinary citizen.

All individuals are expected to have relationships of responsibility to others. Yehudah's repentance sets the model in that sphere. David, in establishing that even kings are expected to have personalized relationships with God, sets a standard in his own right – a standard which is certainly demanding for leaders, but no less so for the ordinary Jew.

almost self-evident, however, that all governments – ostensibly in the endeavor to protect their citizens and act in their best welfare – engage in the kinds of behaviors that we would never tolerate from individuals. It is hard to argue for the morality of violence or spying, yet governments who do not engage in war or covert activities are probably failing their constituencies. Not to mention the morally questionable activities that spies engage in, or how many individuals suffer as a result of the spy's behavior while on a mission.

Rabbi Dr. Alan Kimche

# *Kevod HaBeriyot* and Human Dignity in the Halachah

THE HEBREW WORD "*kavod*" appears often in both biblical and rabbinic literature and represents a general theme in the overall pattern of halachic norms and obligations. This word itself is drawn from the word "*kaved*" (heavy), indicating that someone or something should not be treated lightly. This etymological connection between respect and heaviness is also found in the English use of the Latin word "*gravitas*" where the idea of heaviness is used to express seriousness and dignified status. It is generally translated into various forms of "giving respect" or "honor and preserving dignity," and defines a whole range of obligations, all of which express recognition of the special status of a person, an object, or a place. In the Jewish tradition, its ultimate form is Man's obligation to honor God: *Kevod Shamayim*, literally "the respect of Heaven."

Looking at this "family" of rulings in the halachah, which are all meant to define behavior which expresses *kavod*, we find that in order to properly understand them we need to identify three aspects in each of the relevant situations:

1. Firstly, there is the "object" of the *kavod*, the honoree, that is the person or thing which generates an obligation of respect upon all or some other people.

2. Secondly, there will be a person or group of individuals who are the honorers, the "givers" of *kavod* on whom the obligation to confer respect falls.

3. Thirdly, there is the range of activities, either active or restrictive, which are required as being the halachically prescribed form of expressing *kavod* in this situation.

In all of the cases listed below, the honoree is a special individual, like a parent or a scholar, who merits extraordinary respect on account of his or her status, which is derived from specific relationships and roles that exist in society. Within this spectrum are various social relationships reaching to the highest levels of *kavod* which are due to the most esteemed members of society.

### Five Examples of *Kavod* in the Halachah

#### I.           *Kibbud Av v'Em*

This is the biblical requirement of filial respect in recognition of the status of the parent. In all matters of speech and behavior, the son and daughter are halachically obligated to express special honor and respect to both father and mother. The origin of this imperative is to be found in the Ten Commandments, "Honor [*kaved*; the imperative form of the verb] your father and your mother..." [1]

The Talmud discusses in detail the application of this commandment, and equates the honor due to a parent as being in some way similar to the honor due to God, by stating that there are three partners in the creation of every human being – father, mother and God.[2] The source of this filial honor is that the parent is seen as the source of life itself for the child and the *kavod* of the child's actions express that recognition.

---

1   *Shemot* 20:12 and *Devarim* 5:16.
2   *Kiddushin* 30b–32b.

2.        *Kevod HaIsha* and *Kevod HaBa'al*

Within the marital relationship there is a requirement for mutual *kavod* between husband and wife, each in recognition of the special marital bond through which they are connected. Maimonides requires the laws of mourning to apply for a deceased parent-in-law, both for the wife and the husband to join in the mourning for the other's deceased parent out of mutual *kavod* for each other.[3] The Talmud recommends to the husband that he follows the rule: "... to love his wife as much as he loves himself, and to give her more *Kavod* than he gives himself...."[4]

3.        *Kevod HaTzibur*

This concept is used to describe the way in which communal officials are required to behave in deference to the community, expressing their awareness of the importance of the community and their role as public servants. It is found, for instance, in the Talmud when discussing the way in which the Torah scrolls are to be used in public readings.[5] It is also a consideration regarding which individuals are allowed to officiate in public, as well as requiring them to fulfill their function while standing,[6] and wearing a special garment.[7] Similarly, communal events are designed in such a way that the community participating in the event is not kept waiting unnecessarily or inconvenienced in some other way.[8] To do so would be showing a lack of respect for their status as a community.

---

3    *Mishneh Torah, Hilchot Aveilut* 8:5.
4    *Yevamot* 62b.
5    *Gittin* 60a.
6    *Mishneh Torah, Hilchot Megillah* 2:7 and *Shulchan Aruch, Orach Chaim* 690:1.
7    *Mishnah Berurah, Orach Chaim* 18:5.
8    *Mishnah Berurah, Orach Chaim* 141:22.

4.          *Kevod HaRav* and *Kevod HaTorah*

This category includes all forms of respect due to a Torah scholar and has its origins in the biblical text which states, "You shall rise in the presence of an elder and you shall honor the presence of a sage and you shall revere your Lord, I am God."[9] The Talmud discusses the scope of this requirement and sees the reference to an "elder" as being someone over seventy years old, while the "sage" is anyone with Torah scholarship, irrespective of age.[10] Both these individuals require special *kavod* in the way in which others interact with them. Similarly, the Torah scroll itself as a sacred object, as well as other sacred books and objects, are all required to be treated with the appropriate *kavod*.

5.          *Kevod HaMelech*

This is a special category whereby the monarch requires the respect and obedience of the entire nation. The Talmud derives this from the biblical verse describing the appointment of a king, where the wording implies that the nation must be willing to become subjects of his monarchy in every respect.[11] The extent of this is expressed by Maimonides, who opens a chapter with the words, "Great *kavod* is given to the king and fear, and his fear and respect must be in the hearts of everyone …"[12] and proceeds to spell out special instructions regarding the king's possessions, his wife, his clothing and his rights against others. Interestingly, as part of the checks and balances in the powers of government, Maimonides also rules that, "… it is a mitzvah for the king to give *kavod* to Torah scholars, standing before them and seating them next to him … But this is only in private, while in public he stands before no one." This reflects the idea that the king is himself subject to the rules and values of the Torah and is not a law unto himself.

---

9   *Vayikra* 19:32.
10  *Kiddushin* 32b.
11  *Sanhedrin* 19b.
12  *Mishneh Torah, Hilchot Melachim* 2.

## The Sixth Category of Kavod

In addition to all these categories and, in some respects, distinct from them all, there is a sixth category of *kavod* in the halachah. This is the Talmudic principle of *Kevod haBeriyot*. This term is not found in biblical nor in Mishnaic literature. It is found for the first time in the Talmud.[13] It is widely used as a halachic-legal term in various codifications of Jewish law.

## Three unique features of Kevod haBeriyot

(1) *Kevod haBeriyot* is distinct from all other forms of *kavod* mentioned above regarding the nature and the definition of the honoree. While all these other categories are case-specific in that they relate to an honoree who is a person or situation of outstanding status, the concept of *Kevod haBeriyot* has a much broader scope. It is an attempt to connect with human dignity, which is understood to be a *basic degree of respect or honor due to any person qua human being,* rather than anyone of special status.

(2) All the above categories of obligations to confer *kavod* require special activities to express honor and respect to the particular honoree who has earned special status. In contrast, when we are dealing with *Kevod haBeriyot*, the Talmudic laws are preventative in nature, and we are concerned with *preventing shame and embarrassment,* as opposed to promoting honor. In general, the halachic principle of *Kevod haBeriyot* is designed to protect people from situations which will shame them and in some way undermine their human dignity.

An interesting example of the distinction in the application of this principle can be found in the writings of Rabbi Meir Simcha.[14] He was asked in the late nineteenth century if it was permitted to play musical instruments in the synagogue in honor of the king on a Jewish Festival (*yom tov*) which

---

13  *Berachot* 19b, *Shevuot* 30b.

14  *Ohr Sameach, Hilchot Yom Tov* 6:14, cited by Nahum Rakover, *HaHagana al Kevod HaAdam* (Jerusalem: Misrad haMishpatim, 5738), 79.

coincided with the Russian king's coronation celebrations. In the Talmud it is clear that the playing of musical instruments on Shabbat or any other Jewish Festival is a rabbinic prohibition and, as such, could be set aside by considerations of *Kevod haBeriyot*. However, in his halachic responsa he makes the point that the *Kevod haBeriyot* principle was never used to promote *active* affirmative expressions of honor, only to *prevent* shame, and therefore the prohibition of playing instruments on a *yom tov* could not be overridden by *Kevod haBeriyot*. It appears that his understanding was that *Kevod haBeriyot* only legislates for a person to be protected from being forced to do something which will cause a loss of dignity, but it does not allow *actively* giving *kavod* when to do so violates some other halachic restriction. We will examine this distinction later on.

(3)  A third unique feature of *Kevod haBeriyot* is its universal application beyond the limits of the Jewish people. It is unusual within the halachic system to find definitions of obligations outside the circle of the nation, but clearly, *Kevod haBeriyot* does exactly that.

The universality of the notion of *Kevod haBeriyot* is indicated directly in the choice of language used by the Sages of the Talmud to express this principle. The Hebrew word *"beriyot"* is the most all-inclusive word possible when referring to human beings, and it seems clear that it was chosen to include all mankind, not only members of the Jewish people. This implies the recognition that the human race as a whole is endowed with a special status qua human beings which requires recognition in the form of *Kevod haBeriyot,* the preservation of human dignity.

### First Example of Universality Principle

An example of a relevant source in which this idea is spelled out specifically is to be found in the commentary on the following verse, which introduces the notion that by accepting the responsibility for observing the laws of the Torah, the Jewish people will become the Chosen People.

This is part of an introductory chapter, given as a preamble to the Ten Commandments, in which the Jewish people are charged with a covenant, contingent upon their acceptance of the commandments. The Hebrew word "*segulah*" is the key to this statement, and is variously translated as "treasure" or "chosen," and clearly carries the meaning of being in some way Divinely selected:

> And now if you will surely listen to my laws and guard my covenant you shall become for me a *segulah* from all other nations, for the entire world is mine. And you shall become for me a kingdom of priests and a holy nation . . . .[15]

Ovadiah Sforno briefly deals with some of the implications of this text; in particular the question of whether it is suggesting that the other nations are in some way of lesser Divine concern. He writes as follows:

> Even though the entire human race is more precious to me than all other living beings, since it alone is the purpose of them all; as it is written "how beloved is *Mankind* that they were created in the Image of God"[16] . . . and the difference between you is one of degree, since the entire world is mine, and the *chasidei umot haOlam* (God-fearing gentiles) are precious to me without doubt . . . in this sense you will be for me a *segulah* that you will become a kingdom of priests to teach the entire human race to call in the name of the One God . . .

Sforno is making two very important points in his commentary:

(1) The unique role attributed to *mankind* at Creation by being created "in the image of God" continues to apply to the entire human race even after the moment of Sinai and the Jewish covenant of chosen-ness, just as it did beforehand.

(2) That the notion of chosen-ness refers to a special *responsibility* and mission in life to spread worldwide the belief in ethical monotheism, rather than having been chosen to receive the privilege of some special endowment which is missing in others.

---

15  *Shemot* 19:5–6.
16  *Avot* 3:18.

Clearly, here the uniqueness of the status of all human beings is being categorized together and given a status above other forms of life. We will see that, ultimately, the idea that drives *Kevod haBeriyot* is exactly this special status referred to by Sforno, which requires recognition by all people as a mark of respect.

I suggest that this is why the Talmud refers to human dignity not as some unique respect given to other members of the Jewish people, but rather under the title of *haBeriyot*, a generic word which includes all human beings.

The Mishnah quoted by Sforno reads:[17]

> He [Rabbi Akiva] used to say: How precious is Man (*Adam*) that he was created in the image (*b'tzelem*) [of God]. Greater love was shown to him that he was taught that he was created in the image [of God].

Both the Tiferet Yisrael and the Tosafot Yomtov commentaries on the Mishnah write that this statement of the uniqueness and spiritual nature of Man is a concept applying to all mankind, and they develop the universality of this idea.

### Second Example of Universality Principle

Another very interesting reference to the universal nature of *Kevod ha-Beriyot,* this time from authoritative halachic literature, is to be found in the codification writings of Maimonides. In the following citation he outlines some considerations regarding the way in which Talmudic law empowered rabbinic courts of law with discretionary powers to dispense punishments beyond those of a statutory nature.

Having written that the rabbinic court is also allowed to use custodial sentences, even though this form of punishment is not sanctioned in biblical or Talmudic Law directly, he adds a cautionary note:[18]

… all these matters must be guided by the judgment of the judge (*dayan*) when the situation requires it [these discretionary punishments] and when

---

17   *Avot* 3:14.
18   *Mishneh Torah, Hilchot Sanhedrin* 24:10.

the time is right. In all these matters he must have only intentions motivated by the need to protect the sanctity of the Torah (*l'shem shamayim*) and also [bear in mind] that *Kevod haBeriyot* is not an insignificant matter, as we see it can override all Rabbinic Law, and even more so the honor of the descendants of Avraham, Yitzchak and Ya'akov who preserve the truth of the Torah: he [the judge] must take care not to undermine their dignity [even when meting out these deserved and essential punishments] . . .

From this quote it is clear that Maimonides is addressing himself primarily to the judges in cases where the person to be sentenced is not a member of the Jewish people and reminding them that, in such cases, *Kevod haBeriyot* is an operative principle which must temper their sentencing. Only subsequently does he mention the status of a Jewish person and the additional reason to treat them with dignity.

### Rabbi Bachrach and Rabbi Wasserman: Two Definitions of *Kevod haBeriyot*

A fundamental question to be looked at is what it is exactly about the loss of dignity that drives the halachah to ascribe to it such a special status. To put it a little differently: what exactly is it about the experience of shame or loss of dignity that is so terrible that it justifies overriding other halachic imperatives?

In the writings of the Achronim (latter scholars), we find two schools of thought on this question:

One approach to *Kevod haBeriyot* is simply to focus on the degree of subjective pain and mental agony a person will endure by being shamed or humiliated. On this view, the halachah is aimed at preventing a loss of dignity as a sub-category of the general halachic concern to prevent all types of pain which may be incurred in the performance of any of the obligations of Talmudic law.

The other approach is to understand *Kevod haBeriyot* as a unique category of halachic thinking, which has nothing to do with the mental anguish a person may or may not be suffering. In this view, to violate a person's dignity is seen as an affront to the dignity of *mankind* rather than simply the *kavod* of the individual concerned. According to this second view, we are not concerned with the particular individual's experience of shame, rather we are legislating to preserve the dignity of Man.

## The Personal Suffering Thesis

If it is judged by the personal pain and discomfort experienced by the shamed person, then the laws of *Kevod haBeriyot* are simply saying that halachah takes cognizance of personal suffering, and the *Kevod haBeriyot* principle is designed to minimize it. If this assumption is true, then shame is simply located somewhere on a continuum of the full spectrum of personal suffering that ranges from discomfort at the low end of the range, through pain and shame, all the way to life-threatening dangers. While it is true that the halachic system takes into consideration life-threatening hazards in a very clear and detailed way, it is not so clear to what extent the experience of *tza'ar*, personal discomfort or pain, is considered as an overriding principle in the halachah.

But in what sort of cases is it true that the halachah will accept personal pain to override other halachic obligations? We need to first look at other cases in which the Talmud regards pain as a sufficient justification to override the halachah, in order to be able to see *Kevod haBeriyot* as an experience which qualifies as a type of pain, which would subsequently be the underlying reason for its status.

In the context of the Shabbat laws, we can find an example of this type of override because of pain. The Talmud describes one of the categories of forbidden activities on Shabbat as *"mefarek"* and *"dash."* These activities relate to threshing and winnowing in order to separate the wheat from the husk, and they are extended to include any case where one is removing an edible item from its inedible container. For example, one such forbidden application is the milking of a cow on Shabbat. However we find the following statement in the Talmud:[19]

---

19  *Ketuvot* 60a.

> Rabbi Marinus says: An ill person [who is medicinally in need of milk and
> there is none available] is allowed to extract milk [directly] from the cow
> on Shabbat. Why would we permit it [given that the activity of milking is
> forbidden]? The activity of sucking directly [from the cow's udder] is con-
> sidered to be *k'lacher yad* [i.e., an unusual form of the activity, and therefore
> not biblically forbidden. It is, however, still rabbinically forbidden, but] in
> cases of pain (*tza'ar*) the rabbis did not enforce their legislation. Rav Yosef
> says: The halachic ruling follows the view of Rabbi Marinus.

Tosafot[20] point out that this cannot be referring to a case of life-threatening danger because, in that case, all Shabbat legislation is suspended, even a
full biblical violation, and there would be no need to mention the fact that
it was being done in an unusual way. It must therefore be the case that this is
a non-dangerous pain, but it is sufficient to override the rabbinic law.

However, a fine distinction is drawn between different levels of pain. For
instance, the discomfort of hunger could be seen as a natural part of human
experience, as opposed to the pain of an illness. Tosafot indeed rules that
the pain of hunger would not be sufficient to override other halachic obligations, and that is why the statement here specifies the case of an ill person.[21]

A further application of this principle is also to be found in the context
of the Shabbat laws. One of the Shabbat restrictions is the tying and untying
of permanent knots. In the discussion of what constitutes a permanent knot,
there is a rabbinic law that any double knot should be regarded as such. In
codifying this law, the reservation is made that if the double knot will cause
*tza'ar* by being left tied, one is allowed to untie the knot, because "in a case
of *tza'ar* they did not enforce their laws."[22] No example of what this pain
may be is detailed here, but from the broader context it can be understood
as the laces or straps of a shoe that need to be undone in order to remove the
shoe to sleep, and the pain is, therefore, the discomfort of having to sleep
with shoes on.

From both these sources it seems there is room to see a general principle

---

20   Ibid., s.v. *Goneach.*
21   *Shulchan Aruch, Orach Chaim* 328:33 codifies this distinction.
22   *Remah, Orach Chaim* 317:1.

– that the rabbinic halachah is waived in all cases of significant pain. If this is accepted, then the *Kevod haBeriyot* rule is simply an extension of the concept of pain to include also the mental anguish of loss of dignity and the shame or embarrassment that is thereby experienced.

The following Talmudic source is relevant to our topic, as it compares shame to physical pain: The Talmud debates the process of distributing *tzedakah,* charity to the poor.[23] This subject is analyzed in great detail, explaining various levels of need and the obligations of the trustees of charitable funds that every community is obligated to maintain. One topic deals with problems of authenticating the validity of claims of poverty. In this context, the Talmud looks at a variety of cases where a person asks to be supported by the town's charity fund, but the trustees do not know him, and there is a chance that he may be making a fraudulent claim. However, the delay incurred by making the necessary inquiries will cause hardship to the petitioner. Do the trustees respond to the urgency of his poverty and give him what he needs immediately? Or is it necessary to clarify his eligibility before allocating him funds from the trust, in order to fulfill the duty of the trustees to distribute charitable funds correctly and not to waste them on fraudulent cases?

In this context, the Talmud has to define levels of poverty as a way of quantifying the degree of need. The more extreme cases will be dealt with immediately without investigation, while less pressing cases can wait until the trustees are satisfied with the validity of the claim.

The need of someone who has inadequate clothing is compared with someone who asks for support in order to eat properly.[24] Which of these two is considered more pressing? In the Talmudic analysis, the lack of proper clothing is a matter of public embarrassment, while the lack of sufficient food is a matter of physical suffering. This is an interesting context within which to analyze the question of shame versus physical pain:

---

23   *Bava Batra* 9a.

24   It is clear from the Talmudic debate that neither of these situations are life threatening, otherwise they would be dealt with under different principles.

> Rav Huna says: We must investigate [the claim of a pauper who asks] for
> food [even if this causes delay], but we do not investigate [the claim of a
> pauper who is inadequately dressed and asks] for clothing [rather we supply
> his needs without delay since we do not wish to prolong for even a moment
> his shame at being improperly dressed].

He then offers arguments to prove the priority of loss of dignity over
hunger. This is the worse deprivation, says Rav Huna, and therefore the
need for clothing demands our immediate attention, even before we check
out his credentials.

> Rav Yehudah says: We must investigate [to validate the claim of the pauper
> who asks] for clothing [even if it causes delay], but we do not investigate
> [the claim of the pauper who comes to ask] for food [rather we feed him
> immediately].

He brings arguments to support his view that physical pain is the worse
condition, and therefore the lack of food is the greater need, which must be
remedied without delay.

Thus, according to Rav Yehudah,[25] the need to prevent significant physical pain is considered by Talmudic law to be greater than the need to avoid
embarrassment. If so, one could argue that halachic requirements that are
set aside because of *Kevod haBeriyot* will also be overridden by physical suffering.

We find an authoritative Talmudist and halachist of the seventeenth
century who explored this position in detail. Rabbi Ya'ir Chayim Bacharach
in his response analyses the following situation:[26] a *Kohen* is outdoors in
the freezing cold and needs to find shelter. However, in order to get to the
warmth and shelter of his house he has to go through a building where there
is a corpse. It is biblically forbidden for a *Kohen* to be under the same roof as
a corpse, but in the given case, the halachic violation would be at the level of

---

25   Both Maimonides, *Mishneh Torah, Hilchot Matanot Aniyim* 7:7, as well as the
*Shulchan Aruch, Yoreh Deah* 251:10 rule in accordance with the view of Rav Yehudah
in this context.

26   *Responsa Chavat Ya'ir* 191.

a rabbinic law rather than a biblical law. Is it permitted to override this rabbinic law on account of the physical pain he will have to endure by staying in the freezing cold?

Analyzing the question of whether the pain of the cold is sufficient to permit the *Kohen* to violate this rabbinical prohibition, the rabbi cites a wide variety of sources to defend his view that rabbinic prohibitions would indeed be waived in such a case.[27] One of his arguments is from the halachic discussion of *Kevod haBeriyot*.

He argues as follows: if we rule that physical pain is worse than embarrassment, and if *Kevod haBeriyot* is enough to suspend a rabbinic prohibition, then certainly the sharp pain of freezing wind is also a sufficient reason to override the rabbinic legislation forbidding the *Kohen* to pass through this building.

### The Human Dignity Thesis

This view is firmly disputed by a twentieth century Talmudist and halachist, Rav Meir Simcha of Dvinsk. In his commentary on Maimonides,[28] he argues that it is not possible to rule that all rabbinic legislation is to be set aside because of consideration of physical pain.[29] On the contrary, he says, we find solely regarding the mitzvah to sit in a *sukkah* that "*mitztaer patur min haSukkah,*" that if it is painful to sit in the *sukkah* one is exempt from doing so.[30] From the Talmud, it is clear that this is a unique feature of the laws of *sukkah,* and it is not a general halachic principle.

There is a profound explanation of this thesis in the writings of R. Elchanan Wasserman (twentieth century, Lithuania) in support of the writ-

---

27   R. Bacharach emphasizes that we are not dealing simply with discomfort or the pain of exertion, rather a significant physical suffering.

28   *Ohr Sameach, Hilchot Sanhedrin* 15:1.

29   Using a dramatic statement of rejection: "*veyishtakeach zeh v'lo yomar*," lit.: "let this view be forever forgotten and never be said again."

30   *Sukkah* 27a, *Shulchan Aruch, Orach Chaim* 640:4.

ings of R. Meir Simcha. [31] He suggests that it is a fundamental error of R. Bacharach to derive the exemption of physical pain from the exemption of *Kevod haBeriyot*, since it is not the painfulness of shame which is relevant to *Kevod haBeriyot*. When the Talmud gives priority to *Kevod haBeriyot*, he argues, it is not in order to protect the individual from the mental pain and anguish of humiliation. R. Wasserman's view gets support from the fact that the Talmud treats *Kevod haMet*, the dignity we are obligated to attribute to a corpse, as a subcategory of *Kevod haBeriyot*. Obviously, there is no suffering on the part of the corpse itself if it is treated disrespectfully, so it follows that *Kevod haBeriyot* is not derived from any anguish or pain endured. Rather, the underlying ethos of *Kevod haBeriyot* is the importance of the dignity of *mankind,* which is expressed in this case in the way this particular corpse is treated and would be violated if treated without dignity.

This insight goes to the very heart of the entire *Kevod haBeriyot* topic. R. Wasserman writes in a brief cryptic style, without expounding on this point, but he is clearly putting loss of dignity, experienced as human shame and embarrassment, in a unique category that cannot be compared to other types of physical pain.

An analysis of his position would include two central ideas:

Firstly, that to endure hardship and pain in the service of God is considered a virtue. Indeed, the Mishnah comments *"l'fum tza'ara agra,"* that the reward for a good deed is a function of the amount of *tza'ar* (pain) that is invested in it.[32] Here, the endurance of pain is equated with self-sacrifice. It would be antithetical to this theme in Talmudic literature to claim that the legislation of the rabbis was only obligatory when done without pain and sacrifice.

Secondly, is the question of defining the underlying concept of *Kevod haBeriyot*. He asserts that *Kevod haBeriyot* does not derive its force from a wish to protect a particular individual from suffering of humiliation, but it is rather an expression of the dignity of *Mankind* that is reflected in every human being, even a corpse. This dignity is itself a spiritual dimension of

---

31  *Kovetz Shiurim* on *Bava Batra* 49.
32  *Avot,* end of chap. 5.

mankind, expressed in the biblical statement that Man was created *"b'tzelem elokim,"* in the image of God.[33] Much has been written in attempts to capture the sublime meaning of this phrase, but there is no doubt that it lies at the root of central ethical principles such as the sanctity of human life and human rights.

In this view, it is not a conflict between sensitivity to human suffering on the one hand, and the requirement to live a life that reflects the Divine on the other. This is not a clash between two values, with the Talmud adjudicating which one will be given priority in which cases. Rather, it is a calculation of which course of action will create *greater* Divine honor, *"Kevod Shamayim,"* as reflected in the person's obedience to halachah, or this same honor as it is manifest in the Divine image of mankind.

It is this understanding of *Kevod haBeriyot* as *sui generis* which is the basis for the refutation of R. Bacharach and his comparison with physical pain.

Both R. Bachrach and R. Wasserman offer logical arguments for their positions, but the latter view of R. Wasserman is more attuned to the Talmudic *sugyot*, in the sense that if it were true that shame is simply another type of physical pain, that comparison should have been made as part of the Talmud's discussion.

### Kevod HaBeriyot *vs.* Kevod HaMakom

In the central Talmudic discussion of *Kevod haBeriyot* we find a statement made by Rav that, despite its great significance in halachah, there is an upper limit beyond which *Kevod haBeriyot* is no longer applicable.[34] This refers to those cases where concern for human dignity will result in a desecration of God.

The Talmudic discussion opens as follows:

> Rabbi Yehudah says in the name of Rav: a person who finds *kilayim* in an item of his clothing must remove it [immediately] even if he is in public

---

33  *Bereshit* 1:27.
34  *Berachot* 19b.

[and disrobing in public will cause him embarrassment]. What is the reason [that we will subject him to this embarrassment in order to fulfill the requirement of *kilayim* without delay]? [The answer suggested is:] "There is no wisdom, no understanding, and no counsel [which will prevail] against [the honor o]) God."[35] – [which is understood here to mean that] [Wherever there is a situation which will create] a desecration of God's honor (*chillul Hashem*) we give no respect [to human beings, even] to a scholar.

The Talmud assumes that it does not need to state that ordinarily a person wearing clothing in private which contains biblically prohibited material must remove it. The important feature of this ruling is that it takes place in the public domain and, therefore, creates embarrassment, which is a sign of loss of human dignity. Here, the Talmud has accepted that human dignity is a significant value which is indeed violated by requiring a person to disrobe in public, which would ordinarily be unacceptable. We are paradoxically introduced to the *Kevod haBeriyot* principle by a ruling which sets it aside! However, Rav asserts that when it comes into conflict with the requirement to obey this biblical halachic ruling of wearing forbidden clothing, *Kevod haBeriyot* is of secondary importance and is waived in favor of the fulfillment of the mitzvah of *sha'atnez*.

By requiring a person wearing *sha'atnez* clothing to disrobe in public, Rav is weighing these two imperatives against each other, and he concludes that the importance to protect people from shame does not override the halachah in this case. If we generalize this specific ruling, we would have a rule which states that *all* halachic obligations override loss of human dignity, and it is this proposition which the discussion is clarifying.

What does this crucial statement of Rav mean? Clearly, he is identifying direct active violations of biblical law as a distinct category, and these will never be trumped by the *Kevod haBeriyot* principle. Why is it that despite his acceptance of *Kevod haBeriyot* as a halachic principle that can override other halachic rules, he is unable to set aside biblical law for the sake of human dignity?

---

35  *Mishlei* 21:30.

One of the central ideas that drives this entire discussion is the conflict between the *kavod* which is due to God and that which is due to the human being.

Both types of *kavod* are essential halachic principles that generally function in unison, since the Divine command will usually obligate a person to act in ways that are consistent with human dignity. The question of the Talmud is where to give priority in those cases where the two are in conflict. By using the term *chillul Hashem*, we will see that Rav is putting the problem into a broader perspective, to indicate that the issue here is not *Kevod haBeriyot* versus the other halachic laws, but human *kavod* versus *Kevod Shamayim*, respect for God.

The priority attributed in this discussion to avoiding *chillul Hashem* could be connected to a Talmudic thesis that if we are able to define any single ultimate goal of Creation in any one theme, it is contained in this idea of *Kevod Shamayim*. Whether or not we are able to define God's ultimate purpose in the Creation is a subject of some discussion. It was, for instance, Maimonides who stated categorically that it was beyond human comprehension to grasp the purpose for God's creation.[36] Just as we cannot know anything about the essence of God Himself, similarly His motivations and intentions are beyond the boundary of human thought. However, others hotly dispute this view. Thinkers such as Maharal[37] and Luzzato[38] explain that the Divinely revealed Torah itself gives us the definition of the ultimate purpose of creation, which cannot be reached through rational philosophy alone.


### Kevod Shamayim *in the Mishnah, Talmud and Tanach*

The first statement of this view is found in the brief but dramatic statement made on the occasion of all Jewish marriages. The texts of the seven marriage benedictions, *sheva berachot*, which are made under the *chuppah* canopy are recorded in the Talmud and date back to even earlier Mishnaic

---

36  *Moreh Nevuchim* 3:13.

37  *Derech Chayim* on *Pirkei Avot*, end of chap. 6.

38  Moshe Chayim Luzzato, *Derech Hashem*, chap. 1.

times.[39] After making the *beracha* on the wine, the next *beracha* states "…
*she'hakol bara l'kevodo*," meaning that all Creation was for the sake of His
(God's) *kavod*. Some Rishonim see this as a reference to the first union of
Adam and Eve that took place in the context of a newly created universe,
a universe created in order to manifest the *kavod* of God, the Creator.[40] In
addition, the newly married couple are committing themselves to a marriage that will produce a new generation dedicated to strengthening *Kevod
Shamayim*.

Another important reference to *Kevod Shamayim* is found in a very
significant location in the text of the Mishnah itself. The entire corpus of
Mishnaic text is concerned with the details of the halachic system, but one
small tractate, *Avot,* is dedicated totally to the beliefs and virtues that a
Jewish person is encouraged to attain.

The end of the final chapter reads, "All that the Holy One blessed is He
created in His world, He only created for His *kavod*," followed by a quote
from the verse in *Yeshayahu* mentioned below.[41] The commentary of the
Maharal[42] explains why this statement is specifically made here. Since the
entire final chapter of *Avot* is dedicated to extol the importance of Torah
study, he explains, it was vital to add two points, both of which are emphasized by this final Mishnah:

Firstly, that one should not study Torah for one's own honor, in order
to gain pride and prestige in the eyes of others. Rather, one should be motivated *lishmah*, meaning for the sake of *Kevod Shamayim*, to increase the

---

39   *Ketuvot* 8a. Rashi explains that since a marriage requires the presence of at
least ten adult men, it is considered a public meeting, and this *beracha* is made in order
to articulate the idea that the purpose of this gathering is *Kevod Shamayim*. Possibly
because honor and respect is being given to the bride and groom, their parents and
other prestigious guests, it is important to preface the meeting with an affirmation of
the priority of *Kevod Shamayim*.

40   Meiri on *Ketuvot*, ibid. Also see *Shitah Mekubetzet* in the name of Remah.

41   The sixth chapter of *Avot* is often printed in the Mishnah but in reality belongs
to a collection of Tannaitic material, known as the *Bereita,* which is not part of the
Mishnah itself but originates from the same era. For our purposes, this does not affect
the significance of the citation.

42   Rabbi Yehudah Loew of Prague, sixteenth century.

knowledge of God's Torah. Secondly, in order for Torah scholarship to create *Kevod Shamayim*, the Talmudist, as a religiously prominent individual, is required not only to attain high levels of intellectual scholarship, but also to maintain especially high moral and ethical standards of behavior, even beyond the letter of the law.

The use of *kavod* as the most emphatic verbal description of the worship of God has its origins in the writings of the prophets. This idea can be found in the words of Isaiah: "Everything that is called by My name, I have created for My *kavod*, I have formed it and I have made it."[43] And again in the words of the same prophet, giving an account of his prophetic vision of the heavenly court, the greatest praise that is said about God is: "Holy Holy Holy is the Lord of hosts the whole earth is filled with his *kavod*."[44] Similarly, the prophet Yechezkel has a vision of the angelic praise of God, saying: "Blessed is the *kavod* of God from His place."[45]

We have seen the uniqueness of *Kevod haBeriyot* as a principle of "negative liberty" created by Talmudic law in order to prevent inflicting shame or embarrassment on an individual. It is also clear that the intention of this halachah is to include all human beings, and is not limited only to the Jewish people.

The rationale behind the *Kevod haBeriyot* principle is seen as either a sub-category of the general principle which overrides many halachic rules which could result in suffering pain or, alternatively, it is a new category of a general duty to preserve the dignity of mankind. Either way this is a powerful halachic expression of the sensitivity and human dimension of *Torat Chessed*.

Finally, we have also seen that the application of *Kevod haBeriyot* in halachah is only limited by *Kevod Shamayim*. Therefore, there could be situations in which the halachah will give priority to the prevention of a direct desecration of the honor of God, even if this will entail the individual suffering, shame or embarrassment.

---

43   *Yeshayahu* 43:7.
44   Ibid., 6:3.
45   *Yechezkel* 3:12.

# Professor William Kolbrener

# Ya'akov's Scar[1]

I

In turning to a famous episode in literary history, as well as a famous (and far more recent) episode in literary criticism, this essay foregrounds and examines a central moment in Jewish history. To the moment in literary criticism: my title – "Ya'akov's Scar" – comes as a transformation of the title of Erich Auerbach's "Odysseus's Scar," the opening essay in his *Mimesis*, written in 1935 after Auerbach had been dismissed from his university post at Marburg by the Nazis.[2] The now canonical essay – a *tour de force* of comparative method – elicits the styles of, in his terms, "Old Testament" and Homeric texts, as a means to explore the "literary representation of reality in European culture" (3). The scar to which the title of his essay refers – which takes us to the episode in literary history – is the scar of Odysseus, crucial to the narrative action of Book 19 of Homer's *Odyssey*. Finally, in my argument, the example of Homer's legendary character, Odysseus, serves as a contrast

1    I am grateful to R. Emanuel Feldman, R. Ehud Rakovsky and especially R. Harvey Belovski for their assistance in writing this essay.

2    Erich Auerbach, *Mimesis: The Representation of Reality in Western Literature*, trans. Walter R. Trask (Princeton: Princeton University Press, 1978). Hereafter cited parenthetically within.

to that of the patriarch Ya'akov, who, in the pivotal moment of Jewish history, also suffers a wound – at the hands of the "man" associated in Rabbinic literature with Esav.[3] For Auerbach, it is the *representation* of Odysseus against that of Old Testament figures which functions as the distinction between the styles of classical and Hebraic writings. Taking this distinction as a starting point, this essay moves from issues of representation to the values that underlie them, showing how representational modes distill the competing values of Western and Jewish cultures. That is, different versions of the mimetic not only imply different conceptions of interpretation, as Auerbach himself implies, but also the different sensibilities which inform them. The wounds of both Odysseus and Ya'akov – central to their respective names and identities – mark a difference not only in style, but also in the competing worldviews of the Torah and Homeric epic.

## II

Auerbach's discussion focuses on the discovery of the scar by the aged nurse, Euryclea, upon Odysseus's return to Ithaka. Having survived the ten-year long battle of Troy, as well as ten years of wandering, Odysseus returns to his homeland. Disguised as a beggar, he returns to take vengeance upon the suitors who had overtaken his home during his absence. Penelope, Odysseus's wife, in ignorance of the "beggar's" true identity, commands her housekeeper, Euryclea, to wash the feet of the stranger. As Auerbach recounts it:

> Euryclea busies herself fetching water and mixing cold with hot, meanwhile speaking sadly of her absent master, who is probably of the same age as the guest, and who perhaps, like the guest, is even now wandering somewhere, a stranger; and she remarks how astonishingly like him the guest looks. Meanwhile Odysseus, remembering his scar, moves back out of the light; he knows that, despite his efforts to hide his identity, Euryclea will recognize him ... No sooner has the old woman touched the scar than, in her joyous

---

3   *Bereshit* 32:25, Rashi *ad. loc.*

surprise, she lets Odysseus' foot drop into the basin; the water spills over, she is about to cry out her joy; Odysseus restrains her . . .(3)

Auerbach, as we will see, elicits the significance of Homeric style, his "representation of reality," but the narrative which describes the genealogy of the scar, rendered secondary in Auerbach's account, also requires elaboration. Indeed, how Odysseus received the wound is the subject of the long digression that interrupts the account of Odysseus's discovery by the aged nurse. That is, Homer disrupts the recognition scene (which Aristotle found to be among the supreme examples of the kind) by providing a detailed account of the history of the scar, beginning first with Odysseus's birth, and then a formative event in his youth. In Homer's account, Autolykus, the grandfather of Odysseus, takes the honor of naming the new born child:

> My son-in-law, my daughter, call the boy
> by the name I tell you. Well you know, my hand
> has been against the world of men and women;
> *odium* and distrust I've won. Odysseus
> should be his given name . . . .      (19.436–43)[4]

Autolykus, having himself suffered and caused suffering to others, names the child after himself – or rather with a name which commemorates those qualities which he himself embodies. Odysseus, the chosen name, literally means one who suffers and causes others to suffer (note the translator's attempt to capture this meaning with the word "odium"). The *Odyssey* continually meditates upon the problem of suffering (it is itself a theodicy, part of a genre which Milton in *Paradise Lost* would describe as "justifying the ways of God to men"), associating that suffering with the very identity of the title character. In the passage which follows, Homer recounts a formative moment in the life of Odysseus, a rite of passage which involves the hunting of a wild boar:

---

4  All citations from *The Odyssey*, trans. Robert Fitzgerald (London: Duncan Baird, 1998).

> ... Odysseus
> being on top of him, had the first shot,
> lunging to stick him, but the boar
> had already charged under the long spear.
> He hooked aslant with one white tusk and ripped out
> flesh above the knee, but missed the bone.
> Odysseus' second thrust went home by luck,
> his bright spear passing through the shoulder joint;
> and the beast fell, moaning as life pulsed away.
>
> (19.477–85)

Upon his return home, Odysseus recounts the tale of his own wounding and his ultimate triumph, "spinning out the tale" of "how he got his wound." The incident functions centrally in the *Odyssey*: for the hunter Odysseus, suffering (and making others suffer) is always the prelude to narrative – a self-narration by which he gets to boast of his own prowess, that is his own glory. The wound that Odysseus suffers on his thigh is not only a means throughout the *Odyssey* of identification for Odysseus, but it is a means of identification which ultimately marks off Odysseus in his own glory.

Auerbach, however, is not so much interested in the thematic central-ity of the scar (to which the current essay will return), describing rather the characteristics of Homeric style. For Auerbach, the Homeric narrative emphasizes "delight in physical existence" (13) – achieving such delight through a style which presents a "uniformly illuminated, uniformly objec-tive present," present in the vivid description of detail (like the "basin glittering in the firelight" [11]). From Auerbach's perspective, Homer not only provides uniform illumination by means of "a fully externalized de-scription," but in Homeric epic there is "never a form left fragmentary ... never a lacuna, never a gap, never a glimpse of unplumbed depths" (23, 6–7). Auerbach may underestimate the depth of Homeric narrative, but he does elaborate the particular pleasures of the Homeric style, tied not only to the Homeric representation of "battles and passions" and "adventures and per-ils" – in all of their dazzling "objective" detail – but also to a style which is entirely forthcoming, generous in providing clear relationships between nar-rative events (6). Auerbach calls it a style dominated by "hypotaxes" – where

syntactic subordination and "an abundant display of connectives" lend towards a representation of reality where the narrative is never fragmentary or
half-illuminated (75). The same style which renders the physical in all of its
externalized clarity also provides a narrative where all of the episodes find a
clearly articulated place within the story's structure.

In contrast to the Homeric style of subordination, connection, and
externalization, the Old Testament style is characterized not by subordination, but rather, for Auerbach, the juxtaposition of sometimes seemingly
fragmentary events. Old Testament narratives externalize only that which
is necessary for the purpose of narrative. What lies between those points,
Auerbach writes, "is left in obscurity" (11). Everything about the biblical
narratives "calls for interpretation." In opposition to the Homeric stories,
those of the Old Testament always remain "mysterious" and "fraught" with
a "background" which remains unarticulated (23, 12). In contrast to the
Homeric style of clear and externalized temporal subordination, the Old
Testament courts obscurity and abruptness – always, writes Auerbach,
intimating the "suggestive influence of the unexpressed" (23). The style of
parataxis – not hypotactic subordination, but juxtaposition – is one that,
Auerbach observes, acknowledges "multiplicity of meanings and the need
for interpretation" (23). Had Auerbach not been bound by his own conception of the "Jewish writers" (13) and the documentary hypothesis, he may
have reached the understanding that the parataxis of the Torah is central
to its nature as *Torah SheBichtav* – which through its very nature demands
the activity – the engagement, the *amal* – of *Torah sheBe'al Peh* (indeed it is
Midrash which comes to fill in the temporal gaps engendered through the
paratactic style of the Old Testament).[5]

The differences in styles to which Auerbach calls attention lends to the

---

5   Auerbach describes Augustinian appropriations of the narrative of "Terah and
Abraham" in a way that approximates the methodology of Midrash: "There is visible
a constant endeavor to fill in the lacunae of the Biblical account, to supplement it by
other passages from the Bible and by original considerations, to establish a connection
of events, and in general to give to the specific Biblical episode the highest measure of
rational plausibility" (75).

difference of the *experience* of these Homeric and biblical texts. In the pedagogical contexts of Bar-Ilan University, I have found that student response
testifies to the immediate and accessible pleasures which Homer offers.
Odysseus's return, the reunion with Penelope, the death of the suitors:
these events are "brought to light in perfect fullness," offering immediately
accessible pleasures, externalized in the "objective present" of the Homeric
foreground (6, 7). While the Homeric narrative is always forthcoming, the
lacunae of the Torah – the gaps in narrative – by contrast, call out *darsh-
eni!* – providing not the immediate pleasures of Greek epic, but eliciting
the different and more active (though perhaps less accessible pleasures) of
interpretive engagement.

The pleasures of Homer – especially in the *Odyssey* – are not only
manifest through the style of externalization, but through a parallel narrative emphasis. Although Odysseus may suffer many trials, the blessing
that he receives from the gods are actually bestowed. He, Penelope, his son
Telemachus, and his father, Laertes, revel in the glory manifested through
the epic hero's return to Ithaka. Not only is there an evident transparency
between Divine will and human action – "Zeus, Father!, Gods above!/ you
still hold pure Olympus, if the suitors paid for their crimes" (24.364–5) –
but Odysseus returns home to relish in all of his glory. The homecoming
emphasizes Odysseus in the magnificence of *his* glory – the scar in his
thigh not only a remembrance of his own suffering, but now a mark of his
glory *achieved*. With the bodies of the suitors rotting in the banqueting
hall, Odysseus, having been adorned in his eminence by the gods, basks in
the arms of his beloved wife, celebrating the stories of his sufferings: "The
royal pair mingled in love again and afterward lay reveling in stories ..."
(23.304–5). Homeric style, as Auerbach writes, "only knows a foreground,"
so the glory achieved by Homer's archetypal hero, Odysseus, is one which
is rendered fully – present and immediate – in the epic's closing (7). The
rewards for both Odysseus and the reader are real and immediate.

III

Style and theme are intertwined not only in Homer; but also in the Torah.
Indeed parataxis – foregrounding the incompleteness of what Auerbach

calls Old Testament narratives – is thematized in the description of Ya'akov's confrontation with the *sar* of Esav. While Auerbach makes the discussion of Odysseus's scar central to *Mimesis*, he does not discuss the wound suffered by Odysseus's biblical counterpart, Ya'akov. Indeed, the wound which Ya'akov receives emerges in sharp contrast to the scar of Odysseus described in Homeric legend. What Auerbach describes as the incompleteness of Old Testament style finds a parallel in the literal incompleteness of Ya'akov in his battle with the *sar* of Esav. In this reading, Ya'akov's wound – the dislocation of his thigh – serves as a synecdoche for what Auerbach calls "Old Testament style."

At the beginning of *Parshat Vayishlach*, Ya'akov finds himself terrified at Esav's imminent march towards him (after having lost the blessing of the firstborn to his younger brother). Against the prospect of such forces, Ya'akov sends emissaries with gifts (as a means to appease Esav's wrath); takes special precautions for his family; and then finds himself alone, isolated on the banks of the Yabok River in the middle of the night:

> And Ya'akov was left alone, and someone wrestled with him until break of day. He saw that he could not prevail against him, so he touched the upper joint of his thigh, and the upper joint of Ya'akov's thigh was dislocated as he wrestled with him. And he [the other] said, "Let me go, for day is breaking." But he [Ya'akov] said: "I will not let you go unless you bless me." And he said, "what is your name?" And he said, "Ya'akov." And he said: "Your name shall no longer be said to be Ya'akov, but Yisrael, for you have struggled with God and men and prevailed . . ." The sun rose for him when he passed over Penuel, and he limped upon his thigh. (*Bereshit*, 32:23–33)

According to the rabbis, the dust that whirled up from around these two wrestlers "was a dust that rose up to the Throne of the God" (*Chullin* 71a). As Rabbi Samson Raphael Hirsch explains, this was the prototype of a struggle that continued throughout history. Indeed it is the basic content of world history, what Hegel would call, in a very different context, a truly world-historical struggle.[6] Ya'akov was confronted that night by the *sar*,

---

6    As Hirsch writes, "this struggle was the prototype of a greater struggle that has continued throughout history; indeed it is the sum and substance of all of human history" (*The Hirsch Chumash*, trans. Daniel Haberman [New York: Feldheim and

the angel of Esav, and the battle between the two of them represents the struggle between the ideals of Ya'akov and those of Esav (as Hirsch argues, of Western culture itself).[7] Ya'akov, we note, also suffers a wound. Indeed, the wound is the wound of history, of this world, of *olam haZeh*. In the dark night of *galut* – of exile – Ya'akov suffers under the force of Esav: "his thigh was dislocated." So long as the night of exile prevails, Esav sets the terms. But once day breaks ("let me go, for day is breaking"), it is Ya'akov who must be acknowledged ("I will not let you go until you bless me"). Ya'akov may limp through history, but the sun rises "*for*" him". The healing light for Ya'akov also contains within it the end to the painful traumas of history (and the experience of exile), foreshadowing the days of redemption when the dominion of Esav will come to an end. In *Bereshit*, it is Esav's domination throughout history which is immediate and seemingly complete: Esav receives his inheritance immediately. The inheritance of Ya'akov, however, is always apparently imminent, but never fulfilled. Esav travels directly to Mount Seir (the seat of his inheritance), while Ya'akov builds a temporary structure, a *sukkah*, foreshadowing the path of *B'nai Yisrael* – always to be characterized by wandering, first in the desert, and then throughout history (*Bereshit* 33:17).

Ya'akov's wound, like that of Odysseus, is thus central to his own identity: it is the wound that marks off his exile, but it is also tied significantly to an inevitable change in name. Through that wound, Ya'akov acknowledges himself as subservient – at least partially – to the power of Esav. The *sar* of Esav grants Ya'akov a new name (which God in fact later accords to him: "Your name shall no longer be Ya'akov, but Yisrael shall be your name" [32:28]). He will no longer be known through the name of Ya'akov, but he becomes Yisrael, who even Esav acknowledges as the rightful recipient of the blessing of his father, Yitzchak. Esav had wanted to completely destroy Ya'akov, and declare his supremacy for ever and for all time: but he "could not prevail against him." Which is to say that Ya'akov may limp through

---

Judaica Press, 2002], *Sefer Bereshit*, 661).

7   Rav Dessler, as R. Harvey Belovski informs me, understood that when *Chazal* refer to the '*sar*' of a nation, they mean its ideology.

history under the shadow of the powers of Esav, but even Esav acknowledges that the end of history promises a dawn in which the sons of Ya'akov – that is Yisrael – will be blessed: "And he blessed him there." But that blessing is one which does not come – immediately – to fruition. As the Kli Yakar notes, that Esav was born with hair indicates that, already complete at birth, his portion is the physical realm of *Olam HaZeh*.[8] The *shlemut* – or perfection – of Ya'akov will only come in the world to come, *Olam HaBa*. Indeed, as Rashi explains Ya'akov's refusal of Esav's offer for accompaniment, the latter knows well that he will not catch up with Esav until the end of days, *yamot ha'mashiach* (33:14).[9]

The struggle between Esav and Ya'akov is indeed a world historical struggle: the Torah notes that struggle in a commemoration that takes a very different form from the glory commemorated in the wound of Odysseus. Immediately following the account, the Torah enjoins, "Therefore Yisrael's sons must not eat the sinew of the weakness [*gid haNasheh*] which is on the upper joint of the thigh, to this day, because he touched the sinew of the weakness at the upper joint of Ya'akov's thigh" (32:32). In commemoration of the miracle of Ya'akov's salvation from Esav, God commands an abstention from eating the *gid haNasheh* (the sciatic nerve). The root of the word *nasheh*, in fact, connotes, as Hirsch explains, "submission and powerlessness." Every time a Jew sits down to eat, he is reminded of the admonition to forego the sinew, the symbol of the physical strength of *olam haZeh*.[10] But the embracing of the law of the sinew of submission is not only a concrete means of refusing the powers of Esav – and his desire for immediate glory

---

8    Kli Yakar to *Bereshit* 25:25. In both physical and spiritual terms, Esav is already "*asui*" – that is, "made." His physical appearance at birth – already exemplifying the traits of an adult – reflects a spiritual stasis. The Shem mi-Shmuel points out that the *gematria* of Esav is *shalom*: "from his beginning to his end, he remained what he was at his beginning." Esav's spiritual paralysis, the Shem mi-Shmuel writes further, can be attributed to a sensibility that never "detected any lack in himself" for "all his ways seemed righteous in his own eyes" (Shem mi-Shmuel to *Parshat Toledot*, 5672).

9    For the notion that the one who attains perfection – *shlemut* – in this world will not merit it in the world to come, see Maharal, *Netzach Yisrael* 19.

10    *Hirsch Chumash*, 667.

and power. Rather, the wound of Ya'akov also shows that genuine strength comes not from the physical powers of the natural world, but from the Divine power that bears Israel through history. How different are the responses of Odysseus and Ya'akov! The former's wounding by the boar is precedent to a life of conquest and self-glorification. The latter, however, turns to a practice which as Hirsch writes, allows for the revelation of the "finger of God in history."[11] Odysseus manifests glory through his own powers; Ya'akov brings glory to God through his this-worldly defeat.[12]

Auerbach is right to note the stylistic qualities of the Torah – parataxis, abruptness, mystery. He does not, however go far enough to explain the extent to which the style of Torah – not a historical accident or the mere preference of "Jewish writers" – in fact embodies the central values of Israel. The very "dislocated" style manifested in the Torah is a characteristic embodied in the character of Ya'akov himself, and it is through this means that he transforms into Yisrael. Indeed, the acknowledgement of such incompleteness is the prerequisite not for a narration that will lead to self-glorification as in the case of the hero of the Homeric tale, but for a halachic practice which acknowledges that ultimate well-being and blessing do not depend upon human conquest, but rather upon His Glory. That is, the wound of Ya'akov is a sign of the incompleteness that characterizes Israel throughout history. Odysseus's having suffered a wound on his thigh is an inducement for self-glorification. *Gid haNasheh* is a halachic expression of displacing glory unto its source and origin in the Divine.


IV


The wound suffered by Ya'akov informs a sensibility which acknowledges the imperfections of the world – a world which Esav already understands

---

11   *Hirsch Chumash*, 668.

12   For an extended meditation on the significance of defeat in the life of Israel, see Rabbi Joseph B. Soloveitchik, *Out of the Whirlwind: Essays on Mourning, Suffering and the Human Condition*, ed. David Shatz, Joel B. Wolowolsky and Reuven Ziegler (Ktav 2003), especially the essay entitled, "The Crisis of Human Finitude."

as finished.[13] Ya'akov, himself the paradigm of one who suffers, is open to the demands of an imperfect world, thus refusing Esav's invitation for accompaniment, rather "leading on softly" – accommodating the pace and needs of his "nursing" cattle and "tender" children (*Bereshit* 33:13).[14] Ya'akov recognizes the needs of others; Esav, the hunter, who focuses only on the riches of this world, rapaciously satisfies his own needs. Ya'akov's scar may have healed, but the mark of the lack is left upon the generations which follow.[15] That is, Ya'akov – who himself suffers – learns to heed the suffering of others, and in the process brings glory to God.

In this light, the scar on Ya'akov's thigh is not only paralleled by that of Odysseus, but perhaps even more suggestively by another thigh – that of Esav, and the mark upon it. This mark may further elicit the contrast between the values associated with the West (Esav, as the rabbis tell us, is Rome) and those of Israel. Esav, like Odysseus, is a hunter: indeed, the former's self-serving ideology of immediate gratification from the riches of the world is distilled in the verse, "Esav was a cunning hunter, a man of the field." The *Targum* translates "a cunning hunter" – *yada tzayid* – through the odd word *Nachashirchon*, rendered by Tosefot as simply "a hunter" (*Bava Kama* 92b). Yet the Shelah, relying upon the *mekubalim* takes a different route – faithful to a more literal rendering of the word. *Nachash-irchon* is literally snake-thigh (*nachash-yerech*).[16] In the place where Ya'akov

---

13    For midrashic representation of a later embodiment of the conflict between Esav and Ya'akov in the conflict between Rabbi Akiva and Turnus Rufus, see *Midrash Tanchuma* (*Tazria* 5). To Turnus Rufus's question, "Whose acts are greater – man's or God's?," Rabbi Akiva answers, "man," subsequently asking his Roman interlocutor, "Which are superior cakes or sheaves of wheat?" Turnus Rufus, the descendant of Esav, sees the world as already inherently perfect. Rabbi Akiva, Ya'akov's descendant, sees that both the world and man are refined through adherence to Divine command.

14    On Ya'akov's suffering, see *Bereshit* 43 and Rashi *ad. loc.*

15    On the ramifications of the wound for future generations, see Ramban to *Bereshit* 32:26, and *Sefer HaZohar*. In the latter text, those who would suffer the consequences of the wound are the "upholders of Torah" – the *tamchin d'oraita* – of subsequent generations (*Vayishlach* 171).

16    *Sefer HaShelah HaKodesh* to *Mesechta Megillah, Perek Torah Ohr* 1; see also

suffered the wound at the hands of the *sar* of Esav, Esav himself bears a different mark: the *"demut nachash al yericho"* – an image of the snake. Esav passes through life bearing the imprint of the primal snake that had deceived Chava with the promise of divinity ("you shall be as gods," *Bereshit* 3:4). Ya'akov's wound commemorated in the *gid haNasheh* emphasizes human lack in the face of the Divine. Esav's "mark," by contrast, emphasizes the desire for immediate gratification, pleasure and glory embodied by the *nachash* in *Gan Eden*. In the place of Ya'akov's wound – which stands as a reminder of creaturely imperfection – Esav is adorned with the image of the serpent, which offers the false promise of this-worldly perfection already achieved.

After Esav's figurative defeat in Penuel (having acknowledged Ya'akov to be the true recipient of the blessing of spiritual inheritance bestowed upon him by his father), he is met with his brother's attempt to appease him with gifts. To this request, Esav responds, *yesh li rav* – "I have an abundance," "I have enough" (*Bereshit* 27:9).[17] Stripped of the spiritual blessing, Esav celebrates his self-sufficient command of the material world, declaring his own independence. As Rabbenu Bachaye explains, Esav's words express his "arrogance and haughtiness of heart" which "recount his own self-satisfaction," while Ya'akov "constantly recounts the beneficence of God."[18] Like Odysseus, his counterpart in the Western tradition, Esav is not only one who hunts, but also one who recounts – or narrates – his own sufficiency. Esav's mark of the serpent advertises his belief in this worldly completion

---

*Midrash Yalkut Reuveni*, Warsaw 1883, v. 1, 226 (*Bereshit* 25:25).

17   See *Targum Onkelos* to this verse. Where Esav claims abundance, Ya'akov claims to have everything – *yesh li kol* – understood by Rashi as satisfaction with his lot (see *Bereshit* 33:11 and Rashi *ad. loc.*). For *Chazal*, the attribution of *"kol"* is associated with all three of the *Avot*, and their having functioned as repositories in *Olam HaZeh* for characteristics associated with *Olam HaBa* (see *Bava Batra* 16b).

18   Rabbenu Bachaye to *Bereshit* 33:9. For Ya'akov's mention of Divine beneficence, see *Bereshit*: "… the children which God hath graciously given thy servant" (33:5); "… for therefore I have seen thy face, as though I had seen the face of God, and thou was pleased with me" (33:10); "Take, I pray thee, my blessing that is brought to thee; because God hath dealt graciously with me" (33:11).

and perfection. Ya'akov, by contrast, understanding creaturely imperfection, only mentions the benevolence of Divine providenc

The dislocated style of Torah is thus not a mere aesthetic anomaly, rather it parallels an event central to the life and identity of Israel – the wound of Ya'akov, the figurative scar of which persists throughout the generations. The dislocation of Ya'akov's thigh helps establish the identity of Israel, standing as a concrete manifestation of what Auerbach rightly identifies as the distinguishing characteristics of Old Testament style. Auerbach may have noted that the lacunae of the "Old Testament" intimate "the suggestive influence of the unexpressed," thus demanding a multiplicity of interpretations. Auerbach does not, however, emphasize how this "lack" entails an interpretive humility in the face of a Divine text which can never be fully exhausted (for the engaged hermeneutics of Ya'akov – that of *Torah sheBe'al Peh* – always elicits but never completely represents the Divine). The interpretive humility requisite to the demands of the Torah (and the acknowledgement that the external is never enough as it is for both Odysseus and Esav) is based in the life of Ya'akov, the wound that he endures, and the awareness of creaturely imperfection which it brings. Such awareness leads not to the hunt after glory, but rather to another kind of active engagement, a practice that strives to repair an imperfect world. Ya'akov is thus radically distinct from that of the two hunters of Jewish and Western traditions – the "snake-man" Esav, as well as the "godlike Odysseus" of Homer's epic. Transformed into Israel through his wound, his enduring scar (and the humility it entails) is manifested in both the hermeneutics (*limud Torah*) and practice (*mitzvot*) of his descendant – the means through which, as Hirsch writes, the "finger of God" continues to be revealed.

Professor Elliott Malamet

# Maimonides the Modern? Self and Sensibility in the Twelfth Century

MANY MEDIEVALISTS HAVE labelled the twelfth century "the age of the individual." What they mean by this is a new emphasis on human dignity and virtue, a new concern with self-discovery and psychological self-examination, an increased sensitivity to the boundary between self and other, and optimism about the capacity of the individual for achievement. As the historian Caroline Walker Bynum argues, "if the twelfth century did not 'discover the individual' in the modern expression of unique personality and isolation of the person from firm group membership, it did in some sense discover – or rediscover – the self, the inner mystery, the inner landscape."[1] Sarah Spence extends the claim even further than Bynum when she asserts that "the twelfth-century was witness to the origin of the self as we define it today."[2]

Yet there is a crucial distinction that must be made, a distinction that becomes especially important when considering the work of Maimonides. The

---

1   Caroline Walker Bynum, Jesus as Mother: Studies in the Spirituality of the High Middle Ages (Los Angeles: University of California Press, 1984), 106.

2   Sarah Spence, *Texts and the Self in the Twelfth Century* (Cambridge: Cambridge University Press, 2006), 4.

Middle Ages did not have our contemporary concepts of the "individual." What *they* thought they were discovering when they turned within, what *they* called the soul or inner man, was not what we mean by the individual. As Bynum points out, when *we* speak of the individual, "we mean not only an inner core, a self; we also mean a particular self, a self unique and unlike other selves."[3] In contrast, as John Benton has noted, the twelfth century regarded the discovery of the *homo interior*, or *seipsum*, as the discovery within oneself of human nature made in the image of God – an *imago Dei* that is the same for all human beings.[4] Thus, what the medievals meant by self was not an open-ended process in which one discovers whatever may lie within. Indeed, the twelfth century considered the discovery of the inner person as a quest for a very specific aspect of the self *which was already there* – in everyone – and had been termed by the Bible as the core material of each person. To "find oneself," to use current vernacular, had a very particular and theological resonance in the Middle Ages. It was not left to the discretion of each individual to decide the nature of the self. Rather, one undertook the quest of self-discovery for a purpose, towards a specific – and collectively shared – end. The development of the self was towards God, or more specifically, to try and learn how to align the inner self with the image of God that the Bible had indicated (*Bereshit* 1:26) was the spiritual DNA of every human being.

This stands in marked comparison with modern and postmodern thought. Already Friedrich Nietzsche had examined the possibilities that the notion of unitary self was problematic and that, in fact, the self might not enjoy any guaranteed a priori unity.[5] The Nietzschean current can be seen everywhere at the turn of the twentieth century, echoed in the work of D. H. Lawrence: "our ready made individuality, our destiny, is no more, than an accidental cohesion in the flux of time."[6] The expositor par

---

3   Bynum, *Jesus as Mother*, 87.
4   Quoted in Bynum, 87.
5   Charles Taylor, *Sources of the Self* (Cambridge: Harvard University Press, 1989), 464–65.
6   Quoted in Taylor, 463.

excellence of this fragmentation is surely James Joyce, with his repeated ex-plorations of the fluidity of the human personality and his atomised inves-tigations of selfhood. The trend continues in more postmodern work, such as in the work of the novelist Philip Roth, whose art is grounded in the idea that the contemporary self is a continuously constructed, ever fluid, ever changing apparatus. In his novel, *The Counterlife*, characters that die in one chapter are resurrected in the next, figures that are secular in one part of the text become religiously observant a short time later. The notion of a stable self is continuously undermined. As Roth writes elsewhere, "It's amazing what lies people can sustain behind the masks of their real faces ... People beautifully pretending to be 'themselves.'"[7]

Part of what modern people struggle with all the time is "Who am I? Is there a core self beneath the ebb and flow of my existence, or is my identity changing all the time depending on the flux of my life? What is my identity and how do I define it? Am I what I think? Am I what I do? Am I what I say? Am I what my childhood, especially the first five years of my life, made me? Am I where I come from? Am I some odd mixture of all of these?" The psychoanalyst Erich Fromm tellingly comments on the shift in therapeutic complaints that took place as the twentieth century progressed and con-cludes in stunning fashion:

> At the time of Freud ... people who had a real massive symptom illness, which they could prove by having symptoms, went to a psychiatrist. Today I would say that most people who go to a psychoanalyst are people who suffer what he used to call "*la malaise du siècle*," the uneasiness which is charac-teristic for our century. No symptoms at all, but feeling unhappy, strange, not even sleeplessness, life has no meaning, no zest of life, drifting, a feeling of vague malaise ... There is nothing wrong. *They have everything but they suffer from themselves.*[8]

To have everything and yet to be adrift; to be symptom-free and yet to

7   George Searles, ed., *Conversations with Philip Roth* (Jackson: University of Mississippi Press, 1992), 167.

8   Erich Fromm, *The Art of Listening* (New York: Continuum, 1998), 67–68 (em-phasis added).

be profoundly ill; to be constantly exploring the inner world and yet to feel a floating sense of self; this is the grave modern paradox to which Fromm gives expression.

Is the self a stable entity, which exists prior to our understanding of it – prior to our self-conscious awareness – or is the self a human construction, with no original structure, no core meaning and no goal towards which it must aspire if it is to be called authentic? The debate on such issues has resonated throughout psychological theory for the past century. Even those who believe that there are more fundamental or universal elements to who we are, make relatively modest claims about the *goal* of the self. So, although Freud, for example, does divide the inner man into a tripartite system of id, ego, and superego, he only presents generic prescriptions for what is to be considered the healthy individual.

The questions with which Maimonides grapples in regard to the self are not only ones that have formed the core philosophic issues from the Greeks onwards, but they are of great concern in our existentially anxious age. What are the conditions necessary to fashion the "authentic self," the good life? What are the distractions that deflect people from a life of authentic spiritual and emotional liberation? In a Jewish context, what is the individual's responsibility to his or her community? And perhaps most crucially: If, as Maimonides seems to conclude in *The Guide of the Perplexed* (see, for instance, 1:52), that God is in a fundamental way, unknowable, then what does Maimonides have in mind by linking the search for self to the search for God? What does it mean that we are made in God's image, if, in fact, God is unknowable and inaccessible?

The idea of the self as connected to being a creation of God far predates Maimonides's time. The origin of the idea can be found in the opening chapter of the Bible, and the Midrash (*Bereshit Rabbah* 8:11) likens the image of God to that which is permanent and even eternal within a person. According to the Midrash, human beings occupy a unique median position within creation, somewhere between angel and animal. Our mortality is that which separates us from the angels, but the image of God allows us to transcend an animalistic identity. The traditional Christian concept of self as indicated by Augustine, writing in the fifth century, is that created things receive their form through God, through their participation in God's Ideas. We are not simply self-manufactured selves, but partake of reality insofar as we participate in God's plan for the world. So what is required if we are to really live and bring out the full potential of the self, is to direct the soul at once inwards and yet towards Divinity. Augustine is explicit in this regard: "Do not go outward; return within yourself. In the inward man lies truth."[9]

Augustine's view of selfhood is that the self, almost by a kind of osmosis, will take on the character of whatever preoccupies it. If you think about sexuality, your soul will be absorbed in such. If you are preoccupied by material desires, your soul will take on a material character. In Augustine's words, "Everyone becomes like what he loves. Dost thou love the earth? Thou shalt be earth. Dost thou love God? Then I say, thou shalt be God."[10] This formula for the formation of the self is strikingly parallel to assertions made by the medieval author of the *Sefer HaChinuch*. In a famous comment on mitzvah number sixteen, he states that a "person is influenced according to his actions. His heart and his thoughts are drawn after his deeds in which he is occupied whether good or bad." For the *Chinuch*, as for Augustine, the good for each person is defined by his ability to shift his soul towards seeing and appreciating the Divine order of the world, to direct the inner person away from physical desire and onto spiritual quest. Any other life represents a non-authentic self.

We see an even harsher construction throughout Maimonidean thought, where one's very humanness is basically defined by the intellectual pursuit of God. By this, Maimonides does not mean a sterile concept of the intellect, a mere absorption of information and ideas. Rather, intellectual perfection means a process of first acquiring moral piety, controlling and placing in balance one's passions, mastering Jewish texts and the worlds of math and science, logic and philosophy, removing any form of trivial distraction, committing to the process of reason and the active awareness of God.

In his Commentary on the Mishnah, he writes "Man, before he uses his

---

9    See Taylor, *Sources*, 127, 129.

10    E. Gilson, The Christian Philosophy of Saint Augustine (London: Golancz, 1961), 250.

intelligence and acquires knowledge, can be considered as an animal. When a man chases after lusts and when sensual desires prevail over the conceptual ones, and makes his intelligence subservient to his lusts, so that he recedes to be like an animal which conceives only eating, drinking and copulation for itself, then the Divine capacity, that is intelligence, will not be recognized in him." This is a theme that he repeats in *The Guide of the Perplexed* (3:51), where Maimonides indicates that this person has the "external shape of a man" but his status is like "that of the irrational animals."

The Maimonidean self is thus not a given. The self is the potential to actualize the Divine image within. It is not an accident that the *Guide* begins in Section One, Chapter One, with an analysis of the term "*tzelem elokim,*" the image of God. This image, he tells us, is none other than the human intellect which allows a person to connect with the intellect which flows from God. In the Maimonidean system, which derives from Aristotle, God emanates, as it were, out into reality, and the person who trains himself is able, by virtue of his own intellectual perfection, to become the recipient of this Divine emanation.

This intellectual perception is unique to human beings. Maimonides calls one who does not actualize this intellectual capacity "an animal having the shape and configuration of man" (*Guide* 1:7). Perhaps more troubling still, for Maimonides, is that this animal in human form has the capacity to wreak havoc and destruction: "[Such a man] applies the capacities for thought and perception, which were to prepare him to achieve a perfection that he has not achieved, to all kinds of machinations entailing evils and . . . engendering all kinds of harm." So the distortion of the self in Maimonidean terms, the inability to actualize God's image, leads not simply to mediocrity or mindless physicality, but at the dark end of the spectrum, to unbridled wickedness. It is precisely the intellect gone awry, distorted by a faulty moral sense that leads to evil.

A chilling reminder of this passage of the *Guide* can be found in a recent book by the journalist Ron Rosenbaum called *Explaining Hitler*, in which the author examines those historians who in the past fifty years have tried to explain how such a man could have arisen and what constituted the nature of such evil. Perhaps the most striking part of the hardcover edition is the cover photo of Hitler at the age of approximately two years old. It is a sweet, cherubic face. The photograph is a deliberate attempt to force the reader to encounter what seems like a staggering transition between this innocent child, with his firmly implanted Divine image, to the monster of adulthood. How could *this little boy* have become *Hitler*? The Hitler visage reiterates for the reader why, for Maimonides, intellect without moral guidance is a sterile, empty notion. There is no equation of necessity between intelligence and morality. Only when moral piety has been firmly established in a person, can the true actualization of the intellect begin.

Intellectual perfection is the domain of very few people, not simply because of genetic predispositions, but also because of the enormous pull of distraction in human life. Maimonides was acutely aware of the tragic implications of this. Distraction and truth are really at the opposite ends of the spectrum of life. The American philosopher, Robert Nozick, once created a kind of thought experiment that he called "The Experience Machine." In Nozick's fantasy, a person could "pre-program" their life before entering a kind of tranquillity tank or machine. They would then experience whatever they wanted with whomever they wanted, and it would feel to the person as if it were totally real. Nozick's comment on this process is to ask if the only thing that is important in life is how something *feels*, regardless of whether it is an illusion: "Plugging into an experience machine limits us to a man-made reality, to a world no deeper or more important than that which people can construct. There is no *actual* contact with any deeper reality, though the experience of it can be simulated. Many persons desire to leave themselves open to such contact and to a plumbing of deeper significance."[11]

Nozick's question is more than simply an amusing philosophical diversion. The issue of whether a person prefers pleasant illusion to the often more complex and inevitably more painful fate of real life is one that comes up again and again for all of us. Hence the threat caused by distraction to the achievement of a genuine self is considerable, and for Maimonides, the solutions to this problem are complex and fraught with difficulty. This is because he is always concerned with balance, with an individual achieving

---

11   Robert Nozick, *Anarchy, State and Utopia* (New York: Basic Books, 1974), 42–43.

the best possible conditions for the self but trying to remain attached to the human community, despite all of its frailties. Despite the emphasis on community involvement, Maimonides also takes a kind of "grown-up" view of individual responsibility – one cannot simply blame outside culture for one's lack of focus. Indeed, in the final chapters of the *Guide*, Maimonides stresses that a person's life will ultimately go in the direction that he wishes to turn, and that distraction can easily divert one from the Divine path, "You have the choice: if you wish to fortify this bond [with God] you can do so; if, however, you wish gradually to make it weaker and feebler until you can cut it, you can also do that. You can only strengthen this bond by employing it in loving Him and in progressing toward this, just as we have explained. And it is made weaker and feebler if you busy your thought with what is other than He" (*Guide* 3:51).

What is sometimes overlooked in any cursory reading of the *Guide*, and perhaps should be a mandatory call to attention in the contemporary religious world, is that, for Maimonides, this kind of lack of intense relationship with God is not just the domain of secular people. In the closing chapters of the *Guide*, Maimonides has strong words for those in religious communities who externally carry out commandments but are clearly distracted in their heads. "If you pray merely by moving your lips and at the same time are thinking about buying and selling, or if you read the Torah with your tongue while your heart is set upon the building of your house ... then you should not think that you have achieved the end" (3:51). Such warnings resonate throughout the *Guide* from the Introduction onwards, where Maimonides continually reiterates the limitations of conventional religious instruction and the failure to plumb the depths of the Torah because of a lack of sophisticated training.

The balance between solitude for the self on the one hand, and communion with others on the other hand, is stated in his *Preface to the Commentary on Pirkei Avot*, known as *Shmoneh Perakim* (Eight Chapters). In Chapter Four, Maimonides writes of some of the practices of pious people meant to deflect what they perceived as the negative influence of society, even to the extent of "seeking solitude in the deserts because of the degenerate nature of the people in their city ... they feared that their character traits would also be corrupted through a relationship with them. Therefore they departed from these societies to dwell in the deserts where there are no wicked people."

But for most individuals, solitude is not an ideal at all, but is considered by many sources within the Jewish tradition as an extreme measure, one which should not be adapted by the masses as a means of bolstering the self. Maimonides uses a medical analogy in assessing this behaviour, saying it is like people untrained in medicine who, upon seeing an experienced physician administer certain potions to patients who are dangerously ill and prevent them from eating ordinary food, then apply such a regimen to themselves. But if an ordinary person were to ingest such potions, he would of course become ill. In Judaism one cannot just isolate oneself from others in order to "find oneself." It is the wrong medicine for ailments of the soul. And yet, despite this clear, generally anti-monastic message, Maimonides does offer a reverse message in the *Guide*. He makes it clear that if you really want to achieve a certain spiritual liberation, "it is achieved in solitude and isolation. Hence every excellent person stays frequently in solitude and does not meet anyone unless it is necessary" (*Guide* 3:51). This dual message appears explainable by the fact that Maimonides had a different prescription for different people.

Maimonides sees the very goal of the Torah as the creation of *individuals*, seeing self-perfection as the purpose of all mitzvot. Much of the *Guide* is a discussion of how paganism had infected the world with idolatrous thinking and how the traces of this idolatry remain with us, constantly challenging the individual to rise above conformity and thoughtless devotion to material things in order to achieve selfhood. The pagan mind, which is the antithesis of individualism, thrives on social custom and mindless groupthink. The famous religious theorist Mercia Eliade notes that, in pagan society, reality is achieved through imitating archetypes. He characterizes primitive man as one who "sees himself as real only to the extent that *he ceases to be himself* and is satisfied with imitating and repeating the gestures of another. In other words, he sees himself as real, as truly himself, only, and precisely, insofar as he ceases to be so."[12] For Maimonides, Torah provides the opportunity for attachment to God and hence liberation from conformity.

---

12   Mircea Eliade, Cosmos and History: The Myth of the Eternal Return (New

Yet ultimately, even for the extraordinary individual, the goal is to re-enter society, to come "back to the cave" of Plato's allegory and re-educate the people. The enlightened self has a communal obligation. Hence the irony: one must, in a sense, be free of "collective thinking" in order to come back and liberate the community from its lack of selfhood. For Maimonides, Ya'akov's dream of the angels is an image denoting prophecy, the ascent of the human being to God and then the subsequent re-entry into the human community. He would view the notion of finding oneself in a vacuum where one is divorced from attachments and/or contributions to society as the height of narcissistic irrelevance.

The patriarch Ya'akov himself is a wonderful example of this phenomenon. The Talmud in *Shabbat* relates that after Ya'akov was saved from harm at the hand of his brother Esav, the Torah tells us "Ya'akov arrived complete" (*Bereshit*, 33:18). The Talmud interprets this as the idea that Ya'akov was whole in terms of his body, his wealth, and his Torah knowledge (*Shabbat* 33b). The Torah verse then continues "he encamped before the city," for which the Talmud offers alternative explanations: "Ya'akov established a new coin for the city. Or he established marketplaces for them. Or he established bathhouses for them." So after benefiting from God's grace, and realizing that he has achieved wholeness, he sees it as his duty to contribute to others.

Just prior to this passage, the Talmud relates the cautionary tale of the great sage Rabbi Shimon Bar Yochai. To escape persecution from the Romans, he and his son had escaped and taken up residence in a cave, miraculously nurtured by a carob tree and a water well that is created for them. There, they learn Torah, uninterrupted for twelve years. This is clearly one of the Talmud's core stories regarding the cultivation of solitude for the development of the self. After twelve years, upon being informed by the prophet Elijah that the emperor has died, they re-emerge. Immediately upon seeing a farmer ploughing and sowing, Rabbi Shimon exclaims "They forsake eternal life and instead occupy themselves with temporary life." The Talmud relates that wherever they cast their eyes upon was burnt up, consumed in flames. Immediately, a heavenly voice came forth and said

York: Harper, 1959), 33.

"have you left the cave in order to destroy my world? Return to the cave."
After twelve more months, they are told to leave the cave. This time, Rabbi
Shimon's first question upon leaving the cave is to communal leaders. He
asks "Is there anything here that needs fixing or improvement?" (*Shabbat*,
ibid.).

It takes a full year for Rabbi Shimon to adjust to the level of ordinary
human existence. After being chastised by Heaven for his self-absorbed
perception of life, his inability to integrate his twelve years of Torah study
into a mode where he can contribute to the human community, he finally is
able to emulate the model of Ya'akov and learn a sense of civic responsibility. Rabbi Shimon's initial impulse is ostensibly a healthy one. Faced with an
environment which threatens to crush his Jewish self, he takes drastic steps
to recover time and space and allow himself to cultivate his Judaism. But the
reintegration is difficult.

For many people who have had enlightening or intense experiences,
where parts of themselves previously unexplored have suddenly risen – after
a meaningful trip or interpersonal relationship or absorption of spiritual
wisdom – it is the path afterwards that proves most difficult. The enlightened self must translate his or her understanding of reality into some benefit
for those around them. This is a moral imperative from a Jewish perspective.
The prophet is compelled to return to the Platonic cave and begin a chain
of illumination. With all of the conditions of solitude that a person might
put into place to try and work on self-growth, it is ultimately necessary
to form a bond with "an other" in order to formulate a solid sense of who
we are.

The child psychoanalyst Donald Winnicott, in *Maturational Processes
and the Facilitating Environment*, asserts that the "True Self does not become a living reality except as a result of the mother's repeated success in
meeting the infant's spontaneous gesture." But what of the mother who
does not or cannot reflect her child, whose face instead reflects only her
moods or needs? What does the baby see in such instances? When there is
a regular failure to find the self in the mother, "they look," says Winnicott
and they do not see themselves. They cannot find themselves. If a continu-
ous non-reflective face meets the child, then the child adapts his gestures to

accommodate what is presented. This is the genesis of the False Self, writes Winnicott.[13]

Winnicott's poignant picture of the baby striving to find itself in the mother's face is worth comparing to Eliade's vision of the pagan and also Maimonides's conception of seeking the image of God. The pagan never separates his sense of self from the cultural myths that surround him. Winnicott's baby learns to form a self from the nurturing, mirroring gaze of the mother. And we might say that, for Maimonides, we find ourselves by "looking at" the image of God within us, mirroring our true selves to us. The image of God can thus be seen as the true mirror for the individual, the true model that, if found, reflects back to the person who and what they truly are.

The crucial distinction here is that, for Winnicott, the baby finds herself in an actual tangible physical object, the mother's face. But what is out there, in Maimonides's terms, to be mirrored by? Where is that image of God? How do we know that God is within us if there is no tangible or external trace of God's presence? Although Jewish tradition speaks of God's revelation to the Jewish people, to prophets who receive God's word, and also to Nature as a sign of God, the tradition also emphasizes a God who allows no "trace" of Himself. The rabbis stress that even when performing astounding wonders and miracles, God leaves no evidence of His presence. In *Tehillim* 77, the psalmist sings, "Your path is in the sea, your trails are in the many waters, yet your footprints cannot be known." Even when splitting the Red Sea, the Midrash tells us that the sea quickly returned to its original form, leaving no trace of God's intervention.

God is, to be plain, hard to find. As Jose Faur points out, Rabbi Joseph Ibn Abitur in the eleventh century calls attention to the fact that "traces come as a result of an object resisting a thing 'standing' on it." An example of this would be tracks on mud or snow, where the trace of a presence is recorded by the impact made when ground resists the foot. In other words, a trace of something is an interaction between that thing and whatever it

---

13   D. W. Winnicott, Maturational Processes and the Facilitating Environment (London: The Hogarth Press, 1972).

comes in contact with. But God does not contact humans in that way; no resistance and thus no trace. Reiterating the same principle, Isaac Newton commented that "celestial bodies find no resistance from the omnipresence of God."[14]

Perhaps all of life is an attempt to recover such presence. A good example is a gravestone. A person dies and we erect a sign, a physical trace of them. But can there be a trace of the traceless God? Jacques Derrida once noted "The sign is always a sign of the Fall."[15] In the Garden of Eden, Adam feels God's presence directly. There is no intermediate steps, no signs of God, no substitutions for God. Today, all we have are signs. Even Torah – in the absence of God, we have a text. As Kevin Hart notes, Jesus holds out the hope of the "the one Perfect sign in an imperfect world of signs … unlike other signs, for here the signified – God – is also perfectly expressed in the signifier. He is at once inside and outside the sign system."[16] For Jews, however, this way of closing the gap is off limits for obvious reasons.

Outside of the Christian mythos, one cannot recover presence so easily. The great irony is that we use signs to recover the presence of something, to say *this* is a representation of *that*, but the sign itself guarantees that the real presence is gone. If it were here, we would no longer need the sign of the thing – we'd have the thing itself. So all signs are a sign of "life after Eden," where God's presence is gone. Every sign tells us that things are not perfect. All of life is an attempt to recover presence.

Is the image of God an attempt to compensate for the inability to read the supranatural world? Is God within? Is that the authentic self? One might argue that precisely as God is invisible, traceless, and cannot be found in the actual physical world, the presence of God within, our presence as God's image, is the most authoritative sign of God there can be, or no sign at all. But for Maimonides, the actualized becomes the ultimate pathway to God and perhaps the only means to recover God's presence.

14   Jose Faur, *Homo Mysticus* (Syracuse: Syracuse University Press, 1999), 14.

15   Jacques Derrida, *Of Grammatology*, trans. Gayatri C. Spivak (Baltimore: Johns Hopkins University Press, 1976), 283.

16   Kevin Hart, *The Trespass of the Sign* (Cambridge: Cambridge University Press, 1989), 7–8.

We live in an age of great inward turning, the move to ourselves. Some of this thrust seems to be grounded not simply in a romantic equation between the inner self and a deep truth to be discovered about life, but also in a tremendous suspicion of what is "out there." The twentieth century was a time in which individuals increasingly held public institutions and structures in disregard, from Kafka's nightmare vision of the bureaucratic state to something as mindlessly simple as Timothy Leary's drug-induced chant from the sixties: "Tune in, turn on and drop out."

One of the great ironies of modern life is that we are, on the one hand, mistrustful of what is outside and attendantly obsessed with the self, our individual identities, yet, on the other hand, despite this self-obsession we often feel a great confusion about those identities, about who we really are, a confusion that was not such a common problem in less self-conscious times. As Abraham Joshua Heschel perceptively asserts: "There was never a time in which the need for self-expression was so much stressed. Yet there was never a time in which self-expression was so rarely achieved; in which there was so much pressure to adjust oneself to conventions, clichés, to vogue and standardization. The self is silent."[17]

For Maimonides, the image of God within us is a catalyst to get us to consider ourselves in much larger terms than we are perhaps accustomed to doing in the West. Selfhood is not just an accumulation of private moments of happiness or a life that "works" because I have a good job, a fulfilling marriage and wonderful children, though without question these are important building blocks from a Jewish point of view. Without the quest for God, we become prone to viewing our lives from a socioeconomic perspective, from the possessions we accumulate or even the people by whom we are surrounded. But at the deepest level, Maimonides's search for self begins and ends with the apprehension of God. He forces those of us in contemporary life who take the inner life seriously to think with caution and humility about the loss of God in modern life and the consequent loss of the self.

---

17   Abraham Joshua Heschel, *Quest for God* (New York: Crossroad Publishing, 1990), *xi*.

## Rabbi Dr. Yehuda Schnall

# Philosophy, Poetry, and the Bible[1]

THE SEVENTEENTH CENTURY philosopher and mathematician Blaise Pascal described the Object of his worship as "the God of Abraham, the God of Isaac, the God of Jacob, not the God of the philosophers and the learned."[2] Indeed, it is common to distinguish biblical religion from philosophical theology. The former is characterized by assuming the existence of God, a supreme but personal Being, Who created the world and enters into personal relationships with the human beings He has created. God can achieve anything by simply saying "Let it be so"; yet He commands us to behave in certain ways, and allows us to choose whether we will obey. Like a wise and loving parent, He offers us direction (often backed up by reward and punishment), but gives us the freedom to choose our path in life. He is angry with us when we do wrong, and pleased with us when we do right. He intervenes in human history, bringing down the haughty and raising up the lowly, and generally meting out justice tempered with mercy. Perhaps most importantly, He loves us and wants us to love Him.

---

1   First published in *Philosophy and Faith: A Philosophy of Religion Reader*, ed. David Shatz (New York: McGraw-Hill, 2002). Reprinted here by permission of the author.

2   See his *Pensees*. He was anticipated by the twelfth century Jewish philosopher Yehudah HaLevi in his work *The Book of the Kuzari*, sect. IV.

When we look at the writings of Augustine, Aquinas, and Maimonides, as well as other classic medieval works of philosophical theology which are supposedly based on the Bible, we get an entirely different picture. We find attempts to *prove* that God exists. We find God described in terms so abstract that the theologians themselves admit that they do not know what they are talking about when they use them. God is not merely powerful, He is omnipotent; not just wise, but omniscient; not just good, but omni-benevolent. And far from interacting with His creatures, He is immutable (unchanging), impassible (unaffected by anything), and eternal (outside of time). Furthermore, these and other similarly superlative characterizations do not describe *different* properties that God *has*, the way other beings have their various properties. Rather God *is* His properties and infinitely more, all rolled into one indivisible unity, unlike anything else in existence. Even God's existence is different from the existence of anything else. Thus, the God of the philosophical theologians is not at all what we would ordinarily call a "person"; He is *impersonal*, and so any personal relationship between Him and us is impossible.

So what is the Bible talking about?

One answer offered by philosophical theologians is that the Bible expresses theological truths in ways that are somewhat accessible to the unlearned masses. Most people are not used to abstract thinking, and can understand only what is expressed in concrete terms. One of the essential skills of a prophet, or an author of a book of the Bible, is the ability to express deep, complex, abstract, and generally difficult concepts and truths in the language of ordinary human experience. Biblical narratives and descriptions are often allegories or parables, which (as yet) uneducated people can understand and learn. If and when they become more educated, they can "unpack" the meanings hidden in the allegories and parables and achieve knowledge of theological truths, thus gaining the full benefit of Bible study. And if one never acquires the ability to see the literal truths at which the Bible is hinting, no great harm is done. In fact, it is another aspect of the greatness of the biblical authors (or Author) that their stories make one a better person even if one takes those stories at face value and never discovers the profound truths that lie beneath.

But once we start interpreting the biblical text allegorically, where do we stop? Which statements in the Bible are literally true, and which are mere allegory? Fundamentalists, i.e., those who interpret the Bible as literally true, object to many allegorical interpretations as attempting to rob us of historical truths related in the Bible. Thus, for example, Moses Nachmanides, a thirteenth century Bible commentator, complains of Maimonides's interpretation of several biblical narratives as prophetic visions, rather than as actual events. The allegorists, on the other hand, disparage fundamentalists for taking the Bible at face value and overlooking the deeper meanings that they hold constitute the essential message of the Bible.

However, a compromise is possible. Fundamentalists can admit the validity of allegorical interpretations of biblical narratives, while maintaining the literal truth of those narratives. For example, they can admit that the story of Abraham and Sarah in Egypt (*Bereshit* 12:10–20) is a foreshadowing, or prophecy, of the experience of the Israelites in Egypt several generations later (*Shemot* 1–12). But they need not conclude that the events described in *Bereshit* 12:10–20 never happened. They can say that this prophecy was "acted out" by Abraham and Sarah rather than told to them verbally. Generally, a fundamentalist can admit the importance of the moral and theological lessons taught by the various narratives in the Bible without denying that the events described really occurred. The fact that a story has a moral does not mean that it is merely a fable.

For philosophical theologians, a different kind of compromise is available. It has been suggested by Maimonides and others that God eternally ordains that certain miraculous events occur at certain specific times *as if* in response to human needs at those times. For example, God builds into nature that the Red Sea should split when the Israelites encamp on its shore and find themselves pursued by the Egyptians (see *Shemot* 14). It is not that God *noticed,* at that time, that the Israelites were in trouble, and then *responded* by speaking to Moses and splitting the sea. Rather, it was arranged, from eternity, that the events work out this way. Generally, God does not engage in ongoing interactions with the world. Rather, since He knows all of history from His timeless perspective, He (so to speak) pre-ordained miraculous salvation and punishment, prophets seeing visions and hearing heavenly voices, and the realization of prophecies, to occur at the appropriate times.

Thus, philosophical theologians can accept many of the biblical narratives as more or less literally true, while still maintaining that God is not really interacting with and responding to actions and events in the world.

What remains unclear is whether this latter view sufficiently captures the warmth of the personal relationship that many religious people feel – and many theologians think – exists between us and God. Some will feel that the idea of an impassive, immutable Being outside of time is inadequate to account for the depth of emotion that people feel for God, even if this Being somehow arranges events to occur as if He were responding to our situations. But others will feel that a God Who, from eternity, is there for us, providing us with what we need and deserve, with justice and yet with mercy, calls forth the most profound emotions of reverence and love of which human beings are capable.

Another suggestion about the Bible is that it is neither literal truth nor allegory, but poetic imagery, inspiring us to view the world in a certain way and to behave accordingly. For example, such biblical expressions as "God loves you" (*Devarim* 23:6; see *Malachi* 1:2) and "God created man in His image" (*Bereshit* 1:27) are not to be understood as expressing propositions which can be literally true or false – i.e., which can correspond or fail to correspond to facts or to reality. Rather when we meditate on the expression "God loves you," we will come to accept life's vicissitudes with serenity, and face life's challenges with confidence. And if we keep in mind the words "We were created in God's image," we will develop a deep respect for our fellow human beings, and for ourselves, which will manifest itself in a tendency to always help and never hurt one another. But it is inappropriate to ask, e.g., in exactly what way we are in God's image or to ask for a proof or disproof of God's love for us. The meaning of such expressions is exhausted by their inspiring the appropriate attitudes and behavior; they make no factual claim.[3]

---

3    Such "non-cognitivist" views have been put forward by R. B. Braithwaite in *An Empiricist's View of the Nature of Religious Belief* (Cambridge: Cambridge University Press, 1955), George Santayana in *Reason in Religion* (New York: Charles Scribner's Sons, 1905), and more recently by Howard K. Wettstein, "Awe and the Religious Life:

One could imagine such a suggestion coming from philosophical theologians as a way of accepting the biblical passages in question as somehow valuable, while denying that they are literally true – for example, denying that God is capable of emotions such as love and that God has an image in which He created human beings (or that there is any similarity between God and human beings). However, it has recently come more from opponents of philosophical theology, who claim that philosophical theology distorts biblical religion by analyzing it in terms of a system of propositions about God and His relation to the world and who claim (incorrectly, in my opinion) that their suggestion is closer to the way believers view the biblical texts. It has also come from philosophical atheologians, i.e., philosophers who believe that all statements about God, taken literally, are false (atheists) or meaningless (logical empiricists), but who, for some reason, are looking for some positive role that the Bible can play in their lives. But no matter where it comes from, the suggestion is open to question.

First of all, it should be noted that the fact that biblical passages can, do, and even should, affect our attitudes and our behavior does not in any way indicate that those passages are non-propositional poetic imagery. Our propositional or factual beliefs affect our attitudes and behavior in much the same way as it is suggested that these poetic images do. To use the above examples, one who firmly held the factual belief that God really loves us, would have at least the same serenity and confidence as one who meditated on the poetic imagery of God's loving us is supposed to have. His belief would be a *reason* for having such attitudes, in the sense that if someone were to ask him *why* he is so serene and confident, he could answer, "Why shouldn't I be? After all, God loves us, so whatever happens is certain to be for the best." Similarly, one who held the factual belief that we were created in God's image, i.e., that we resemble God in some specific, important way,

---

A Naturalistic Perspective," in *Midwest Studies in Philosophy XXI: Philosophy of Religio,* ed. Peter A French, Theodore E Uehling, Jr. and Howard K. Wettstein(Notre Dame: University of Notre Dame Press, 1997), and "Poetic Imagery and Religious Belief," in *Philosophy and Faith: A Philosophy of Religion Reader*, ed. David Shatz (New York: McGraw-Hill, 2002).

would naturally feel respect for others and tend to behave accordingly, at least as much as someone who meditated on the poetic figure "God created man in His image."

More importantly, it is not at all clear that viewing biblical passages as non-propositional poetic imagery is consistent with being inspired by them. It is difficult to see how an expression that has no propositional content can inspire us.[4] At least it seems that if we *know*, or *believe*, that a given expression has no propositional content, it cannot influence our attitudes and behavior. For example, unless we believe that in actuality God loves us, how can meditating on the words "God loves us" help us accept troubles with serenity or face challenges with confidence? And if we do not believe that human beings really resemble God in any morally relevant way, then how can meditating on the words "God created man in His image" give rise to respect for human beings? It seems that to the extent that such images inspire, they must have propositional content which is believed. Then the poetic expression of these propositions can further help bring about the inspirational effect.

Thus, even if we view the main function of the Bible as influencing our attitudes and behavior, it is more plausible to say that it performs this function by instilling propositional beliefs than that it does so by providing us with non-propositional poetic imagery.

One might object that I underestimate the power of poetry, and of fictional literature in general, to influence us. After all, fictional literature has had profound effects on people's attitudes and behavior. For example, presumably no one believed that the events described in Stowe's *Uncle Tom's Cabin* actually occurred. Yet the book is said to have had a tremendous influence on attitudes toward slavery and to have led people to fight against it in the years preceding the American Civil War. And the romantic poetry of Keats, Byron, and Shelley has changed people's lives, even though this

---

4 See, e.g., William P. Alston, "Religious Language," in *The Encyclopedia of Philosophy*, ed. Paul Edwards (New York: MacMillan, 1967), VII:173; and Eleonore Stump, "Awe and Atheism," in *Midwest Studies in Philosophy* vol. XXI (University of Notre Dame Press, 1997).

poetry is not the propounding of propositions for the reader to believe. So perhaps the majestic prose and poetry of the Bible can influence us in the way suggested, even if it is, on the literal level, fiction.

The question of how literature influences us is much too broad and deep for us to settle here. Besides, it seems to be a question best discussed by experts in literature and psychology, as opposed to philosophy and religion. But a few brief remarks seem called for. So speaking as a philosopher, my opinion is that though fictional literature does not *state* propositions for the reader to believe, it usually *implies* propositions for the reader to believe. For example, consider Shelley's poem "Ozymandias," in which he describes the ruined remains of a once great statue with an inscription arrogantly boasting of the grandeur of the surrounding structures, when all that remains in the area is barren sand. The poem tends to make us take less seriously our own and others' pride and ambition, and perhaps makes us pause in our pursuit of "the biggest and the best." We need not believe that the scene described in the poem ever existed. However, it is not non-propositional poetic imagery alone that influences us. Rather it is the *implied proposition* that this *sort* of thing *can* happen, and *has* happened, on one scale or another, countless times: people accomplish things of which they are so proud that they think their reputation will live forever, but in fact they are soon forgotten. The suggestive descriptions, the irony, and the other poetic devices used by Shelley help us to conceive the implied proposition more vividly and to think of aspects of our experience that corroborate it. We believe the implied proposition, and it is this belief that primarily influences our attitudes and behavior, the poetic imagery merely facilitating that influence. I think that most cases of fictional literature's influence on us can be analyzed this way.

I may be accused of generalizing from a single, self-serving example. I plead guilty, with the excuse that I cannot do much more in this context. I recommend that all those who are interested in the issue try to apply this analysis to whatever work of fiction or poetry has influenced them, to see if they can find an implied proposition to which the primary influence can be attributed. (I suspect that existentialist works will pose a bit of a challenge.) But to conclude my argument: This analysis does not seem to work for "God loves us" and similar expressions. The only proposition I can see that is involved in this sentence that could give us serenity and confidence is the proposition *stated* by it – i.e., that God loves us. If I'm right, then it is only by belief in the literal truth of "God loves us" that one can achieve the serenity and confidence that this central sentence of the Bible can provide.

Rabbi Dr. Eliezer Shore

# Torah from the Heart: Chassidic Insights into Spiritual Education

W
HEN THE CHASSIDIC movement first made
its appearance among Eastern European Jewry
in the mid-eighteenth century, it found itself
addressing a fairly stable, well-established community almost seven hundred years old. True, the golden age of Polish Jewry had ended with the
Chmelnicki Massacres (1648–1649) and the subsequent breakdown of the
Council of Four Lands. Still, the community's social structure, its legislative
processes, its hierarchy of rabbis and communal officials, and its religious life
had remained intact despite the series of catastrophes.[1]

Into this scene came the Ba'al Shem Tov and the Chassidic movement.
In many ways, this revivalist movement that quickly conquered most of
Eastern Europe was not new at all. The social structures remained in place,[2]

---

1   The influence of the *Haskalah*, with its civic, educational and dress reforms
clearly had a greater effect on the structure of Eastern European Jewry than the
Chassidic movement.

2   Though control was transferred to the Chassidim. See also Moshe Rosman,
*Founder of Chassidism: A Quest for the Historical Ba'al Shem Tov* (Berkeley: University
of California Press, 1996), who claims that the Ba'al Shem Tov simply filled an
established communal position of doctor and *ba'al shem*. While this opinion clearly
ignores the creative contribution of the father of Chassidism to the movement, it does

and many of the central ideas underlying the movement had existed previously.[3] What did happen, however, and what shook Jewry to its core, was a restructuring of the *values* of Jewish life.[4] While many of the central tenets of Chassidism have been shown to exist in pre-Chassidic writings, it was their unique combination, their popularization, and their embodiment in the figure of the Tzaddik that transfigured Jewish life. What Chassidism did was re-order and re-prioritize Jewish values – the Tzaddik over the scholar, prayer over Torah study, immanence over transcendence.[5] No longer was attachment to God the exclusive property of the *talmidei chachamim* and kabbalists. Rather, it was equally available (at least in theory) to the broad spectrum of Jews. God was "close to all who call upon Him; to all who call upon Him in truth" (*Tehillim* 145:18). This was the curative for a society that, to many of its members, had lost its vision and inspiration.[6]

Almost three hundred years later, the influence of the Chassidic movement has not abated. This is not only evident in the remarkable post-war rebirth of traditional Chassidism, with its unique mode of dress, its Rebbes and courts, and its tight-knit communities. Rather, conceptually, the transformation in values that the Ba'al Shem Tov initiated has remained a powerful spiritual force, expressing itself in a variety of ways, whether Martin Buber's existential Chassidism of the early twentieth century or the counter-culture Chassidism of Rabbi Shlomo Carlebach, which continues to inspire people a decade after his passing.

---

affirm that the Ba'al Shem Tov was less radical than previously thought in terms of his communal position. On the transfer of communal authority to Chassidic leaders in the first generations of the movement, see Glenn Dynner, *Men of Silk: The Chassidic Conquest of Polish Jewish Society* (New York: Oxford University Press, 2006).

3   See Mendel Piekarz, *The Beginning of Chassidism: Ideological Trends in Derush and Musar Literature* [Hebrew] (Jerusalem: Bialik Inst., 1978).

4   A good synopsis of the various issues under debate (albeit presented from a reactionary, traditional point of view) is Dov Eliach, *Sefer HaGaon* [Hebrew] (Jerusalem: Moreshet HaYeshivot, 2002).

5   See A. Green, "Typologies of Leadership" in *Jewish Spirituality I*, ed. Arthur Green (New York: Crossroads, 1987), 127–156.

6   See S. Dresner, *The Zadik* (New York: Schocken, 1960).

One of the significant areas in which Chassidism changed traditional values was in the fulfillment of *mitzvot* and the study of Torah. No longer was it sufficient to perform these acts out of mere servitude to God. Rather, they became means to the goal of *deveikut* – mystical clinging to the Divine. Selfless learning, *limmud Torah l'shemah* – for the sake of Heaven – became learning *l'shem hey* – for the sake of the letter *hey*, representing the *Shechinah*. In other words, a person learns Torah in order to uplift and return the Divine Presence to God, which entailed, as well, a transformation in human consciousness.[7]

This change in focus is precisely where Chassidism has the power to speak to us today. Not necessarily in its emphasis on mystical experience (though renewed interest in that area may also be occurring), but in the change in focus from the rote performance of *mitzvot* and Torah study to that which engenders a sense of personal meaning.[8] It offers us a different

---

7   On the Chassidic approach to Torah study, see Moshe Idel, *Hasidism, Between Ecstasy and Magic* (Albany: SUNY Press, 1995), 171–188. On the connection between prayers for the *Shechinah* and the uplifting of the consciousness, see my doctoral diss., *Letters of Desire: Language, Mysticism, and Sexuality in the Writings of Rabbi Nahman of Bratzlav* (Bar-Ilan University: 2005), 121–122.

8   Of course, it is unlikely that the early Chassidim would have understood themselves in this way, as the idea of "personal meaning" was not yet in their vocabulary. They too developed a theory that *deveikut* was for the sake of a higher, objective good – the restoration of the Divine Presence, an act which entails the negation of the self, not its enrichment. Nevertheless, when one looks at the sociological response to the early movement and the enthusiasm with which it spread, it is clear that a renewed sense of personal meaning lay at its heart. This approach was given explicit voice in later generations of Chassidic teachers, such as in the statement of R. Klonymus Kalmish Shapira, the Piazeczna Rebbe, in his work *Tzav v'Ziruz*: "Emotion is the food of the soul; it is as much of a need of the soul as food is to the body. A person who fulfills this need with emotional prayer and study is nourishing the soul correctly. Prayer and study without emotion will leave a vacuum that will force the soul to search for emotion anywhere, even in sinful behavior."
  It is possible to read the issue of "self-fulfillment" as part of Rabbi Chaim of Volozhin's critique of the Chassidic movement, in the fourth chapter of his work, *Nefesh HaChaim*. There, he rails against those individuals who seek spiritual experience over the straightforward, selfless fulfillment of the commandments or Torah

approach to the fulfillment of the tradition than is currently practiced.[9] In other words, the underlying principles that Chassidism originally advanced are still available to us – such as an emphasis on experience over knowledge, or a sense of closeness to the Divine. These can be used to further the spiritual renewal of the Jewish people.[10]

### SPIRITUALITY IN JEWISH EDUCATION

The idea that education should be a spiritual experience, and not merely an intellectual one, is receiving increasing attention of late.[11] There are, of

---

study.

For a contemporary example of this debate, see David Bleich's discussion of women's prayer groups in *Contemporary Halachic Problems,* vol. III (New York: Ktav, 1989), especially his comment on p. 119.

9    For a discussion of the perennial disagreement between the Chassidic movement and the Mitnagdim, as it has played out in contemporary Judaism, see Shaul Magid, "Hasidism, Mithnagdism, and American Jewry," in *The Cambridge History of Jewish Philosophy*, ed. Martin Kavka and David Novak (Cambridge: Cambridge University Press, 2009).

10    Chabad-Lubavitch Chassidism has banked on this idea over the last forty years in their outreach work. Furthermore, the current, widespread interest in Kabbalah is really, to my mind, an interest in Chassidism (though not explicitly identified as such), since authentic Kabbalah is generally so complex and abstract that the average person would derive little satisfaction in learning it. Chassidism, however, developed the practical and pyschological implications of Kabbalistic ideas. This was also the goal of Rabbi Yehuda Ashlag, the *Ba'al HaSulam,* in his reinterpretation of the *Zohar* and the Lurianic system (though his system differs widely from that of Chassidism). This may explain why R. Ashlag's teachings have lent themselves to such popularization of late, such as in Philip Berg's Kabbalah Centre in America, and Michael Laitman's "Bnei Baruch" in Israel.

11    Several important titles on this topic are: *Education as Transformation: Religious Pluralism, Spirituality and a New Vision for Higher Education in America,* ed.V. Kazanjian and P. Laurence (New York: Peter Lang, 2000); *The Heart of Learning: Spirituality in Education,* ed. Steven Glaser (New York: Penguin Putnam, 1995); Palmer, Parker, *To Know as We Are Known: Education as a Spiritual Journey* (San Francisco: Jossey-Bass, 1993). See also the "Spirituality in Higher Education"

course, numerous definitions of the term "spirituality," among them many that seem vague or catchall.[12] Alan Brill,[13] however, lists five criteria for an authentic spiritual experience: (A) It is concerned with living experience over religious doctrine. (B) Spirituality is *not* to be confused with ethics. Rather, "ethics are the applications of the Divine imperative to life."[14] (C) Spirituality includes a practical discipline, such as meditation or prayer. (D) It deals with the extra-ordinary – that which transcends normal life – while at the same time; (E) it makes these states or concepts personally

---

initiative of UCLA, at www.spirituality.ucla.edu.

From the Jewish perspective, see Asher Friedman, *"K'Gananim b'Gan Hashem* – As Gardeners in the Garden of God: Chassidic Thought and its Implications for Teacher-Student Relationship," in *Wisdom From All My Teachers: Challenges and Initiatives in Contemporary Torah Education*, ed. Jeffrey Saks and Susan Handelman, (Jerusalem: Urim Publications and ATID, 2003); Zvi Leshem, "The Translation of Chassidic Educational Philosophy into the Contemporary Educational Landscape" at www.nishmat.net; Jeffrey Saks, *Spiritualizing Halakhic Education* (Jerusalem: Mandel Foundation, 2006); Ron Wacks, "Emotion and Enthusiasm in the Educational Doctrine of R. Klonymus Kalmish Shapira of Piazeczna," [Hebrew] *Hagut b'Chinuch Yehudi* 6 (2004), 71–88. Philip Wexler, *Mystical Interactions: Sociology, Jewish Mysticism and Education* (Los Angeles: Cherub Press, 2007). A recent issue of *Jewish Educational Leadership* (5:2 Winter 2007) published by the Lookstein Center for Jewish Education, Bar-Ilan University, is devoted to this topic.

On the role of emotions in learning, see Israel Scheffler, *In Praise of Cognitive Emotions* (New York: Routledge, 1991), 3–17, although none of his emotional categories quite fit that which Rabbi Tzadok refers to.

12    See Alan Brill, "Dwelling with Kabbalah: Meditation, Ritual and Study," in *Jewish Spirituality and Divine Law*, ed. A. Mintz and L. Schiffman (New Jersey: Ktav, 2005), 142.

13    Brill, ibid., 128–144, based upon Louis Bouyer, *A History of Christian Spirituality: Volume One: The Spirituality of the New Testament and the Fathers* (New York: Desclee Co., 1963). Bouyer himself cites P. Pourrat, *Christian Spirituality* (London: Burns, Oates, and Washbourne, 1922), v.

14    Brill, ibid. This is opposed to the approach of *Tikkun* magazine editor, Michael Lerner, who conflates these two aspects, following his general socio-political approach to the topic. See, for instance, Michael Lerner, *Jewish Renewal: A Path to Healing and Transformation* (New York: Putnam, 1994) and *Tikkun* 13, 6. September/ October 1998).

relevant. The words of Ewert Cousins sum up these last points: "This spiritual core is the deepest center of the person. It is here that the person is open to the transcendental dimension; it is here that the person experiences ultimate reality."[15] In other words, spirituality is both transcendent and deeply personal. It can be understood as a sense of *ultimate context*, within which the broadest dimension of existence is able to connect with the deepest levels of the soul.

In the following article, I would like to briefly examine the works of one of Chassidism's greatest thinkers, Rabbi Tzadok HaKohen of Lublin (1823–1900). Rabbi Tzadok is unique in the Chassidic movement not only for the depth and breadth of his thought,[16] but also on account of his personal history. Growing up in a traditional Lithuanian rabbinic family, he became a student of the Chassidic master, R. Mordechai Yosef Leiner – the *Mei HaShiloach* – in his early twenties. Throughout Rabbi Tzadok's life, he maintained his incredible love for and intensity of learning, and even today, his writings are highly esteemed by both Chassidim and Lithuanian scholars alike.[17] As a Torah scholar of the highest caliber, Rabbi Tzadok's writings on *limud Torah* shed light on the uniqueness of the Chassidic approach to study. Though his writing on the topic of Torah are vast and complex,[18] I would like to focus here on one particular aspect – Torah study with heart – a goal toward which many of us, as educators (or even just parents), should

---

15   Ewert Cousins, "General Editor's Introduction to the Series" in *World Spirituality: Christian Spirituality: Origins to the Twelfth Century*, ed. Bernard McGinn and John Meyendorff (New York: Crossroads, 1985), xiii.

16   See Alan Brill, *Thinking God* (New York: Yeshiva University Press, 2002) for a discussion of much of Rabbi Tzadok's thought, particularly his approach to mystical experience.

17   Many important twentieth century rabbinic personalities were influenced by Rabbi Tzadok's thought, among them R. Yitzhak Hutner, author of the *Pachad Yitzhak*, R. Eliyahu Dessler, author of *Michtav m'Eliyahu* and R. Avraham Yitzchak Kook.

18   The most thorough work on this topic is Amirah Liwer, *Oral Torah in the Writings of R. Tzadok haKohen of Lublin* [Hebrew] (doctoral diss.: Hebrew University, 2007). Especially relevant is chap. 9. See also, Brill, ibid., chap. 10.

strive in our efforts to make Torah study a more vibrant and spiritual experience for today's youth.

Before discussing the path of Torah study itself, I cite here a teaching of Rabbi Tzadok on the nature of human thought. This is a necessary preface to understanding how Torah study should ideally be conducted.

### INNERMOST THINKING

At the beginning of the book *Machshavot Charutz*, Rabbi Tzadok discusses a passage from the Kabbalistic work, *Tikkunei Zohar*:[19]

> How many thoughts there are, one higher than the other, one above the other, as it is written: "for one higher than the high watches, and there are higher than they" (*Kohelet* 5:7). And above all of them is the most hidden thought of all (*machshavah setimah*), the highest of the high, of which no other thought is higher. And how many thoughts there are, one enclothing the other.

Although the *Tikkunei Zohar* uses the term "thought," the broader context of the discussion shows that it is actually referring to the supernal worlds[20] or *sefirot* – the Divine hypostasis that underlie reality. The text is stating that these worlds can be envisioned in two ways, either hierarchically, one higher than the other, or concentrically, one within the other, so that the most recondite can also be considered the most high. This highest, innermost world is called *machshavah setimah* – hidden thought, which Kabbalistically, corresponds to the dimension of *Adam Kadmon* ("Primordial Man"), the first emanation from the Godhead.[21]

On this passage, Rabbi Tzadok comments:

---

19   *Tikkun* 69, p. 115a.

20   The envisioning of supernal worlds in anthropomorphic terms is characteristic of Kabbalah, from among the earliest texts, such as the *Sefer Yetzirah*, down to Lurianic writings. Chassidism reversed this trend, as will become evident below.

21   According to the commentary *Metok m'Devash* (Jerusalem: Machon Da'at Yosef, 1991), 1064.

It is known that whatever is above also exists below in the human soul, which is "in our image and our likeness"[22] . . . Human thought also has numerous levels. And there is the deep beginning of thought, which is hidden and concealed from a person, from which all thoughts are drawn. This is the hidden thought, whereas the lowermost garment, which is the revelation of thought in actuality – the various thoughts and musings that pass through the mind – is not essential thought, which is always considered Wisdom (*Chochmah*), which is the essential man, *ko'ach mah* ("the potential of what"), as stated in the *Tikkunim* 22.[23] This has the numerical value of "Man" – "Adam" (מה = אדם), as is known. And this is the thought that makes a mark on the mind and spreads immediately to the heart and from there to the entire body. For *Abba* and *Imma* ("Father and Mother") are "two companions that are never separate."[24] For thought that touches the root of *Abba* alludes to the wisdom of the mind, as is known. It is joined to Understanding (*Binah*), which is in the heart, and causes the birth of the potential for action, in the manner of "the eye sees, the heart desires and the vehicle of action completes [the process]."[25]

Rabbi Tzadok is stating that just as there are multiple levels (or garments) to the worlds, so there are numerous levels of human thought. The thoughts we are most familiar with – the fleeting cognitions of the mind – are only the outermost shell of essential thought. Even moments of concentrated thought may still be superficial, since true thought – *machshavah setimah* – is unique in that it maintains a continual connection to the heart. Rabbi Tzadok cites the Zohar,[26] which calls *Abba* and *Imma*, "two companions that never separate." Kabbalistically, this refers to the constant union of the two uppermost sefirot, *Chochmah* and *Binah*, which engenders a continual downflow of energy that maintains the creation. Rabbi Tzadok applies this

---

22  *Bereshit* 1:26. Here, Rabbi Tzadok uses the familiar Chassidic principle of the psychologization of Kabbalistic cosmology. On this, see Moshe Idel, *Hasidism, Between Ecstasy and Magic* (Albany: SUNY Press, 1995), 227–238.

23  P. 67a.

24  See *Zohar* 2:56a, 3:4a.

25  See Rashi on *Bamidbar* 15:16.

26  Alternative names for the *sefirot Chochmah* and *Binah* when functioning as *partzufim*.

principle to the cognitive dimension. *Chochmah* corresponds to intellect, *Binah*, to the heart.[27] Just as in the upper worlds, *Abba* and *Imma* are never separated, so on the innermost level of consciousness – what Rabbi Tzadok calls the essential person – an inseparable connection exists between the mind and the heart, so that what a person knows, he immediately feels, with the result of this union being the birth of appropriate actions.

> There are also many levels in the feelings of the heart. There are also superficial feelings that are not in the depths and inwardness of the heart at all, for from the heart "is the outpouring of life" (*Mishlei* 4:23). A total emotion is that which touches the depths of one's life. This is the root of Understanding (*Binah*) of the heart, which is drawn from the depths of the Wisdom (*Chochmah*), which is in the mind. And this type of thought, upon which the essential point of life of the heart depends, is the essential person; not the other, superficial thoughts, which are garments to the inner and essential thought.

This innermost point of Wisdom and Knowledge, thought and feeling, are hidden from a human being – *machshavot setimah* – yet they underlie and generate all other thoughts. They are the spring from which true knowledge and meaning continually flow outward.

At this primal level of essential thought and emotion, explains Rabbi Tzadok, a human being is engaged in a continual, contemplative union with God. All of one's thoughts and feelings are directed to the Source. Here, Rabbi Tzadok echoes a teaching of the Ba'al Shem Tov, which states that at the root of all mundane desires and emotions is the love or experience of God. Rabbi Tzadok is stating that even mundane thoughts bear within them a spark of Torah, which is at every moment touching the heart, though the deeper one's thoughts go, the more the heart is aroused.

Although, according to Rabbi Tzadok, only the rarest individuals can access this most recondite part of the soul (for to do so permanently would be to repair the sin of Adam), nevertheless, everyone can approach it to some degree. Thus, he offers a model of cognition that should be of significance

---

27  This is a common distinction in Chassidic texts, based upon the *Tikkunei Zohar* 17a.

to Jewish educators, for it implies that the natural consequence of "deep thought" is its ability to touch the heart and bring about a corresponding change in action, whereas a superficial understanding of Torah will have little effect on the heart or deeds. A teacher should perhaps ask him or herself if the material he or she presents reflects such a union of mind and heart. Does it reach out to unite the minds and hearts of his or her pupils (as the rabbis have said: "Words that come from the heart enter the heart"). Does it inspire them and lead them to action, or do the ideas remain cold and irrelevant? And if so, how can this natural link between our minds and our hearts be uncovered, to whatever degree possible.

### TORAH OF THE HEART

In *Tzidkat HaTzaddik*, Rabbi Tzadok's earlier,[28] more renowned work, he discusses the idea that Torah study must include an affective dimension.[29] He writes:

> The words of Torah that pass through a person's heart, which the heart feels and becomes enthused by, are called a "Tree of Life" and an "elixir of life." For the heart is the source of life, as it states: "for from it are the issues of life."[30] And when it is aroused, the very source of one's life is aroused by means of the words of Torah, which engender life in a person.[31]

To Rabbi Tzadok, it is not sufficient to merely understand Torah, there must be an emotional experience as well – a person must be moved by the words of Torah and by what they signify. To be more precise, it is not merely an emotional experience that is being suggested here, but a deep

---

28   See Brill, *Thinking God*, 384–385.

29   One should not make the mistake that Rabbi Tzadok saw Torah study as *only* an act of the heart. Indeed, Rabbi Tzadok developed a comprehensive intellectual mysticism, in which Divinity is grasped through the mind, in the act of Torah study. For a critique of superficial emotionality and enthusiasm in the spiritual life, see Brill, "Jewish Spirituality," 143.

30   *Mishlei* 4:23.

31   *Tzidkat HaTzaddik* 225.

*internalization* of the topic being studied: A sense of truth and affectiveness of which emotion is only one part. The traditional appellation of the Torah as a "Tree of Life"[32] means just that: when a person learns Torah with heart, the Divine life-force within him – his very vitality – becomes aroused. Herein lays the Torah's power to change a person for the better, as the rabbis have said: "The light in it causes him to become good."[33] According to Rabbi Tzadok, this ability is implied in the very word "Torah," which he sees as related to the word *"moreh,"* as in *"moreh derech"* – a guide.[34]

To Rabbi Tzadok, this type of knowledge is the very definition of wisdom, and the interiorization of Torah is the goal of all learning: "The main wisdom and understanding is when it is absorbed in the heart."[35] It is captured by the rabbinic statement: "The Compassionate One desires the heart"[36] – meaning, it is not that God simply desires our emotions, but that our knowledge of Him, gained through the Torah, should affect us in the most heartfelt way.

### The Need for Need

Experience shows that this process does not happen automatically. Not every word of Torah penetrates the heart of the listener, nor is every heart naturally open to hearing the deeper strata of words of Torah. Rabbi Tzadok thus identifies the most important criterion for being able to hear deeply the meaning of the words as a feeling of lack for what the Torah is coming to teach.

> The main words of Torah are those that enter the heart. And which ones enter the heart? When a person is thirsty and greatly longs for them, as it

---

32  "It is a tree of life for all those who cling to her" (*Mishlei* 3:18).

33  *Eichah Rabbah*, Introduction, *piska* 2.

34  *Tzidkat HaTzaddik* 133.

35  *Divrei Sofrim* 15. This is Rabbi Tzadok's understanding of the verse: "And I have given wisdom to all those of wise heart" (*Shemot* 31:6).

36  See *Sanhedrin* 106b and Rashi *ad. loc.* See also *Zohar* 2:162, 3:218b.

says: "And I ate it, and it was sweet as honey to my mouth" (*Yechezkel* 3:3),[37] which is the matter of: "Your Torah is within my innards" (*Tehillim* 40:9). Meaning, it is absorbed in one's entire body.[38]

Words learned without longing and a sense of spiritual or existential emptiness do not penetrate the heart or affect a change in the student. They remain external to a person, as Rabbi Tzadok writes: "This is not the case [when Torah is studied] with coldness; when [the words of Torah] do not pass through the heart. For even though he understands their wisdom intellectually and grasps matters of Divinity and the words of Torah, the heart is completely unaffected, as though he were studying secular wisdom,[39] to which he has no connection."[40] Not only do such words of Torah fail to change a person for the better, they may propel him away from a true connection to God, as the Talmud says: "If a person deserves it, the Torah becomes a potion of life; if not, it becomes an elixir of death."[41]

Rabbi Tzadok defines this sense of lack as "fear of God" or "fear of sin." This is a dramatic reinterpretation of the traditional understanding of these terms, which usually implies fear of transgression or fear of punishment.[42]

---

37  Notice how Rabbi Tzadok plays with the meaning of the verse. In the original context, Yechezkel saw a scroll containing prophecies of doom. The rabbis, however, identify it with the Torah. Rabbi Tzadok goes one step further and points to its sweetness ("... so I ate, and in my mouth it was as sweet as honey") – the Torah that one learns must be sweet to the mouth.

38  *Tzidkat HaTzaddik* 133. Rabbi Tzadok also writes here: "This thirst comes from the existence of a lack; that a person feels lacking in something, and he needs the words of Torah to fill it." See, also *Tzidkat HaTzaddik* 211: "The Torah was only given to those who lack, and recognize their lacks and request God to deliver them."

39  Lit., "external wisdom" – *chochma chitzonit*. See Rabbi Tzadok's work, *Likutei Emorim*, p. 42a for a further discussion of the nature of this type of wisdom.

40  *Tzidkat HaTzaddik* 225.

41  *Yoma* 72b.

42  *Shabbat* 31a; *Yoma* 72b; *Avot* 3:17. On the concept of fear of God in Chassidic thought, see Alan Brill, "Moving Beyond Lightness and Confronting Fears: Chassidic Thought on the Fear of Heaven" in *Yirat Shamayim: The Awe, Reverence and Fear of God*, ed. Marc Stern (New York: Michael Scharf Publication Trust of the Yeshiva University Press, 2008).

Here, Rabbi Tzadok interprets them to mean the inherent sense of lack and dissatisfaction that so often accompanies the pursuit of worldly pleasures. The point, however, is not to annul these desires, but to direct a person to seek fulfillment from the words of Torah.

This reflects an important concept in early Chassidism, found in statements of the Ba'al Shem Tov, that physical desires are not inherently evil, as often implied in pre-Chassidic ethical treatises, but contain within them the potential for good – a spark of divinity. As the Ba'al Shem Tov taught, "It is proper for a man to have physical desires, for through them he will come to desire the Torah and the service of God,"[43] and "Every commandment or act of holiness starts with thoughts of physical pleasure."[44]

The point is that desires, even mundane ones, actually reveal a longing in a person's heart for God. They lay the ground for all deep, positive learning and should thus be encouraged. This may be the very opposite of every educator's personal experience. The worst thing for a teacher is to face an unruly class, whose students are given over to their every whim and desire. A "good class" is usually defined as one in which the students are quiet and attentive. However, to Rabbi Tzadok, this situation might indicate precisely the opposite – the lack of an "evil inclination" on the part of students indicates a lack of desire and feeling, and ultimately, a lack of interest. Such students lack the basic prerequisite for Torah to enter their hearts – the potential to feel and transform their own shortcomings. They lack a feeling of lack. Rather, the educator must know that when faced with a class of challenging, difficult, and unruly students, he is addressing a group of individuals who have the greatest potential to hear his words. As the Zohar states: "If it were not for the evil inclination, there would be no joy from Torah."[45]

---

43   R. Ya'akov Yosef of Polnoy, *Ben Porat Yosef,* 66b quoted in David Biale, *Eros and the Jews* (New York: Figures Basic, 1992), 131. See Esther Liebes, "Love and Creation: The Thought of Rabbi Baruch of Kosov" [Hebrew], (doctoral diss., Hebrew University, 1997), 270–275; Tishby and Dan, "Chassidism," in *Encyclopedia Hebraica* [Hebrew] (Jerusalem: Poalim, 1988), XVII: 1405, 1408; Weiss, "Beginnings of Chassidism" [Hebrew], *Zion* 16 (1951), 46–105.

44   *Toldot Ya'akov Yosef,* 151a, quoted in *Eros,* 131.

45   *Midrash HaNe'elam, Toldot* 138a. Quoted by Rabbi Tzadok in *Tzidkat*

Obviously, this does not mean that the students should remain on the level of gross desires. Fear of God – the sense of lack – is the indispensable key for transforming these emotions into something positive. How an educator can instill this feeling, how he can somehow extract his students from the enticements and distractions of modern society is a challenge and a question unto itself. The point we will remain with here, at least, is that the students who are the most difficult to address may actually be the ones with the greatest potential for heartfelt learning. Needless to say, the words of Torah that the teacher offers must be able to quench this thirst. They must be of equal potency to the desires that rack the students' hearts.

### TORAH FROM THE LIPS

Does this mean that any Torah study that is not accompanied by deep-heartedness or interiorization is worthless? Yes and no. On the one hand, learning Torah without "fear" may lead to an inner dichotomy in which knowledge of religious truths and unredeemed material desires exist simultaneously, with the former unable to redeem the latter. In such a case, the lower desires can eventually influence and corrupt the mind, leading to a misconstrual of the Torah's authentic meaning. Rabbi Tzadok identifies this as the problem with such biblical and Talmudic characters as Doeg HaEdomi, Bila'am or Elisha ben Abuya (*Acher*), who were Torah scholars (or prophets, as in the case of Bila'am), yet who rebelled against God. It is particularly a problem for Torah scholars, who must struggle with greater desires than the average person.[46] Thus, Torah, if not properly channeled through the heart after the prerequisite of fear-lack, becomes an "elixir of death."

On the other hand, in a related teaching, Rabbi Tzadok clearly states that fear of God is not an absolute prerequisite for studying Torah:

---

*HaTzaddik* 133.

46   See *Tzidkat HaTzaddik* 45; *Divrei Sofrim* 19. It is precisely this inclination, when transformed, which propels them to greatness.

Each person is able to grasp wisdom and words of Torah, even though he does not have the preceding fear of sin and the arousal from below that stimulates the study and understanding of Torah for the sake of the honor of His name, and recognizes that [the Torah] is God's Torah. Nevertheless, God is always ready to constantly bestow words of Torah, even without a lower arousal. And this is: "In His goodness, He constantly renews each day the work of creation."[47] Just as the act of creation did not have a lower arousal, for Adam had not yet been created, so, constantly, each day, He renews [creation] in His goodness alone, without any prior lower arousal ... However, the "work of the chariot" is when God reveals Himself to one who arouses Him.[48]

In discussing the dynamic relationship between the upper and lower worlds, Chassidism often speaks of *hitarutah d'l'tatah* – the lower arousal, and *hitarutah d'l'eylah* – the upper arousal, with the former being preferable to the latter. In other words, in the symbiotic relationship between the upper and lower worlds, there is a difference as to which dimension of reality initiates the process that ultimately leads to an outflow of *shefa* – spiritual bounty from above to below. Ideally, spiritual outflow should be initiated by human endeavor, which triggers a corresponding downward movement. There are times, however, such as during the creation of the world, when there was no source of "lower arousal" with which to start the process of outflow – mankind having yet to be created.[49] At that time, God had to begin the process from above. Subsequently, only after the creation of Adam, could the proper sequence be established.

In general, Kabbalah and Chassidism see this model as applying to every act in the relationship between God and the creation. Every human act

---

47    From the morning prayers, in the blessings before the recitation of *Keriyat Shema.*

48    *Tzidkat HaTzaddik* 226.

49    This is only until the creation of Adam, of which the verse states: "Now, no shrub of the field was yet on the earth, nor had any of the herbs of the field yet sprung up, because the Lord God had not brought rain on the earth, for there was no man to work the soil" (*Bereshit* 2:5). That is, once man would be created, Adam's prayers for rain (the lower arousal) could initiate a supernal response.

triggers some Divine reaction.[50] However, Rabbi Tzadok points to a section of the morning prayers which states: "In His goodness, He constantly renews each day the work of creation." In other words, there is an aspect of creation that is constantly being generated by God, even without human influence. This "upper arousal" is an ongoing dimension of reality, not a one time event. Whereas human events can initiate the supernal outflow – effectively generating and justifying the ongoing existence of creation – there is another, parallel dimension in which God is constantly, gratuitously creating the world, regardless of human actions.[51]

Rabbi Tzadok applies this idea to the way we understand Torah. Ideally, Torah should be learned from "the bottom up." A "lower arousal" – the fear of sin that produces the sense of emptiness and lack – should drive a person to seek fulfillment from the words of Torah, which descend from Above. However, even when that prerequisite is lacking, God is always ready to bestow Torah upon the individual, in the same way that He is always creating the world anew, from above to below, without any lower impetus. By "Torah" Rabbi Tzadok does not mean the simple act of book learning, but a creative interaction with the text, and a degree of Divine influence that enhances one's ability to understand the subject and develop *chiddushim* – new understandings of the material being studied.

The difference as to whether Torah comes first from above or in response to a movement from below is the difference as to whether the words of Torah affect a person's heart or not. In the "above to below" model, the words of Torah remain external to a person, registering in his intellect alone. When the arousal comes from below, however, as a result of the

---

50   See *The Palm Tree of Devorah* by R. Moshe Cordovero, for several examples of this.

51   Rabbi Tzadok would say that this reflects the paradox of God's omniscience and human free will. Both sets are true, although they do not overlap. We can regard human actions as products of human free will. In that case, Divine providence plays no role in them. Or, we can regard all activities as being ordained from above, in which case, free will is irrelevant. Rabbi Tzadok says (*Tzidkat HaTzaddik* 40) that both are true, each in its own, independent dimension.

fear-lack nexus, words of Torah can penetrate a person's heart and lead to transformation.

Rabbi Tzadok applies to this distinction the terms *Ma'aseh Bereshit* and *Ma'aseh Merkavah* – the Work of Creation and the Work of the Chariot. The Talmud speaks of these as two early schools of mystical knowledge: "One should not explain ... the Work of Creation to two [students] and the Work of the Chariot to one, unless he is wise and understands it by himself."[52] *Ma'aseh Bereshit* refers to the secrets of the creation of the world, alluded to in the opening chapters of *Bereshit*, whereas *Ma'aseh Merkavah* refers to the mystical secrets contained in Yechezkel's prophetic vision (*Yechezkel* 1:4–26).[53]

According to Rabbi Tzadok, these categories correspond to the two different approaches to Torah study mentioned above. *Ma'aseh Bereshit* refers to the Torah novellas that descend each day as part of God's ongoing creation of the world,[54] whereas *Ma'aseh Merkavah* refers to God's presence that rests itself upon an individual who has prepared himself for the encounter, leading to a personal and transformative understanding of the Torah:

> God "rides" upon and leads a person who works hard [at Torah study] and prepares himself... And this is the subject of the second blessing before the *Keriyat Shema*[55] – to grasp the words of Torah derived from the wisdom of the Work of the Chariot, which is what God bestows upon us individually ... in as much as we wait and long for Him, and with our lower arousal.[56]

---

52   Mishnah *Chagigah* 2:1.

53   *Tosafot Yom Tov* on the Mishnah. See Maimonides, *Commentary on the Mishnah*, for a different approach.

54   Rabbi Tzadok interprets the Midrashic statement that "God looked into the Torah and created the world" as an ongoing phenomena. God is constantly "looking into the Torah" and creating the world, on a daily basis. As a consequence, just as the world is new each day, so there are new revelations of Torah that descend from heaven. See *Tzidkat HaTzaddik* 90 and 216.

55   As opposed to the ongoing, autonomous and universal emanation of the worlds and the Torah, which is alluded to by the words of the first blessing of *Keriyat Shema*: "In His goodness, He constantly renews each day the work of creation."

56   *Tzidkat HaTzaddik* 226. See also ibid., 189: "There are two ways of apprehending Divinity, one from the perspective of creation, in that one recognizes that

In another early work,[57] in the context of a discussion of Kabbalistic texts and mystical experience, Rabbi Tzadok defines these terms somewhat differently: *Ma'aseh Bereshit* is the study of *any* text whose purpose is to merely describe the ontological structure of reality (primarily the supernal worlds). *Ma'aseh Merkavah*, on the other hand, is not the *description* of the cosmos, but an *experience* of divinity. In other words, even the Lurianic corpus, often considered as the most recondite and esoteric school of Kabbalah, still falls only in the category of *Ma'aseh Bereshit*, in that it describes the operation of the worlds.[58] *Ma'aseh Merkavah*, on the other hand, is the living experience of God.

If we juxtapose this teaching with the one from *Tzidkat HaTzaddik* discussed above, we find an interesting parallel. In both cases, *Ma'aseh Bereshit* refers to the acquisition of knowledge on the intellectual realm, whereas *Ma'aseh Merkavah* means experiencing the knowledge in an inner way. The latter is considered the deeper of the two approaches, thus making experience, whether mystical or heart-felt, to be the true goal of Torah study.

Practically speaking, we can say that while true Torah study is that which is preceded by a sense of lack, and not merely that which is learned intellectually – "from the lips and outward," as Rabbi Tzadok calls it – there is still some validity to Torah taught as an objective discipline. This parallels God's ongoing act of creation, which begins from above without human initiation.[59] Still, if Torah is to be more than *Ma'aseh Bereshit* – a mere *description* of reality – it must eventually enter the hearts of its learners as a response to their seeking and longing.

---

there is a Creator. This is called *Ma'aseh Bereshit*. The second from the perspective of stewardship (*hanhagah*) and this is called *Ma'aseh Merkavah* – how God 'rides' on the creation." See, also, *Dover Tzedek*, 117 and *Sefer HaZichronot*, 58ff.

57   *Divrei Sofrim*, 66ff.

58   At least, when these texts are taken at face value. For an interpretation of the Lurianic corpus as a vast meditative system, see Menachem Kallus, *The Theurgy of Prayer in the Lurianic Kabbalah* (doctoral diss.: Hebrew University, 2002).

59   Even in this case, there must be an element of newness and originality in the material presented, in that it corresponds to the energies of creation, which are renewed each day. See n. 54 above.

CONCLUSION

What do these ideas mean for us, besides informing us of the deeper, truer levels on which we should study Torah?

As an educator, I believe they have important repercussions as to the nature of both the study and instruction of Torah. Rabbi Tzadok's words present an ideal and a challenge. They tell us that the ultimate expression of Torah study is that which joins the mind and heart on the innermost level, so that one's knowledge and feelings are united in a way that naturally leads to action – to the inspired service of God. On the other hand, they also tell us that the prerequisite for this connection is a heart that thirsts – at first, for anything, but ultimately, for the words of the living God. One needs a feeling heart, a passionate heart, even a heart filled with worldly lusts, which can be transformed and redirected.

A teacher not only has to connect deeply to the subject he presents, he must recognize, and even elicit, the gnawing existential sense of lack in his students. As Abraham Joshua Heschel wrote: "Religion is an answer to man's ultimate questions. The moment we become oblivious to ultimate questions, religion becomes irrelevant, and its crisis sets in."[60] The students have to first hear the question; only then can they begin to hear the answer.[61]

---

60   Abraham Joshua Heschel, *God in Search of Man* (New York: Meridian Books and the JPS, 1959), 3.

61   Attention should be brought here to a pedagogical technique called Problem-based Learning (PBL), in which small groups of students must solve challenging, open-ended problems, with the teacher acting as a "facilitator." This has been shown to be highly effective in generating student involvement, particularly on the secondary school level. See Janice Skowron, *Power Lesson Planning: Every Teacher's Guide to Effective Instruction* (Thousand Oaks, CA: Corwin Press, 2006), 109ff. See the author's comment on p. 10: "Problem-based learning activities that engage students in personal and interesting ways can increase motivation and the desire to learn. Classrooms can be dynamic places where students and teachers are energized about learning, but it takes more than just a problem to excite students. Teachers need to share their own passion for learning, know how to relate to students, and provide the setting and resources that allow students to pursue meaning."

Rabbi Prof. Avraham Wijler
and Dr. Akiva Wolff

# A Jewish Approach to the Quality of the Environment

### INTRODUCTION

O NE OF THE problems faced by modern society is the degradation of our physical environment. The environment is our life support system, supplying us with everything we need to survive and function in this world. Unfortunately, many of our activities have destructive effects on the environment. Environmental degradation seems to be increasing, and the capacity of our life support system to sustain us and future generations is increasingly in doubt.

There are differences in opinion as to where the blame and solutions for environmental degradation lie, but almost everyone focuses on three main areas. Some believe that overpopulation is the main culprit, and the solution is to reduce the human population. Others believe that the main cause of the problem rests in the excessive consumption and materialism of modern society, and want to reduce these substantially. Some believe that inappropriate use of technology is the main culprit and want to put better controls on new and existing technologies. Virtually everyone agrees that all three of these factors play an important role in causing environmental problems and that the solutions lie in addressing these factors.

We would like to suggest a different way of looking at the problem and perhaps to the solutions to environmental problems. This approach will utilize traditional Jewish values in contrast to the modern Western values through which the problems are normally viewed. The biblical prohibition of *bal tashchit*[1] (do not destroy) plays an important role in this approach, as we will see. To help introduce this approach and to try to bridge the gap between different value systems, we'll start with a little scientific background.

### PHYSICAL LAWS RELATING TO THE DEGRADATION OF THE ENVIRONMENT

Scientific discoveries over the past two and a half centuries have changed the way we look at our environment – the physical world around us. In the mid-eighteenth century, the *law of conservation of matter* established that matter, the substance making up the physical world, is indestructible. The quantity of matter in the environment remains basically constant. While we cannot destroy this matter, we can change it into different forms. It is the *form* in which matter exists which determines our relationship with it – such as whether we consider it to be useful or not; or whether it is a resource or a pollutant.

The establishment of the first and second laws of thermodynamics in the nineteenth century also influenced our understanding of the physical world. Similar to the law of conservation of matter, the *first law of thermodynamics* states that energy can be converted from one form to another, but can be neither created nor destroyed.

One of the formulations of the *second law of thermodynamics* states that when energy flows from a high concentration to a lower concentration or when energy is changed from one form to another, some of the useful energy is always degraded to higher entropy,[2] less useful energy.

---

1   *Devarim* 20:19.
2   "Entropy" is commonly defined as a measure of the disorder in a system.

## Relationship between Energy and Matter

At the beginning of the twentieth century, Einstein established that energy and matter are closely related and, in theory at least, interchangeable.[3] Does the second law, the law of increasing entropy, apply also to matter? When matter is changed from one form to another, is some of the matter degraded to lower-quality, less useful matter? This is still unclear.[4] Experience shows that when we change matter from one form to another, for example, in virtually any production process, there seems to be an inevitable loss in the *usefulness* of some of the matter. One of the expressions of this is the inevitable creation of waste materials, which are a primary cause of environmental problems.

## Introduction to "Quality" of Matter

G. Tyler Miller writes:

> From a human standpoint, we can classify matter according to its quality or usefulness to us. Matter quality is a measure of how useful a matter resource is, based on its availability and concentration. High quality matter is organized, concentrated, and usually found near the earth's surface, and has a great potential for use as a matter resource. Low quality matter is disorganized, dilute, and often deep underground or dispersed in the ocean or the atmosphere and usually has little potential for use as a matter resource.[5]

For example, bauxite, the ore from which aluminum is extracted, is low quality matter – the aluminum that it contains is difficult to access, highly

---

3   $E = mc^2$; where E = energy, m = mass, and c is a constant representing the speed of light.

4   Daly and Farley cite the late Nicholas Georgescu-Roegen who claimed that the entropy law also applies to matter and proposed that this be recognized as the fourth law of thermodynamics. See Herman E. Daly and Joshua Farley, *Ecological Economics* (Washington: Island Press, 2004), 66.

5   G. Tyler Miller Jr., *Living in the Environment*, 10th ed. (Belmont: Wadsworth Publishing Company, 1998), 76–77.

dispersed, and not in a useable form. An aluminum can, on the other hand, is high quality matter, in that the aluminum in it is accessible, concentrated and very useable.

The concept of matter *quality*, as described by Miller, is an important tool for understanding environmental problems. There is a natural degradation of the quality of matter – from higher to lower quality – in virtually all interactions between an organism and its environment.[6] Environmental problems result from the degradation of the *quality* of matter making up our environment. For example, water pollution is the degradation of the quality of a body of water, from a higher quality (more pure) state to a lower quality, polluted state. A water shortage can be described as the dispersal of available fresh water to a less available, lower quality state. Environmental protection, then, is essentially concerned with protecting the *quality* of the matter making up a given environment.

The problem is, virtually every time we interact with our environment, we inadvertently end up degrading the *quality* of some, if not all, of the matter that makes it up. And it's not only us – almost all living organisms negatively affect the *quality* of their surrounding environment. As Miller writes: "All forms of life are tiny pockets of order (low entropy) maintained by creating a sea of disorder (high entropy) in their environment." [7]

In other words, all living beings maintain their life at the expense of their surrounding environment, which they degrade by withdrawing from their environment relatively high quality material (usually in the form of food and water) and expelling back into the environment lower quality material (usually in the form of wastes).

It is important to clarify that the physical laws described above operate

---

6    Even though some living organisms may concentrate and increase the quality of certain materials in a specific location, this usually comes at the cost of an overall decrease in quality in the entire system – as will be discussed below.

7    Miller, 84. Miller is apparently echoing Physicist and Nobel laureate Erwin Schrödinger who wrote: "Thus the device by which an organism maintains itself stationary at a fairly high level of orderliness (= fairly low level of entropy) really consists of continually sucking orderliness from its environment." From Erwin Schrödinger, *What is Life?* (1944), archived at: http://home.att.net/~p.caimi/Life.doc.

primarily within a *closed* system. That is, a system that is materially closed to its surroundings. The ecological system (ecosystem) of our planet operates as a closed system in terms of physical matter. There is virtually no exchange of physical matter between our planet and the surrounding universe.[8] It appears, therefore, that our planetary ecosystem should be inevitably moving towards dissolution and chaos. And yet we see that this is not necessarily so. In many cases, we see the opposite process – movement away from degradation and toward greater organization. The processes of life itself appear to work against this natural degradation. The key seems to be the importation or utilization of an energy source from *outside* of the system which counteracts the natural degradation of quality (organization, structure, concentration) within the system.

### INCREASING QUALITY AGAINST THE TENDENCY OF DEGRADATION

To reverse the natural degradation – to increase or simply to maintain the quality (organization, purity, availability) of material in this world requires tremendous energy. This energy comes from either "consuming" other material within the closed system (for example, burning fossil fuel) – which causes an increase in quality in one place at the expense of an overall decrease in quality within the closed system – or from the importation of energy from *outside* the system.[9]

---

8 Relatively insignificant amounts of matter may enter or leave the system outside of the influence of man, and man has become increasingly capable of transferring material from place to place, including outside of the earth's ecosystem (for example with space exploration). Furthermore, matter can be transformed into energy and vice versa ($e = mc^2$). Nevertheless, these exceptions are not considered significant in the scope of this discussion.

9 The source of the physical energy necessary for counteracting the natural degradation is the sun, which provides the constant flow of energy necessary for life. While the sun's energy warms the planet, it cannot be used directly as a source of energy by most living beings (with the exception of the photosynthesizers as described below). The sun is also the source of the energy contained in fossil fuels such as coal, oil and

There are two primary agents that are able to "import" energy from outside the system in order to counteract the natural dissolution and destruction of all order that makes up life as we know it.

The first agents are the *photosynthesizers.* Photosynthesizers – primarily green plants, phytoplankton, and certain bacteria – are able to import (actually to utilize what is already there but otherwise unavailable) some of the radiant energy from the sun, energy that is not otherwise utilized. Photosynthesizers transform this sunlight, along with other relatively low quality (diffuse) inputs – atmospheric carbon dioxide, and soil water – into oxygen, chemical energy, and biomass which form the basis for other forms of life on the planet. In other words, photosynthesizers transform high entropy, largely unusable energy and material into low entropy resources that are vital for life as we know it.

The second agent – at least in potential – is actually us, the human race. Through proper application of our unique intelligence we are able to increase the quality (organization, structure, availability) of matter within the earth's ecosystem. For example, we are able to creatively innovate and develop more efficient ways of growing food – a high quality, low entropy resource – from lower quality material. Humans have demonstrated an amazing ability to overcome challenges and limitations posed by the natural degradation of material resources. On the other hand, as we all know, humans can be, and often are, a very destructive force in the environment. As we said earlier, most of our interactions with our environment have a negative effect on the quality of matter. The difference seems to be how human intelligence is applied in relation to the world around us.

How do we differentiate between a proper application of human intelligence that increases the net quality and improper applications that degrade the net quality of our environment? Is there any formal structure for guiding the application of man's intelligence and his activities in such a way as to ensure that his activities result in a net increase in 'quality?'

---

natural gas – which are thought to originate from decomposed plant and animal matter that became buried beneath the earth's surface.

## BAL TASHCHIT – A PRO-QUALITY COMMANDMENT

In the Jewish tradition, there is a commandment known as *bal tashchit* which *prohibits wasting or needlessly destroying any object or material that humans can benefit from*. From the physical laws mentioned above, we know that man cannot actually destroy matter – he can only degrade its "quality." Therefore, the prohibition of *bal tashchit* may be more accurately described as a prohibition against unnecessarily degrading or corrupting[10] the quality of useable resources. Rabbi Samson Raphael Hirsch said as much a century and a half ago when he wrote, "*Shachat* (the root of the word "*tashchit*") is the conception of corruption, not destruction. It is the overthrow of a good condition, and the impeding of progress, and the changing into the opposite of anything which was meant to thrive and prosper."[11]

In other words, *bal tashchit* can be expressed as the prohibition against causing a *net* loss in *quality*. This appears to be consistent with the definition of Maimonides, who wrote that the unnecessary causing of any loss enters into the prohibition of *bal tashchit*.[12]

Hirsch's definition also introduces another crucial element to our discussion. According to Jewish tradition, man and his world are meant to be progressing towards a better future.[13] *Bal tashchit*, as well as the other commandments, is meant to help guide us there, in a systematic, step-by-step fashion.

---

10 The *Random House New World Dictionary* defines "corruption" as: foulness, pollution, contamination; made inferior by errors or alterations. See *Random House Webster's Unabridged Dictionary*, 2nd ed. (New York, 1998).

11 R. Samson Raphael Hirsch, *The Pentateuch, Translated and Explained*, trans. Isaac Levy (Gateshead: Judaic Press Limited, 1982), I:138–139, on *Bereshit* 6:11.

12 Maimonides, *Sefer Hamitzvot*, ed. S. Frankel (Jerusalem, 1995), negative command no. 57, p. 308.

13 See for example *Yeshayahu* 2:2–4.

THE PATH TO PROGRESS – CONSISTENT PROFIT

As we discussed above, virtually every time we interact with our environment – even our very existence – causes a corruption or degradation in the quality of the matter in our environment. This is inevitable, but this is only part of the equation. The other part of the equation – and a crucial factor – is the *benefits* that result from our activities. We can still bring profit – increasing the net quality of the system – as long as the benefits from our actions are greater than the costs.

In other words, the degradation of useful resources, which is prohibited by the commandment of *bal tashchit*, is the corruption or the decrease in the quality of the resources *without commensurate benefit* to compensate for this loss.[14] As long as the overall benefits to the system, even if expressed in a different location within the system, exceed the overall costs, there is a *net gain* in "quality." In other words, the whole system has profited, and is progressing towards its destiny.

A key issue in the determination is the pre-examination of our actions. What benefits will likely accrue from our actions and do the benefits outweigh the costs in terms of the loss of *quality* caused by our actions? A related question is, where the actions of an individual or group bring them a profit, how does this affect other individuals or groups within the system? Perhaps more importantly, what is the *net* result – how does this affect the entire system? Is there an overall profit or loss within the system?

How do we measure profit to the system? Is there a satisfactory way of measuring both the net costs – in terms of the decrease in the quality of matter in the environment and the net benefits – in terms of increase in quality – that result from our actions? This is in some ways similar to conventional cost-benefit analysis. We need an accounting system for *quality*

---

14    The Talmud (*Bava Kama* 91b) rules that if a fruit tree is more valuable (*m'uleh b'damim*) as a source of wood than as a source of fruits, then it may be cut down for its wood. While cutting down the fruit tree is a destructive act – it causes a loss in the quality of the material – the benefits derived more than compensate for this loss. Therefore, there is no violation of *bal tashchit*. This principle applies to any resources.

– wherein we can measure gains and losses in quality and thereby compare the benefits and costs.

The usual unit of measurement for profit is monetary equivalent. The monetary equivalency is an expression of the market value of a resource, and can be, at least under ideal market conditions, a useful indicator of the quality of the resource. Benefits derived from resources can also be expressed in monetary units. All other things being equal, the higher the quality of a resource, the higher the monetary value the resource should fetch. This may correspond with the understanding of the prohibition of *bal tashchit* of several of the medieval Jewish scholars.[15] For example, Rabbi Isaiah Ditrani, a thirteenth century scholar, writes that with *bal tashchit* we are most concerned with preventing the loss of the *monetary value* of resources.[16]

## THE BIGGER PICTURE – *TIKKUN OLAM*

It may be, then, that the underlying meta-principle of *bal tashchit* is to ensure that the world is constantly progressing – moving towards perfection – and that all resources are being dedicated to this goal and not wasted in improper uses. While consistent with protecting the environment, *bal tashchit* goes beyond environmental protection. *Bal tashchit* addresses the bigger picture – beyond trying not to destroy the world and its resources, what is the positive direction towards which our use of resources should lead us? What is the goal and how do we progress in that direction? Similarly, *bal tashchit* goes beyond the concept of *sustainability* – of leaving the world in as good a shape as we found it – it raises the bar to leaving the world improved. Jewish tradition provides a goal – *tikkun olam* (perfecting ourselves and our world) – and instructions on how to get there – the Torah. Looked at this way, we can say that *bal tashchit* is a mechanism for progressively reaching the goal of *tikkun olam* by properly using our physical resources.

There is a well-known argument in environmental circles that is related to our discussion. The "neo-Malthusians," represented, for example, by

---

15    Including *Tosefot haRid, Yereim, Smag* and *Rosh*.
16    Commentary of *Tosefot haRid*, on *Bava Kama* 92a.

Paul Ehrlich, claim that we are rapidly destroying our environment and exhausting our natural resources.[17] They correctly state that man's activities degrade the quality of his environment. Therefore, with a rapidly growing population, over time, this should lead to destruction of the environment and disaster for man. The other side of the argument claims that the neo-Malthusians either ignore or greatly underestimate a vital factor: the unique ability of man to properly utilize his intelligence to adapt, innovate, and compensate – and sometimes more than compensate – for the naturally destructive effects of his activities. This position, represented for example by the late Julian Simon, predicts a progressively better future for humanity and for man's relationship with his environment.[18]

The future is in question. It is possible that both sides are conditionally correct. If man uses his resources properly, Simon's scenario – which is not entirely inconsistent with the Jewish tradition's point of view described above – may prevail. Simon predicts that as the human population in-creases, the environmental quality (which he claims is already improving in much of the developed world) will continue to improve. On the other hand, if man doesn't properly use his intelligence – if his intelligence is exploited as a servant to his lower impulses – Ehrlich's predictions may finally pan out. Ehrlich predicts that the quality of the environment will continue to worsen, and the expected (but delayed) disaster is imminent. Either way, man has a strong and growing influence on his environment and it is likely that our actions – how we use our resources – will have a significant effect on the quality of our environment life-support system.

---

17   See for example: *Limits to Growth* by the Club of Rome, New York, 1972; or Paul Ehrlich's *The Population Bomb* (Berkeley: Sierra Club Books, 1968) or any number of other related books and articles by Ehrlich and his colleagues.

18   See for example: Julian Simon, *The Ultimate Resource 2* (Princeton: Princeton University Press, 1996); and Bjørn Lomborg, *The Skeptical Environmentalist* (Cambridge: Cambridge University Press, 2001).

# Contributors

**Rabbi Dr. Nathan Lopes Cardozo** is the Founder and Dean of the David
Cardozo Academy in Jerusalem, an institution established in 2000 to
revolutionize Jewish spirituality and learning. A world-renowned lecturer and prolific author, Rabbi Lopes Cardozo's books and essays are
read by laypeople, rabbis and academicians of Jewish and non-Jewish
persuasion. Educated in Amsterdam with roots in the Portuguese and
Spanish Jewish community, Rabbi Lopes Cardozo received his rabbinical degree from Gateshead Talmudic College, studied at Yeshivat Mir
in Jerusalem, and holds a Doctorate in Philosophy. He pens a weekly
"Thought to Ponder," available on the David Cardozo Academy website.

**Rabbi Dr. Norman Lamm** was elected President of Yeshiva University
in August 1976. He served as the university's third president and
first native-born American. In June 2003, he was elected Chancellor
of the university. He also continues to be Rosh haYeshiva at the
university's affiliated Rabbi Isaac Elhanan Theological Seminary.
During the 17 years preceding his election as president, Rabbi Dr.
Lamm served on the Yeshiva University faculty, culminating in his
appointment as the Erna and Jakob Michael Professor of Jewish
Philosophy in 1966. He was in the Rabbinate for 25 years, serv-
ing as spiritual leader of The Jewish Center in Manhattan and,

earlier, as rabbi of Congregation Kodimoh in Springfield, MA. Dr. Lamm has authored 11 volumes and edited over 20 volumes.

**Rabbi Francis Nataf** is the former Educational Director of the David Cardozo Academy, and had previously held many senior educational positions in Israel and the United States. Rabbi Nataf was ordained at Yeshiva University and also holds degrees in Jewish History and International Affairs. He has written numerous articles for a variety of important Jewish periodicals and websites and is also the author of *Redeeming Relevance in the Book of Genesis* (Urim,) and *Redeeming Relevance in the Book of Exodus* (Urim).

**Rabbi Yitzchok Adlerstein** is the Director of Interfaith Affairs for the Simon Wiesenthal Center. He holds the Sydney M. Irmas Adjunct Chair in Jewish Law and Ethics at Loyola Law School and also serves as a faculty member at Yeshiva of Los Angeles and its high schools. Rabbi Adlerstein is a contributing editor to the quarterly *Jewish Action*, and the Founding Editor of Cross-Currents.com, an internet Journal of Orthodox thought. He has also authored an adaptive reading of the Maharal's *Be'er HaGolah* for Artscroll.

**Prof. Yehuda Gellman** recently retired from his professorship in Philosophy at Ben-Gurion University of the Negev. He is the author of *Experience of God and the Rationality of Theistic Belief* (Cornell University Press), *The Fear, the Trembling, and the Fire: Kierkegaard and Hassidic Masters on the Binding of Isaac* (University Press of America), *Mystical Experience of God, a Philosophical Enquiry* (Ashgate Publishers, London) and *Abraham! Abraham!* (Ashgate Publishers, London). He is also a frequent guest lecturer at the David Cardozo Academy.

**Rabbi Dr. Alon Goshen-Gottstein** is director of the Elijah Interfaith Institute as well as of the Center for the Study of Rabbinic Thought at Beit Morasha College. Ordained as a rabbi in 1977, he holds his B.A. and his Ph.D. from Hebrew University in Jerusalem. Stanford University Press published his *The Sinner and the Amnesiac: The Rabbinic Invention of Elisha ben Abuya and Eleazar ben Arach* in 2000. His *Israel* *in God's Presence: An Introduction to Judaism for the Christian Student* is forthcoming from Hendrickson Press. He is also a frequent guest lecturer at the David Cardozo Academy.

**Rabbi Zvi Grumet** is a teacher and thinker who served the American Jewish community for more than two decades before he made aliyah. He now teaches at Machon Pardes and Yeshivat Eretz HaTzvi, and is a senior member of the educational team at The Lookstein Center for Jewish Education at Bar-Ilan University. He has published numerous articles on Bible, Jewish Thought and Education, is Editor of *Jewish Educational Leadership* and is working on a new commentary on *Bereshit*. Rabbi Grumet was ordained at Yeshiva University and has a M.A. in Educational Administration from the Azrieli Graduate Institute. Rabbi Grumet is also a senior faculty member of the David Cardozo Academy.

**Rabbi Dr. Alan Kimche** is the spiritual leader of the Ner Yisrael community in London. He studied at Yeshivat Kol Torah in Jerusalem under the mentorship of R. Shlomo Zalman Auerbach as well as at the Mirrer Yeshiva. Rabbi Kimche holds a Ph.D. in Philosophy from University College, London and received his Ph.D. from London University.

**Prof. William Kolbrener** is a professor of English Literature at Bar-Ilan University and writes widely on the poetry, politics and theology of the early modern period in England. His *Milton's Warring Angels* was published by Cambridge University Press in 1997, and his *Mary Astell: Reason, Gender, Faith* by Ashgate in 2008. In addition to his work on the early modern period, Prof. Kolbrener has published on rabbinic hermeneutics and epistemology as well as on the philosophical works of R. Joseph Soloveitchik. His *Open Minded Torah: Of Irony, Fundamentalism and Love* was published by Continuum in 2011. Prof. Kolbrener is also a senior faculty member of the David Cardozo Academy.

**Prof. Elliott Malamet** received his Ph.D in English Literature from the University of Toronto where he taught for several years. Prof. Malamet is currently assistant professor of Jewish Education at York University in Toronto and co-director of the Torah in Motion organization. Prof. Malamet's work in the field of spiritual education has been featured in the leading Canadian newspapers and he has appeared many times on Canadian radio and television. Whenever in Israel, Prof. Malamet offers stimulating lectures for the David Cardozo Academy.

**Rabbi Dr. Yehuda Schnall** teaches philosophy at Bar-Ilan University. He is a prolific writer whose articles frequently appear in a variety of scholarly journals. Rabbi Schnall's ordination is from Yeshiva University, and he taught Jewish Studies for over a decade at David Shapell College of Jewish Studies in Jerusalem. Among his areas of specialization are the philosophy of science and the philosophy of religion. Rabbi Schnall is also a senior faculty member of the David Cardozo Academy.

**Rabbi Dr. Eliezer Shore** teaches and writes on topics in Chassidut and Spirituality. He teaches at the Rothberg International School of Hebrew University, Bar-Ilan University and several other institutions of higher learning. Rabbi Shore earned his Ph.D. from Bar-Ilan University, having written on the topic of Language and Mystical Experience in the writings of R. Nachman of Breslav. He is also a senior faculty member of the David Cardozo Academy.

**Rabbi Prof. Avraham Wijler** is a lecturer in physics and materials engineering at the Jerusalem College of Technology. His current research involves the characterization of a new thermoplastic leather material that has been developed at JCT, the role of Introns in DNA, and a Jewish perspective on environmental problems. He is also an ordained rabbi.

**Dr. Akiva Wolff** works as a therapist/coach/consultant helping people improve the quality of their lives and the environment. He has a doctorate from Leiden University in the Netherlands, and a masters degree in energy and environmental studies from Boston University. He previously served as the director of the Environmental Responsibility Unit of the Jerusalem Center for Business Ethics and taught environmental management at the Jerusalem College of Technology. Dr. Wolff is a guest lecturer at the David Cardozo Academy.